SOCIAL STRUCTURE IN SOUTHEAST ASIA

VIKING FUND PUBLICATIONS IN ANTHROPOLOGY
Number Twenty-Nine

SOCIAL STRUCTURE
in
SOUTHEAST ASIA

Edited by
GEORGE PETER MURDOCK

QUADRANGLE BOOKS · CHICAGO · 1960

This volume comprises one of a series of publications on research in general anthropology published by the Wenner-Gren Foundation for Anthropological Research, Incorporated, a foundation created and endowed at the instance of Axel L. Wenner-Gren for scientific, educational, and charitable purposes. The reports, numbered consecutively as independent contributions, appear at irregular intervals.

SOL TAX
UNIVERSITY OF CHICAGO
Editor, Viking Fund Publications in Anthropology

Copyright © *1960 by*
WENNER-GREN FOUNDATION FOR ANTHROPOLOGICAL RESEARCH, INC.

First published 1960
QUADRANGLE BOOKS, INC., *119 West Lake Street, Chicago 1, Illinois*

Printed in the United States of America

To
The Hospitable People of Thailand

PREFACE

THE editor was asked to organize a symposium on Social Structure in Southeast Asia at the Ninth Pacific Science Congress, which met in Bangkok, Thailand, from November 18 to November 30, 1957. The present volume is the result. Most of the contributors attended the Congress and delivered papers or briefer summaries at the symposium, later expanding them to their present form. Two of the contributors, Professor Koentjaraningrat and Professor Ruey, though invited to participate in the symposium, were unable to attend the Congress but nevertheless prepared papers which were presented *in absentia* and subsequently expanded. Two participants, Dr. W. R. Geddes of the University of Sydney (then of Auckland University College) and Professor R. Lauriston Sharp of Cornell University, delivered short papers on the social organization of the Land Dayak of Sarawak and of the Thai, respectively, but have been unable to expand them for inclusion in the present volume.

The symposium aroused great interest among the anthropologists attending the Congress and led to lively discussions. The participants asked the organizer to edit the papers, to arrange for their separate publication so as to achieve a wider circulation, and to write an introduction to the collective volume. This he gladly agreed to do because of his conviction of the very high level of quality of the contributions and of their important potential significance for the understanding of social organization in Southeast Asia.

The descriptive and analytic studies presented herewith include contributions from anthropologists of seven different nationalities: American, Australian, British, Chinese, French, Indonesian, and Japanese. Yet they all clearly represent a single international scientific tradition and reflect an encouragingly uniform frame of reference. They cover thirteen separate social systems [Professors Mabuchi and Wei have dealt with six distinct systems among the Formosan aborigines]. Two of these are patrilineal—the Bunun of Formosa and the Miao of China. Two are matrilineal—the Ami of Formosa and the Mnong Gar of Vietnam. The Mnong Gar are especially interesting since they represent, to the best of the editor's knowledge, the first matrilineal society of the Crow type to be described for the entire Eurasiatic continent.

The other nine social systems, despite striking individual differences, all belong to the general type which has been variously called "ambilateral," "bilateral," "cognatic," and "nonunilineal." Social structural analysis over the past century has been concerned very largely with unilineal systems, i.e., those characterized predominantly by either matrilineal, patrilineal, or double descent, and with respect to these has achieved a level of scientific understanding that is highly gratifying. In comparison, social systems in which unilineal descent either is absent or is not the major organizing principle have received little attention, and precise knowledge of their structuring is still relatively rudimentary. The contributions to the present volume seem to the editor to add a major increment to our scientific knowledge of the subject. He has therefore chosen to devote his introductory chapter exclusively to analyzing and comparing the nine nonunilineal social systems described in this volume in relation to one another and to comparable systems described elsewhere in the ethnographic literature.

In this enterprise he has relied upon two principal resources. For comparative data he has drawn upon materials assembled in his own files on some 200 nonunilineal social systems from all parts of the world. For theoretical enlightenment and intellectual stimulation he has drawn heavily on the papers and discussions in a Seminar on Nonunilineal Kinship Systems held during the winter and spring of 1959 at the Center for Advanced Study in the Behavioral Sciences at Stanford, California. This seminar was organized by Fred Eggan, Raymond Firth, Meyer Fortes, and the editor with the objective of achieving some measure of common understanding of the basic problems and range of variation in nonunilineal social systems and with the hope of finding some collective agreement with respect to terminology and appropriate modes of analysis. Besides Eggan, Firth, and Fortes, other participants among the Fellows at the Center, notably Edward P. Dozier, Lloyd Fallers, Clifford Geertz, and George C. Homans, made significant contributions to the seminar. To all of them the editor feels a deep sense of obligation.

The editor must also acknowledge, with gratitude and appreciation, the help and cooperation of the many people who contributed in various ways to the organization and success of the Bangkok symposium. He and the participants owe a special debt to Air Marshall Muni M. Vejyant Rangsrisht, President of the Congress; to Dr. Charng Ratanarat, Secretary-General of the Congress; to Professor Phya Anuman Rajadhon, Organizing Chairman for Anthropology and Social Sciences; to Mr. M. R. Chakratong Tongyai, Vice Chairman of the Publications Committee; to Dr. Bernard P. Groslier, Vice Chairman of the Standing Committee for Anthropology and Social Sciences; and to Miss Brenda Bishop, Secretary of the Pacific Science Association.

THE EDITOR

TABLE OF CONTENTS

PREFACE vii

1. COGNATIC FORMS OF SOCIAL ORGANIZATION 1
   By George Peter Murdock

2. THE MNONG GAR OF CENTRAL VIETNAM 15
   By Georges Condominas

3. THE SAGADA IGOROTS OF NORTHERN LUZON 24
   By Fred Eggan

4. THE EASTERN SUBANUN OF MINDANAO 51
   By Charles O. Frake

5. THE IBAN OF WESTERN BORNEO 65
   By J. D. Freeman

6. THE JAVANESE OF SOUTH CENTRAL JAVA 88
   By R. M. Koentjaraningrat

7. THE SINHALESE OF THE DRY ZONE OF NORTHERN CEYLON 116
   By E. R. Leach

8. THE ABORIGINAL PEOPLES OF FORMOSA 127
   By Toichi Mabuchi

9. SUPPLEMENTARY NOTES ON THE FORMOSAN ABORIGINES 141
   By Wei Hwei-Lin

10. THE MAGPIE MIAO OF SOUTHERN SZECHUAN 143
    By Ruey Yih-Fu

NOTES 157

BIBLIOGRAPHY 165

INDEX 175

CHAPTER 1

COGNATIC FORMS OF SOCIAL ORGANIZATION

GEORGE PETER MURDOCK
University of Pittsburgh

THE various forms of social groups which have in common the fact that membership is acquired through one parent only—either exclusively through the father or exclusively through the mother, not through both at the same time nor optionally through either—are today universally called "unilineal." This term embraces the two alternative categories of "patrilineal" and "matrilineal" as well as so-called "double descent," which is not an independent rule of affiliation but refers to societies which have two or more types of kin groups, some of which are characterized by patrilineal and others by matrilineal descent. There is also widespread acceptance of "lineage" as the most general term applicable to all consanguineal groups resulting from unilineal descent. Unilineal kin groups are differentiated as "patrilineages" or "matrilineages" in terms of the two alternative organizing principles, and as "minimal," "minor," "major," or "maximal" lineages in terms of their increasing generation depth from the common ancestor of their members. A maximal lineage with geographically dispersed membership, with few if any corporate characteristics, and with an unknown or merely postulated or traditional common ancestor is often distinguished as a "sib" (in British usage a "clan"). If an entire society is divided into two very large sibs, these are called "moieties."

Since lineages are almost universally characterized by exogamy, their members can rarely reside together as a local group. Localization necessitates some compromise between the prevailing principle of unilineal descent and the fact of co-residence. In the overwhelming majority of unilineal social systems this compromise is achieved through adherence to a "unilocal" rule of residence—patrilocal, matrilocal, or avunculocal—which is consistent with the rule of descent. What results is a local group having as its core the adult members of a lineage of one sex only, to whom are added the inmarrying spouses of these members and from whom are subtracted their adult siblings of opposite sex who have departed to join their spouses in other local groups. British social anthropoligists have not recognized or named this very important type of kin group. I have elsewhere (Murdock, 1949, pp. 65-78) suggested reserving for it the term "clan," and have named the three alternative forms in which it occurs "patriclans" (with patrilineal descent and patrilocal residence), "matriclans" (with matrilineal descent and matrilocal residence), and "avuncuclans" (with matrilineal descent and avunculocal residence).

At least a third of the societies of the world are not unilineal, in the sense that they do not employ either patrilineal or matrilineal descent as a major organizing principle in the grouping of kinsmen. Despite significant pioneer efforts, notably by Davenport (1959), Firth (1957), Freeman (1958), and Goodenough (1955), there still exists no solid consensus regarding organizational principles, typology, or terminology comparable to that achieved for unilineal social systems. This paper will attempt a clarification on all these points, drawing heavily upon the contributions of the above-mentioned men and on those of the contributors to the present volume.

First of all, there is need of a general term, contrasting with "unilineal," which can be applied to any grouping of kinsmen organized by genealogical ties without particular emphasis on either patrilineal or matrilineal connections. The term "nonunilinear," employed by Davenport and Goodenough, has the disadvantages of being negative rather than positive in its connotations and of not implying kinship affiliation; any voluntary association is "nonunilinear." The "multilineal" of Parsons (1943, p. 24) is inappropriate since, as will be indicated below, many such systems, including the American, are not in fact "lineal" in any sense. The "ambilineal" of Firth and the "bilateral" of current American usage seem better reserved for special subtypes of nonunilineal systems. I therefore propose the adoption of the one remaining familiar alternative, "cognatic," which is also the choice of two contributors to the present volume, Freeman and Leach. The word connotes appropriately "akin by birth." Its sole disadvantage, a minor one, is its former secondary meaning of "related on the mother's side," for which "uterine" is today the preferred synonym.

Analysis of cognatic social systems may begin with a consideration of five of those described in the present volume, which share a very large number of common features that align them with a recognized and widespread subtype, called "Eskimo" (Murdock, 1949, pp. 226–228). In all of them a small domestic unit is the most important social, economic, and landholding group—fully corporate in every sense. The Iban, Sagada, and Yami observe strict monogamy, and the Javanese and Subanun, though permitting polygyny, practice it to only a very limited extent. The domestic unit is an independent nuclear family in three instances, a stem family in two; one child continues to reside after marriage with his or her parents among the Iban and Javanese. Extended families occur in none of the five societies. Residence is ambilocal[1]—more often patrilocal than matrilocal among the Yami, more often matrilocal among the Javanese, equally balanced among the Iban, Sagada, and Subanun, never strictly unilocal. Neolocal residence also occurs as an alternative among the Javanese and as the norm in later life among the Subanun.

The Javanese and Sagada possess functionally insignificant ambilineal descent groups of a type to be analyzed later, but the only important grouping of kinsmen other than the dominant small family unit is the aggregation of near relatives to which Rivers (1924, p. 16) gave the name "kindred." All five of the societies in question possess kindreds, and in every case these embrace close lineal and collateral kinsmen regardless of whether the connecting links are male or female. The collateral range of the kindred varies. It embraces first but not second or remoter cousins among the Yami, but among the Iban the kindred includes fourth cousins though its effective range usually terminates with second cousins.

The domestic unit is always exogamous, the kindred only rarely so. The Iban, Javanese, and Subanun permit marriage with a first cousin; the Sagada and Yami forbid such unions but allow marriage with any second cousin. No group makes any distinction between cross and parallel cousins. The same holds true of the kinship terminology, which clearly reflects the influence of both the family and the kindred. One set of terms is typically confined to members of the family unit, and a different set is employed for collateral relatives who are members of Ego's kindred but not of his family. This results in lineal terminology on the first ascending generation and in Eskimo terminology for cousins. The five societies reveal only two exceptions, both partial. The Javanese employ lineal terminology only for uncles, extending the term for mother to maternal and paternal aunts, and Frake reports that the Subanun apply either Hawiian or Eskimo terminology to cousins depending upon the "level" of discourse. The two remaining principles of classification—bifurcate merging and bifurcate collateral (Lowie, 1928)—find no expression in any of the five societies.

The two types of kin groups—the small family and the kindred—whose relative importance in the social structure characterizes these and other societies of the Eskimo type, demand meticulous analysis. A family is created by marriage, a universal human phenomenon, which establishes an affinal link between husband and wife and indirectly between their respective consanguineal kinsmen. A child acquires membership in a family by birth, or more technically and accurately by "filiation," which Fortes (1959, p. 206) defines as "the relationship created by the fact of being the legitimate child of one's parents" and correctly characterizes as "universally bilateral." Rules of inheritance, succession, and descent are compounded out of filiation links, usually by some selective preference for "patrifiliation" or "matrifiliation." For present purposes, however, the important point is that the small domestic unit is fundamentally a bilateral kin group. It must therefore be defined in such a way as to exclude any lineal principle. Of the various forms of the family or household recorded in ethnography, only the following fall within such a definition:

1) the independent monogamous or nuclear family composed of married parents and their children;
2) the polygamous family (with either polygyny or polyandry), which links the children by two or more spouses to one common parent;

3) the stem family, which links the family of procreation of one married child to his family of orientation in a common household;
4) the lineal family,[2] which links the families of procreation of several married siblings to their common family of orientation but which dissolves with the death of their parents.

Any type of family or household organization which embraces two or more married siblings in its senior generation constitutes an "extended family" and must necessarily be based on a lineal principle—either patrilineal, matrilineal, or ambilineal—rather than exclusively on bilateral filiation. An extended family is essentially a minimal clan or localized lineage and, as such, should be sharply differentiated from a genuine domestic group.

The kindred should also be recognized as a bilateral kin group. It is always Ego-oriented, i.e., composed of persons related to a particular individual (or group of siblings) bilaterally (literally "on both sides"). The members of a kindred, other than the core individual and his siblings, need not be, and frequently are not, related to one another. In any society, kindreds necessarily overlap one another endlessly. They are not discrete units; a society can never be divided into separate kindreds as it can be segmented into discrete families, lineages, clans, or communities. From the point of view of the core individual or siblingship, the membership of the kindred can be defined in terms of serial links of filiation produced by the ramifying intersection of families of procreation and orientation. The membership cannot be defined, however, in lineal terms by descent from a common ancestor. A kindred therefore is not, and cannot be, a descent group. There are, to be sure, certain types of descent groups, ancestor-oriented rather than Ego-oriented, which bear a superficial resemblance to kindreds, and they will be analyzed below. At this point it suffices to note that they are invariably ambilineal rather than bilateral.

Because of its lack of discreteness a kindred cannot be a corporate group.[3] The concept of corporateness, as used in the ethnographic literature, is confused and ambiguous, and urgently needs clarification. On the whole, I agree with Leach that it would be desirable to return essentially to Maine's original definition of a corporation as an estate comprising rights over persons and various forms of real, movable, and incorporeal property in whose assets a number of individuals share in accordance with their respective statuses. Thus defined, a corporate group is one whose members share an estate, especially one consisting of land, dwellings, or other material resources which its members have the right to use or exploit according to culturally accepted rules of tenure. As a practical matter, I would restrict the concept to groups whose rights are regularly rather than sporadically exercised, especially rights to the land (and its improvements) on which the members live and from which they extract their economic livelihood. I would not exclude, of course, incorporeal rights which have genuine significance in the everyday ceremonial, social, or artistic life of a people, such as the crests and associated privileges of Haida lineages. I would, however, prefer to treat as though they were noncorporate all groups whose collective rights and associated responsibilities are seldom exercised and are inconsequential in the total cultural context, e.g., the Sagada descent groups described by Eggan with collective rights in the pine trees planted by a common ancestor or the *alur walis* of the Javanese with its collective responsibility for the intermittent care of ancestral graves.

If the proposed definition is acceptable, kin groups can be conveniently classified in three categories:

1. *Corporate kin groups.* Families, lineages, and clans (in the sense of Murdock, 1949) are almost universally corporate.
2. *Occasional kin groups*, i.e., those which, according to Firth (1959), become operative only on specific occasions, even though they may sometimes be corporate in a technical sense. Firth cites as an example the modern Scottish clan with its periodic reunions.
3. *Circumscriptive kin groups*, i. e., noncorporate groups which never function as units, even on sporadic occasions, but which merely serve to define the limits of certain rights and duties of their members. The sib, for example, is often only a circumscriptive group. Thus in the central Caroline Islands, where sibs are widely dispersed among peoples with differing languages and cultures and only lineages are corporate groups, common sib membership serves only to set limits to the obligation of exogamy and to the right to receive food and overnight hospitality when away from home.

In this classification, kindreds are occasional groups, not only in the five societies under discussion but seemingly in every society where they occur. Sometimes, as in the northern Philippines and in early Europe (Phillpotts, 1913), they become operative on occasions for blood vengeance or the distribution of wergild. In most societies, however, they function primarily at crises in the life cycle of the core individual, especially in naming, initiation, wedding, and funeral ceremonies. In unilineal societies, comparable services are often rendered by what Eggan has called "skewed kindreds," i.e., *ad hoc* groups composed of two or more lineage segments like the Tikopia *kano a paito*.

To return to the case material, all five of the societies under consideration are characterized by the presence of important kin groups of only two types—always the same two—namely, small domestic groups and kindreds. The former are invariably corporate, the latter occasional. Neither, however, is a descent group. Both are bilateral rather than lineal. Davenport, Firth, and Goodenough have already suggested segregating kin groups of the kindred type from other forms of cognatic organization. I accept their suggestion, and propose that the term "bilateral" be reserved for the former. For those who favor the application of such terms to entire societies, rather than rigorously confining them to types of kin groups, it would seem appropriate to speak of a society as bilateral if it has no functionally significant descent groups, either unilineal or cognatic, and possesses only kin groups of the bilateral type such as small families and kindreds.

Discussion of the world distribution of bilateral societies will be limited to those with social systems closely resembling the Iban, Javanese, Sagada, Subanun, and Yami, i.e., to societies of the Eskimo type which conform to the following eight definitive criteria:

1) Prominence of small domestic units and absence of any form of extended family.
2) Prevailing monogamy with no more than a limited incidence of polygamy.
3) Ambilocal or neolocal residence, i.e., with no invariable unilocal rule.
4) Absence of any functionally important descent groups, unilineal or ambilineal.
5) Presence of bilateral kindreds or at least no specific report of their absence.
6) Absence of distinctions in the marriageability of different kinds of first cousins.
7) Cousin terminology of the Eskimo type.
8) Avuncular terminology of lineal or bifurcate collateral type, i.e., no extension of parental terms to uncles or aunts.

The societies mentioned below include only those for which my own files contain sufficient information for classification, and among these only those which conform to the above eight criteria in every respect. References are cited, however, only for published sources of a quality adjudged to be commensurate with the contributions in the present volume.

Bilateral societies of the Eskimo type are not uncommon in the general region of Southeast Asia. To the five described in this volume must be added the Bontok (Keesing, 1949), Kalinga (Barton, 1949), Sugbuhanon, Tagalog, and Tagbanua of the Philippines; the Land Dayak (Geddes, 1954) of Borneo; the Andamanese, Nicobarese, and Selung; and the Cambodians. The acculturated Chamorro of Saipan (Spoehr, 1954) are the sole representatives in Oceania east of the Philippines. In overwhelmingly unilineal Africa, only the Khoisan hunters have bilateral systems, and among them only the Kung Bushmen (Marshall, 1957 and 1959) are adequately described. Except for the Albanians and some Yugoslav groups, all modern European societies and those of European derivation have social systems of the Eskimo type, and my files contain specific reports of kindreds for the Americans, Argentinians, Czechs, Dutch (Keur, 1955), English, French, French Canadians, Hutsul, Irish (Arensberg and Kimball, 1940), Jamaicans, Lapps (Pehrson, 1954, and Whitaker, 1955), Lithuanians, and Russians. Essentially similar systems prevail in eastern Asia among the Japanese and in parts of the Ryukyu Islands, and in northeastern Asia among the Ainu, Chukchee (Bogoras, 1907), and Koryak (Jochelson, 1905-08). The Eskimo, from North Alaska (Spencer, 1959) east to Greenland, represent, so to speak, the type specimens. The similar systems of the Catawba and Penobscot in eastern North America possibly reflect acculturative influences, but those of the Tewa and Tiwa pueblos of the Southwest are clearly indigenous. In South America, systems of the Eskimo type are reported for the Carinya of Venezuela, the Cayapa of Ecuador, the Camba of Bolivia, the Abipon of Argentina, and the Ona and Yahgan of Tierra del Fuego, although in the last two instances patrilocal residence may preponderate too strongly to warrant this classification.

The degree of identity in diagnostic characteristics among the peoples mentioned is extraordinary—the more so since they range from simple hunters and gatherers, through intermediate tillers, to European and Asiatic societies of the highest complexity. It seems clear, therefore, that modes of subsistence, technological attainments, elaboration of status distinctions, and levels of political integration exert little differentiating influence. However great or slight its social and cultural complexity in such respects, if a society for any reason maximizes the small domestic unit and minimizes lineal descent groups it tends automatically to arrive at a single uniform configuration of marriage rules, kin alignments, and kinship nomenclature. The similarities go far beyond the features specifically analyzed. Thus payment of a bride-price, the overwhelmingly predominant mode of obtaining a wife throughout the world as a whole, is customary only among the Abipon, Cambodians, Caribou Eskimo, Subanun, and Sugbuhanon of all the societies mentioned or indirectly alluded to in the foregoing discussion.

The social structure of the Sinhalese, though clearly more cognatic than unilineal in its basic organizing principles, contrasts with the bilateral systems analyzed above on practically every essential point. Small domestic units, instead of being prominent and independent, are absorbed in a larger extended family, the *watte* or "co-resident compound group." Among the wealthy, these groups tend to be characterized by patrilocal residence and patrilineal succession, and to approximate the structure of patrilineages, although the patrilineal principle is neither fully elaborated nor universally operative. Bilateral kindreds are either absent or too insignificant to seem to Leach deserving of consideration. Cousins are not equally marriageable or non-marriageable. The Sinhalese forbid unions with a parallel cousin but permit them with a cross-cousin; indeed they utilize cross-cousin marriage as a means of reuniting portions of an estate fragmented by bilateral inheritance. In harmony with this, they employ cousin terminology of the Iroquois type, which, unlike Eskimo terminology, distinguishes cross from parallel cousins. In the first ascending generation, instead of lineal terms, they use bifurcate merging terminology, reflecting the patrilocal and patrilineal tendencies in the organization of the extended family.

In all the respects in which the Sinhalese social system differs from cognatic structures of the Eskimo type it approaches norms characteristic of patrilineal systems of the well-known Dakota type (Murdock, 1949, pp. 236-238). It might thus be called "quasi-patrilineal." Even the rule of residence—predominantly patrilocal, but matrilocal in *binna* marriages—falls somewhere between the prevailing norms for societies of the Eskimo and Dakota types. Among the societies elsewhere in the world which closely resemble the Sinhalese in structural features are the Bacairi, Camayura, and Wapishana of South America; all are characterized by predominantly patrilocal residence, by extended forms of family organization, by the absence or unimportance of kindreds, by symmetrical cross-cousin marriage, by cousin terminology of the Iroquois type, and by bifurcate merging avuncular terms. The same continent also contains a number of "quasi-matrilineal" societies, e.g., the Motilon, Panare, Yabarana, and Yekuana, which are identical to the foregoing in all respects except that the residence rule is predominantly matrilocal. They approach matrilineal societies of the Iroquois type in precisely the same way as the Sinhalese approach the patrilineal Dakota structural type. In the classroom I have used the term "Carib type" to embrace both unilocal variants of cognatic systems with unilineal features, and have distinguished them from the more strictly cognatic "bilateral" and "ambilineal" subtypes.

Social systems of the Carib type are in many instances demonstrably transitional forms in the evolution of unilineal from cognatic structures, or *vice versa*. Their unusual frequency in aboriginal South America, however, suggests that, at least under certain circumstances, they may achieve a relatively stable equilibrium, which would warrant regarding them as an independent type and not merely as phases in a process of change. The distribution of cognatic systems of the Carib type is by no means confined to South America. Some of those which most closely resemble the Sinhalese in their diagnostic features merit special consideration.

The Aleut and the Nunivak Eskimo (Lantis, 1946) of western Alaska retain the bifurcate collateral avuncular terminology of other Eskimo groups but agree with the Sinhalese in adhering to patrilocal residence, in having extended families, in possessing incipient and agamous patrilineages, in permitting cross-cousin marriage, and in using cousin terminology of the Iroquois type. The Polynesians of Rennell Island, whose social system is presumably derived historically from an ambilineal rather than a bilateral form of cognatic organization, have bifurcate merging avuncular terminology as well as extended families, cross-cousin marriage, and Iroquois cousin terms. The Fort Jameson Ngoni (Barnes, 1951), who have settled amongst and intermarried with matrilineal peoples in Northern Rhodesia, and have thereby lost all except a few vestiges of their original patrilineal organization, agree with the Sinhalese in having patrilocal residence, cross-cousin marriage, Iroquois cousin terminology, and avuncular terms of bifurcate merging type. Their quasi-patrilineal system is thus in the process of change from a unilineal toward a cognatic structure rather than *vice versa*.

Because they are so commonly transitional, and thus tend to preserve certain features of their earlier structure, systems of the Carib type show more variability than do those of the Eskimo type. What they all have in common is some degree of dependence, whether vestigial, incipient, or relatively stable, upon a unilineal principle of organization. Thus the Coos and Siuslaw of Oregon, the Maidu and Shasta of California, and the Havasupai (Spier, 1922 and 1928) and Pima of the Southwest have patrilocal residence, extended families and sometimes other elements of patrilineal organization, and Iroquois cousin terminology but lack cross-cousin marriage and bifurcate merging avuncular terms. In all cases, however, the unilineal principle of organization remains subordinate to the cognatic principle. Social systems of the Carib type must thus be grouped in the general category of cognatic systems. They nevertheless differ in so many respects from cognatic systems of the bilateral or Eskimo subtype, as well as from the ambilineal systems next to be analyzed, and still reveal so many common features, that it seems advisable to segregate them as a distinctive subtype, for which the descriptive term "quasi-unilineal" is herewith proposed.

In his analysis of Sinhalese society, Leach reaches the conclusion that "social structures are sometimes best regarded as the statistical outcome of multiple individual choices rather than as a direct reflection of jural rules." With this point of view I must register hearty and enthusiastic argreement. Leach amply demonstrates the validity of this approach in analyzing the processes which produce structural continuity and adaptation to underlying economic and technological facts in Sinhalese life. The available evidence on other quasi-unilineal systems seems to me to corroborate his interpretation. I would even go further and assert that social structures are always best regarded in the same light, and that jural rules themselves are the "outcome of multiple individual choices" in situations where one kind of choice is likely to be appreciably more strongly or regularly rewarded than possible alternative choices. This point of view, which seems to me generally shared by American students of social structure, accounts for my own sense of discomfort with the analyses of certain extreme British structuralists who assert the opposite, especially those who reify the concept of structure and speak, for example, of structural principles as exerting pressures upon individuals. Leach's position seems to me to have the enormous advantage of making possible the utilization of psychological principles and of scientific knowledge concerning the dynamics of cultural change in the interpretation of social systems. It has both realism and flexibility, and gives promise of substantial future progress in social structural research.

Of the nine cognatic social systems described in the present volume, those of three Formosan groups treated by Mabuchi—the Atayal, Paiwan, and Puyuma—reveal a series of distinctive structural features which distinguish them alike from the five bilateral societies and from the quasi-unilineal Sinhalese. They are characterized most strikingly by the presence and functional importance of corporate descent groups of the type which Firth has called "ambilineal." Both Firth (1957 and 1959) and Davenport (1959) have subjected this kind of group to penetrating analysis, which requires only minor clarification, especially in regard to terminology, to become fully acceptable.

In a recent article, Fortes (1959) departs from modern usage in two respects in his interpretation of ambilineal descent groups. He confuses the concepts of descent and kinship, referring twice in a single paragraph to "kinship or descent" and once to "descent or kinship" (p. 211). He thus abandons the clarifying contribution of Rivers (1924, p. 86), who first disentangled the two concepts and proposed applying that of descent "to membership of a social group, and to this only." Secondly, when other students of social structure have long since ceased to use marriage rules, such an exogamy and endogamy, as defining attributes of kin groups, Fortes insists that a "bilateral descent group . . . would have to be strictly endogamous" (p. 211). He thus refuses to class the Maori *hapu* (Firth,

1929 and 1957) and "the kind of land-owning groups described by Goodenough" (1955) as descent groups but, curiously enough, regards "the Jews in an East European Ghetto, or a caste, as long as it is coupled with obligatory endogamy" (p. 206) as acceptable examples. He even compounds his confusion by proposing "kindred groups" as an appropriate term for ambilineal structures. In preference to Fortes, the subsequent discussion will follow Goodenough, Firth, Davenport, and the contributors to the present volume.

The Atayal, Paiwan, and Puyuma are characterized, in addition to their ambilineal descent groups, by monogamy, by the extension of marriage prohibitions to all second as well as first cousins, by the application of sibling terms to cousins, by avuncular terminology of the generation type (except among the Atayal), and by ambilocal residence, with matrilocality predominating among the Puyuma and patrilocality in the other two tribes. An individual's membership in a descent group is usually determined by his parents' choice of marital residence, and affiliation is not ordinarily maintained with the natal group of the parent who has shifted residence. In the case of the "ritual groups" of the Puyuma, however, Mabuchi notes certain exceptions—examples both of dual affiliation and of affiliation with a group other than that of residence. Such exceptions do not occur in connection with the comparable groups among the Paiwan. Because of the high incidence of patrilocality among the Atayal, each ritual group consists of a core which resembles a localized patrilineage and of a much smaller fringe affiliated on the basis of matrilocal residence. In all three tribes the descent groups are clearly ambilineal, since affiliation in each successive generation is acquired through either parent and depends, not on filiation links radiating outward from an individual as in the case of a bilateral kindred, but on chains of filiation links converging upon a common ancestor, from whom land rights are derived and in whose name collective rituals are performed.

These Formosan descent groups conform in basic structural respects to the Bellacoola *minmint* (McIlwraith, 1948), the Gilbertese *kainga* (Goodnenough, 1955), the Kwakiutl *numaym* (Boas, 1897), the Lozi *mishiku* (Gluckman, 1950 and 1951), the Mangaian *kopu* (Buck, 1934), the Maori *hapu* (Firth, 1929), the Nukuoro *te-haka-sa-aluna*, the Samoan *'ainga sa* (Ember, 1959), and the old Scottish clan, the essential features of all of which have been summarized by Davenport (1959) and need not be repeated here. Before citing additional examples from my own files, I should like to propose certain clarifications in respect to terminology.

I have already recommended the adoption of Firth's term "ambilineal" to denote descent groups of this type in contradistinction to "quasi-unilineal" for those of the type found among the Sinhalese and to "bilateral" for the Ego-centered rather than ancestor-centered kindred. The three terms serve adequately to differentiate three distinct variants of cognatic as opposed to unilineal organization. Along with "Eskimo type" and "Carib type" for societies characterized primarily by bilateral or quasi-unilineal structures, respectively, I propose "Polynesian type" for those in which ambilineal structures are emphasized. Such systems are especially prevalent in Polynesia. The alternative, "Hawaiian type," although it has some currency, seems less suitable since the indigenous social system of Hawaii is not yet fully described and may well deviate in important respects from the pattern under discussion.

As a general term for ambilineal descent groups Davenport (1959) uses "sept," borrowed from Boas. Firth (1957, p. 6), however, proposes a revised definition of the term "ramage," and this seems to me clearly preferable, despite the unquestioned priority of "sept," because of its resemblance to "lineage," the accepted general term for unilineal descent groups. Ramages are the precise functional equivalents of lineages. They are equally consanguineal in composition, and they are equally susceptible to segmentation. Just as the core of a unilocal extended family is called a minimal lineage, so the core of an ambilocal extended family may be termed a minimal ramage. A ramage confined to a ward or similar subdivision of a community may similarly be called a minor ramage, and one coexistent with the community a major ramage. The term "sept" might be retained for a maximal ramage, in parallel to "sib" for a maximal lineage, i.e., for a kin group substantially exceeding the bounds of a single community. Like lineages, ramages occur in both pure or consanguineal and in compromise or localized forms. If the latter are called clans (patrilocal, matrilocal, or avunculocal) in unilineal societies, it would be appropriate in ambilineal societies to designate them as "ambilocal clans." This would, incidentally, return the word clan to its original meaning.

Two alleged distinctions between lineages and ramages deserve consideration. Davenport (1959, p. 566) notes that lineages are regularly "exclusive" in the sense that an individual can belong to only one group of the same category at the same time, whereas ramages are often "nonexclusive" with dual or even plural memberships. Firth (1957, p. 5) points out that affiliation with a lineage is regularly "definitive," i.e., determined by a fixed rule of descent, whereas ramage membership is "optative," i.e., allowing for a choice among alternatives. While both allegations are unquestionably correct, comparative evidence somewhat qualifies their significance. Many ambilineal societies do not permit plural memberships; once the choice of ramage affiliation has been made, it is in an important sense exclusive since the alternative memberships either become latent or lapse entirely. Freeman (1958) calls such a rule of affiliation "utrolateral." I suggest a category of "optative-exclusive" to contrast with "optative-nonexclusive." Although the ramages of the Bellacoola, Kwakiutl, Maori, Puyuma, and Samoans, for example, are essentially optative-nonexclusive, those of the Gilbertese, Lozi, Mangaians, Nukuoro, and Paiwan are optative-exclusive.

Wherever kin-group affiliation is nonexclusive, an individual's plural memberships almost inevitably become segregated into one primary membership, which is strongly activated by residence, and one or more secondary memberships in which participation is only partial or occasional. A similar situation, indeed, often prevails in unilineal societies, where individuals, through what Fortes (1953 and

1959) calls "complementary filation," commonly acquire and retain certain subsidiary rights and duties of participation in the lineage of the parent through whom descent is not reckoned. Unilineal descent does not even invariably exclude an optative element, since not a few unilineal societies permit full affiliation through complementary filiation under special circumstances. In addition to the widespread practice called "ambil-anak," two specific cases will illustrate the point. The patrilineal and patrilocal Mongo peoples of the Belgian Congo (Hulstaert, 1938) accord to a man who has no paired sister whose bride-price can be used to provide him with a wife the right to remove to the village whence his mother came, to affiliate permanently with her patrilineage, and to receive a wife from his maternal uncle. The matrilineal and matrilocal Trukese of Micronesia (Goodenough, 1951) encourage a woman with insufficient "mothers" and "sisters" to operate an efficient matrilocal extended family to join the extended family of her husband's mother and sisters; if the situation cannot be rectified within a generation, her offspring become permanently affiliated with their father's matrilineage. As opposed to the usual "definitive-exclusive" mode of kin-group affiliation in unilineal societies, that of the Mongo and Trukese can be regarded as conditionally optative.

The data in my files indicate the probable presence of minor or major ramages in a number of societies not mentioned by Davenport (1959). In Polynesia, they are suggested by the "paternal descent groups" reported by Métraux (1940) for the ambilocal Easter Islanders; by the "exogamous clans" reported by Kennedy (1931) for the ambilocal Ellice Islanders; by the *kutunga* or lineage-like landowning groups with optative-nonexclusive affiliation described by Burrows (1936) for the Futunans; by the landholding groups reported by Buck (1938) for the ambilocal Mangarevans; by the landowning "families" described by Loeb (1926) for the ambilocal Niueans; by the patrilineal exogamous "joint families" with 10 per cent matrilineal affiliation described by Hogbin (1934) for the Ontong-Javanese; and by the ambilocal long-house group inhabiting a "district" which Henry (1928) reports for old Tahiti. Although the Palauans of Micronesia tend strongly toward matrilineal descent, Force (1960, pp. 46-48) states specifically that a person "always had membership (or at least membership potential) in both the lineage of his father and the lineage of his mother and . . . he might elect or be forced by circumstances . . . to accept membership in his father's lineage. . . . If a man did follow his paternal lineage he then brought his wife to live with him on land inherited from his father's *keblil* [sib]." In Melanesia, the exogamous *taviti* or "kindred" of Eddystone Island described by Rivers (1926, pp. 71-94) may conceivably be actually a ramage; the *komu* or ambilateral "kindred" which Ivens (1927) reports as inhabiting a Ulawan hamlet is almost certainly such; and Goodenough (1957) specifically compares the *gaabu* and *unuma* of the Bwaidoga to the segmentary ramages of the Maori.

Outside of Oceania the incidence of indubitable ramages becomes sporadic. In northwestern North America, Goldman (1940) reports bilateral crest groups with a patrilineal bias among the Alkatcho Carrier, and similar groups are to be inferred from the description by Teit (1906) of the Lillooet. In Africa, bilateral clusters of extended families with a patrilineal bias among the Jukun, which Meek (1931) calls "kindreds," are undoubtedly ramages, and recent information cited by McCulloch (1950) for the Sherbro of Sierra Leone indicates that the *ram*, formerly held to be a matrilineage, is actually a localized ambilateral group with patrilineal as well as matrilineal affiliation.

All thirty of the ambilineal societies thus far considered—3 from Mabuchi, 12 discussed by Davenport, and 15 from my own files—are characterized by Hawaiian cousin terminology and the extension of marriage prohibitions to at least all first cousins, as well as by ambilocal residence and major or minor ramages. A series of agricultural peoples in Mexico, e.g., the Aztec, Mazatec, Mixe, Popoluca, Totonac, Yaqui, and Zapotec, should perhaps be added to this list. All are predominantly patrilocal but definitely nonunilineal. All possess Hawaiian cousin terminology and prohibit marriage with any first cousin. Although strong acculturative influences have obscured the indigenous social organization, early accounts nearly everywhere describe villages as subdivided into "barrios," which may conceivably have been ramages. Only in the case of the Aztec *calpulli* have these been thoroughly analyzed from early records, and Monzon (1949) has demonstrated that the *calpulli* were neither unilineal nor exogamous.

If ambilocal extended families are to be regarded as minimal ramages, the list of ambilineal societies can be extended to include the Hawaiians and Tongarevans of Polynesia; the Ingassana of Sudan; the Chorti and Terena of Central and South America; and the Alsea, Arapaho, Caddo, Cheyenne, Comanche, Hukundika Shoshone, Hupa, Karok, Kiowa Apache, Kutenai, Sinkaietk, Southern Ute, and Yurok of North America. It is noteworthy that these peoples, without exception, also possess Hawaiian cousin terminology and prohibit cousin marriages.

Careful analysis of the data in my files on all nonunilineal societies which do not fall obviously into one or another of the three types already distinguished—the Eskimo or bilateral, the Carib or quasi-unilineal, and the Polynesian or ambilineal—fails to reveal any additional comparable configurations. Many groups differ from a particular type in only one of a half dozen criteria, and the rest share features of two cognatic types. This is, of course, no more surprising than that societies with double descent combine features of both the matrilineal and the patrilineal varieties of unilineal organization. The Ifugao of the Philippines will serve as an example. As Eggan has shown, they possess ambilineal ramages as well as the bilateral kindreds reported by Barton (1919). Their Hawaiian cousin terminology and avuncular terms of the generation type accord with the former; their small domestic units with the latter; their ambilocal rule of residence with both.

By way of conclusion and summary, the principal structural features which differentiate the three basic subtypes of cognatic social organization may be presented in tabular form.

Structural feature	Bilateral (Eskimo)	Quasi-unilineal (Carib)	Ambilineal (Polynesian)
Small domestic units	Invariably prominent	Rarely prominent	Rarely prominent
Extended families	Invariably absent	Nearly always present	Usually present
Bilateral kindreds	Usually present	Nearly always absent	Occasionally present
Ambilineal ramages	Usually absent	Invariably absent	Nearly always present
Rule of residence	Always neolocal or ambilocal	Usually unilocal	Nearly always ambilocal
Marriage with first cousins	Often allowed	Allowed with cross-cousins	Invariably forbidden
Marriage with second cousins	Usually allowed	Usually allowed	Commonly forbidden
Kinship terms for cousins	Nearly always Eskimo	Nearly always Iroquois	Nearly always Hawaiian
Avuncular terminology	Usually lineal	Usually bifurcate merging	Commonly of generation type

CHAPTER 2

THE MNONG GAR OF CENTRAL VIETNAM
(Les Mnong Gar du Centre Viêt-Nam)

GEORGES CONDOMINAS
École Pratique des Hautes Études (Sorbonne)

THE Mnong Gar are a Mon-Khmer tribe of the forested and mountainous interior of Vietnam (see Map 1). They subsist by shifting rice cultivation and reside in impermanent villages of 100 to 150 inhabitants each. The basic economic, ceremonial, and property-holding unit is the nuclear family. Several related or friendly families, however, occupy separate apartments in a common long house. Marriage involves an exchange of gifts, mainly provided by the family of the groom, and is preferentially arranged with a matrilateral cross-cousin, the mother's younger brother's daughter. Descent is matrilineal, and residence normally matrilocal. Deviations from the residence pattern nevertheless occur with sufficient frequency, e.g., patrilocal residence in cases where the bride's family is very poor, so that the matrisibs, though exogamous, are not localized, and a number are represented in each village. Kinship terms are classificatory, and reflect differences in relative age on both Ego's and the first ascending generation. Cousin terminology conforms to the Crow pattern widely characteristic of matrilineal societies.

The foregoing editorial summary in English will suffice to introduce the text, presented, as it was written and delivered, in French. (Ed.)

LA TRIBU, LE VILLAGE, LA "MAISON-GRENIER"

Les zones montagneuses de l'Asie du Sud-Est continental—ou péninsule indochinoise—ont servi de refuges à des populations au mode de vie archaïque que les peuples évolués des régions basses désignent sous les vocables péjoratifs de Moï, Kha, ou Pnong (mots viêtnamien, thai, et cambodgien signifiant "sauvage" ou "esclave"), dénominations sous lesquelles ces populations sont connues dans la littérature qui leur est consacrée. Outre que ces termes de caractère injurieux sont rejetés par les intéressés, ils ne peuvent avoir que des utilisations locales, d'ailleurs imprécises (les Jörai, par exemple, dont l'aire tribale chevauche sur deux pays, seront appelés Moï au Viêt-Nam et Kha au Laos; par contre, le mot Kha pourra servir au Laos ou en Thaïlande à désigner non seulement des tribus

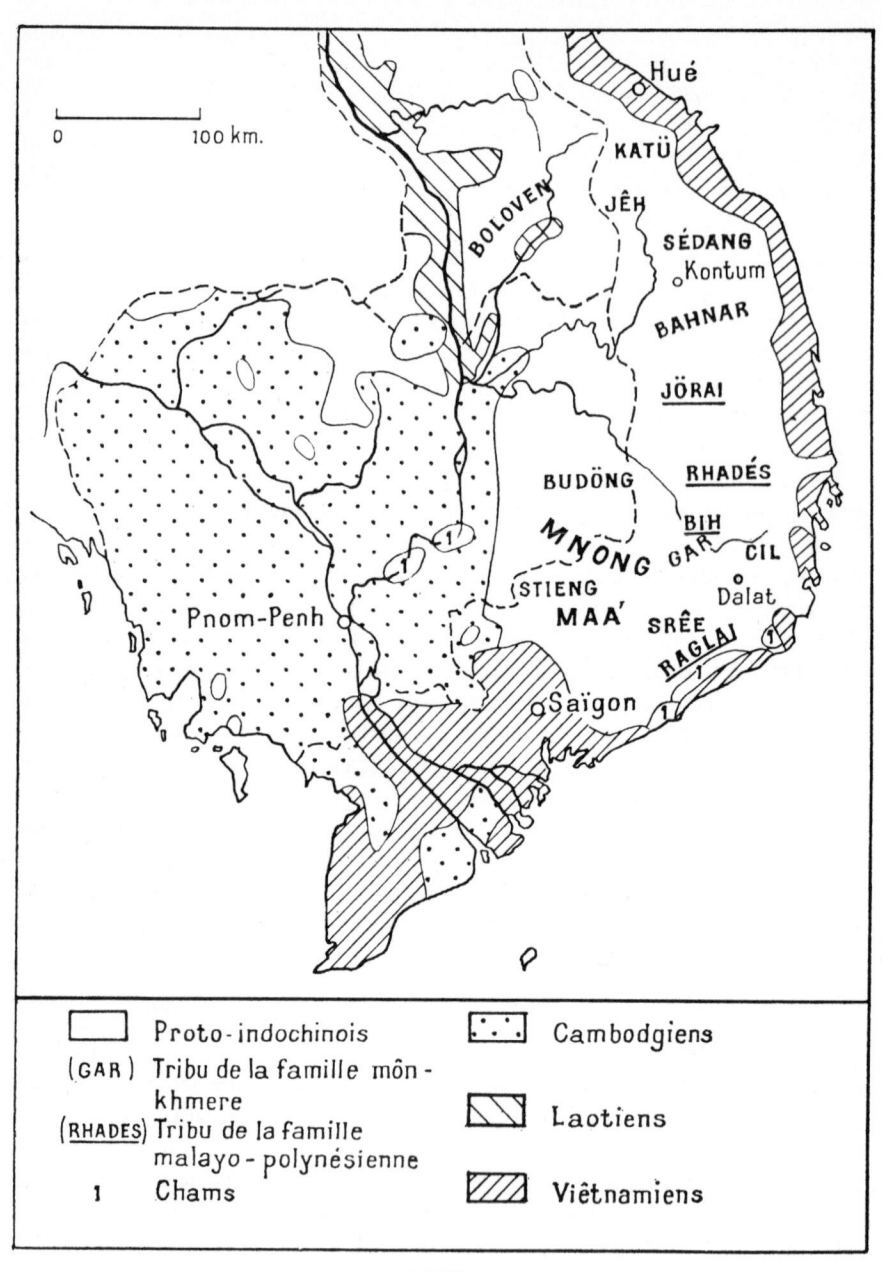

MAP 1
PEUPLES ET LANGUES DE L'INDOCHINE

de parler môn-khmer, mais aussi des peuplades parlant un dialecte thai et dont le niveau de vie est moins évolué que celui des Laotiens ou des Siamois). Aussi nous a-t-il paru, à M. A. G. Haudricourt et à moi-même, plus utile de forger un terme général, Proto-Indochinois, qui pût inclure sous une seule dénomination l'ensemble des tribus disséminées à travers la péninsule indochinoise—de la Birmanie au Viêt-Nam—dont elles représentent le stock humain culturellement les plus archaïque.[1]

C'est dans le vaste pays montagneux et couvert de jungles du Viêt-Nam central et méridional que les Proto-Indochinois présentent le plus grand nombre et la plus grande variété de tribus. La linguistique permet d'y distinguer en gros trois groupes principaux. Les tribus de parler malayo-polynésien (Rhadé, Jörai, etc) en s'insérent dans la masse des tribus de parler môn-khmer ont divisé celles-ci en deux blocs: celles du nord comprenant entre autres les Bahnars, Sédangs, et Jên et celles du sud dont font partie les Mnong, les Maa', etc. C'est à ce groupe méridional des tribus de parler môn-khmer que les Mnong Gar appartiennent; ils habitent au sud de la cuvette du lac Darlac, entre Ban-Mê-Thuot et Dalat, le pays montagneux que traverse d'est en ouest le cours moyen du Krong Knô, affluent de la Srêpok, elle-même affluent oriental du Mékong.

Ce sont, comme la plupart des Proto-Indochinois, des agriculteurs semi-nomades pratiquant la culture itinérant sur brûlis du riz de montagne. Leurs relations commerciales reposent sur le troc. Le vie religeuse—ils sont animistes—se trouve son point culminant dans le sacrifice du buffle.[2]

L'organisation social traditionnelle repose sur le village qui dispose d'un territoire de forêt dont il "mange" (*saa brii*) chaque année un pan différent pour y faire ses cultures. Chaque village est habité par des membres de clans différents. Mais si le clan joue un rôle capital pour la position de l'individu au sein de la tribu, le noyau de la vie villageoise reste la famille restreinte. Aucun mnong gar ne demeure fixé de longues années sur le même emplacement; q'une épidémie entraîne un grand nombre de décès, ou que le cycle itinérant des cultures éloigne par trop les champs et l'on reconstruit le village dans un endroit jugé favorable et pour lequel les génies ont donné leur accord. Le village mnong gar est constitué par de longues maisons (*root*)[3] divisées en autant de "maisons-greniers" (*hih nam*), logements d'un couple et de ses enfants. C'est en fait la *hih nam* qui constitue l'unité économique et rituelle de base de la société mnong gar. C'est elle, et non le clan, qui, en fait, possède les biens meubles et les lopins de terre; c'est elle qui met ceux-ci en valeur (ou les loue à d'autres *hih nam*) à l'intérieur du grand *miir* (du champ sur brûlis) où sont regroupés, pour des raisons de commodité et de sécurité, les lopins de toutes les *hih nam* du village. Chaque foyer possède ses plantes magiques (*gun*) et exécute individuellement les rites l'intéressant en propre notamment au cours des rites agraires d'aspect collectif (où en dehors d'une partie intéressant le village, en tant qu'entité, l'autre, la plus importante consiste dans le déroulement d'un même rite exécuté par chaque foyer l'un après l'autre).[4] Le groupement en longue-maison de plusieurs foyers n'est pas déterminé par les seuls liens de parenté, mais également par ceux de l'amitié, même si celle-ci n'a pas été couronnée par l'échange de sacrifice du buffle dit *tam boh;*[5] d'ailleurs à chaque reconstruction du village le regroupement des *bih nam* subit des changements.

Bien que se soit la famille de l'homme qui fasse la demande en mariage et qui, dans les échanges de dons que celui-ci occasionne, fournisse la part la plus importante semble-t-il, c'est cependant l'homme qui vient, en principe, habiter chez les parents de sa femme. Toutefois les parents du garçon peuvent obtenir l'accord de la famille de la fiancée—notamment si celle-ci est très pauvre—pour que le jeune couple s'établisse chez eux, mais ils devront pour cela offrir un sacrifice supplémentaire. A la mort de l'un des conjoints, les enfants vont, soit avec leur mère suivivante, soit dans la famille de celle-ci, si c'est la mère qui est morte. Quant aux biens, après défalcation des apports qui retournent aux familles d'où ils proviennent, les acquêts sont partagés pour moitié entre les enfants et la famille de la femme (ou la femme elle-même si c'est elle la survivante), d'une part, et "les soeurs et la mère" de l'homme, d'autre part.

Le village, et non la tribu, constituait l'espace socio-politique maximal. De la masse des habitants—c'est à cent cinquante individus au maximum—trois, parfois quatre, hommes, élus parmi les plus influents, émergent: ce sont les *croo weer töóm brii töóm bboon* ("les hommes sacrés dans la forêt et le village"). Leur rôle essentiel restant celui de guides, non seulement pour les rites agraires ou de reconstruction du village, mais pour les questions de propriété foncière. Cependant leur rôle essentiel semble être en apparence tout au moins, surtout rituel. C'est cette organisation archaïque qui survit sous la nouvelle structure administrative rigide née de la colonisation et qui a élargi considérablement l'horizon sociopolitique des Mnong Gar.

LE *MPÖOL* OU CLAN

Le *mpôol*[6] est constitué par l'ensemble des individus se réclamant d'un ancêtre commun en ligne maternelle, c'est à dire que le nom de clan se transmet de mère à enfants. Nous avons vu que le mari réside chez sa femme. Nous avons donc, selon la terminologie de Lévi-Strauss,[7] un système harmonique (de type matrilinéaire et matrilocal) puisque la filiation et le lieu de résidence sont déterminés par la même lignée (en l'occurence la lignée féminine).

Du clan paternel on ne retient comme parents que les très proches parents du père, alors que tous les membres du clan maternel, aussi éloignés fussent-ils du sujet, sont considérés comme ses parents. La principale conséquence en est que le mariage est absolument prohibé avec tout membre du clan maternel. Et la preuve de relations sexuelles entre deux membres du même clan (c'est à dire dont les mères respectives appartiennent au même *mpôol*) entraîne une mise en jugement pour inceste avec sacrifice expiatoire, amendes, et séparation des coupables.[8] Signalons cependant que la parenté du côté paternel crée un empêchement à mariage lorsqu'elle est établie en ligne directe, et pour des collatéraux, seulement pour deux individus dont les pères respectifs sont frères ou demi-frères entre eux. De même la fils du frère ne peut, en principe, épouser la fille de la soeur. Mais il y a mariage préferentiel lorsqu'il s'agit de cousins croisés matrilatéraux. On pour suivre l'énoncé plus restrictif de la théorie mnong gar "suivre la fille du frère cadet de la mère" (*têng koon kôony*) mais en fait ce mariage préférentiel du fils de la soeur cadette avec la fille du frère aîné. Le *kôony* (le frère cadet de la mère) en effet constitue le véritable "élément de parenté"[9] celui qui représente l'élément à la fois exceptionnel et dynamique du système (cf. Fig. 1).

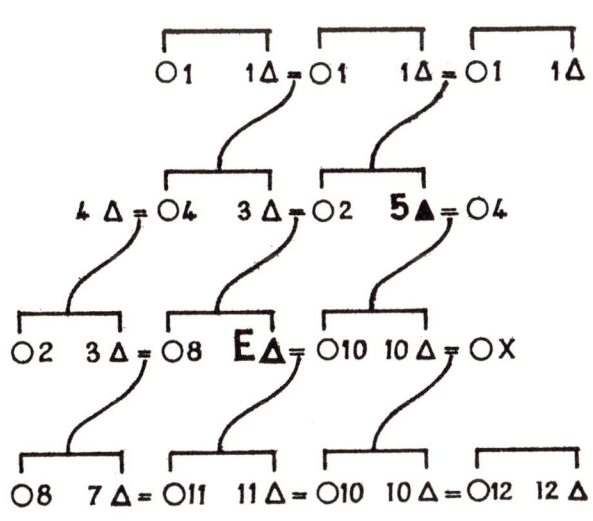

FIGURE 1
Système de Parenté Mnong Gar

LA NOMENCLATURE DE PARENTÉ

La nomenclature de parenté mnong gar est d'une remarquable économie.[10] Elle n'utilise que quatorze termes élémentaires auxquels il faut ajouter deux terms attributs: *êet* ("petit") et *pii* (servant de déterminant aux alliés du type *tam köih*), dont l'un (*êet*) est d'ailleurs facultatif et très rarement employé. Il existe un troisième terme attribut dont on peut se demander s'il n'est pas qu'un simple doublet eurythmique: *see* dans l'expression *soo see* plus élégante que *soo*, "les petits-enfants."

Cette nomenclature est classificatoire par générations. Celle des grands-parents ne comprend qu'un terme: *yoo*. De même celle des petits-enfants: *soo* (ou, pour faire élégant, *soo see*).

Pour la génération d'Ego et celle de ses père et mère, l'âge relatif (par rapport à Ego dans sa génération, par rapport à son père ou à sa mère dans la leur) et le sexe relatif interviennent comme éléments déterminants. C'est aisi que pour la génération des père et mère on a *mei* (mère) et *baap* (père), auxquels s'ajoute l'attribut facultatif *êet* ("petit") pour spécifier qu'il s'agit de "mère" ou de "père" classificatoires; *waa*, frères et soeurs aînés de la mère et du père (et aussi, non seulement leurs conjoints, et la femme du *kôony*, mais les conjoints des aînés d'Ego); *kôony*, frère cadet de la mère. Dans le génération d'Ego, on a *mii*, frères et soeurs aînés; *oh*, frères et soeurs cadets; *rôh*, soeur (homme parlant); *tlau*, frère (femme parlant); enfin *uur* (femme) et *sae* (mari).

Dans la génération des enfants d'Ego on a un terme général: *koon*, enfant, avec, comme réciproque à *kôony*, le terme *moon* qui désigne les neveux et nièces utérins d'un homme, ou plus spécialement les enfants de la soeur aînée d'un homme. Mais du fait de la situation particulière du frère cadet de la mère et de son corrélatif, la soeur aînée du père, les enfants de ces deux individus subissent un décalage de génération qui se répercute sur l'ensemble du système. On a donc affaire, selon la typologie adoptée par Murdock et reposant sur la terminologie des cousins-croisés, à un système Crow,[11] mais un système Crow "orienté," si je puis dire, puisque la dichotomie entre aînés et cadets constitue l'une des bases mêmes du système mnong gar.

LES ALLIÉS (*OH WAA*)

Cette dichotomie entre aînés et cadets se répercute sur le plan des alliés. Alors que les rapports d'un individu avec les cadets de son conjoint sont libres, ceux qu'il entretient avec les aînés de son conjoint (comprenant outre les parents de sa génération, ceux des générations supérieures) sont limités par une serie d'interdits dont la sanction mystique est le *nôot* qui se traduit par un grave amaigrissement. Sur le plan de la nomenclature ces rapports se traduisent par l'adjonction du terme attribut *pii* à un terme élémentaire, par exemple, *waa pii*. On dit qu'on est avec cette catégorie d'alliés en rapport de *tam köih* alors qu'avec les autres alliés et avec les parents on se trouve en rapport de *tam khual* ou de *khual lam* ("appellation simple, normale").

Cette distinction entre alliés joue un rôle capital dans la vie mnong gar. Les alliés avec lesquels on est en rapport de *tam khual* sont assimilés à des parents, et mieux à des cadets de votre génération ou des générations inférieures, avec lesquels on peut non seulement plaisanter mais chahuter et qu'on appelle par leur prénom. Or, on ne peut même pas appeler par son prénom un personne que l'on *tam köih*, mais par la formule "mari (ou femme) de X" ou, si elle a déjà un enfant, "père (ou mère) de X." De plus, on ne peut même pas employer, en parlant d'elle le pronom personnel singulier masculin, *kan* ("il"), ou féminin, *dee* ("elle"), mais seulement le pluriel, *nae* ("ils, elles, eux"). Ce pronom personnel pluriel[12] n'a pas d'autre utilisation au singulier (sinon on n'aurait pu le considérer comme un terme de respect); à propos d'un parent très âgé on emploiera comme pour les autres *kan* ou *dee* selon son sexe. Peut-on y voir un signe comme quoi les *tam köih* sont considérés comme membres d'un group, plutôt que comme individus.

En contrepartie de cette réserve que l'on doit observer vis à vis des gens qu'on *tam köih* ce sont ces derniers qui fournissent la base même de la plus grosse plaisanterie—en même temps que la plus populaire—que connaissent les Mnong gar. Elle consiste simplement à attribuer à un individu comme flirt ou conjoint un aîné de celui-ci, c'est à dire un personne que cet individu *tam köih;* bien qu'il s'agisse là d'une plaisanterie archi-usée celui qui en est l'objet ne sait que répondre "Tu mens! tu mens!" alors que toute l'assistance éclate de rire.[13]

Par contre, la plus grande liberté règne vis à vis des cadets du conjoint. C'est parmi les "soeurs cadettes" de sa femme qu'en général—lorsqu'il est assez riche— un home prend sa seconde èpouse. Bien mieux la règle du remplacement du conjoint décédé *tam trok* permet au veuf (ou à la veuve) de demander au clan de son conjoint dèfunt de lui donner comme remplaçant un cadet de celui-ci (le fils de la soeur ou le frère cadet si le defunt est le mari, la fille de la soeur ou la soeur cadette si c'est la femme qui est morte). Cette coutume rappelle celle qui existe chez les Rhadés[14] où elle est appliquée avec une rigueur inconnue chez les Mnong gar, car elle permet de prolonger indéfiniment ce lien solide entre deux clans que représente le mariage dans la grande tribu malayo-polynésienne.

LISTE DES TERMES DE PARENTE

1 *yoo:* grands-pères et grands-mères maternels et paternels; les frères et soeurs de ces grands-parents; les ascendants des grand-parents; les ancêtres maternels; les enfants de la soeur aîné du grand-père maternel ou paternel (soit des individus de la génération, non pas des grands-parents, mais des mère et père d'Ego et dont la position fait en quelque sorte écho à celle qu'occupe un homologue les enfants du frère cadet de la mère).

yoo pii: les *yoo*, *mei* et *baap* (précis ou classificatoires) du conjoint.

2 *mei:* mère, à la fois terme précis et classificatoire, mais pour le terme classificatoire on pourra obtenir la spécification suivante:

mei êet: soeurs cadettes de la mère et du père (mais principalement toutes les femmes membres du clan maternel, plus jeunes que la mère); fille de la soeur aînée du père (soit la *moon* du père, c'est à dire la femme dont celui-ci est le *kôony* et qui est de la même génération qu'Ego); chez les alliés: les femmes de *baap êet* (frère cadet du père et fils de la soeur aînée du père). *Nota:* Le mot *êet* veut dire "petit." Il n'est employé dans la nomenclature de parenté q'avec *mei* et *baap*, et il est presque toujours sous-entendu. Je n'ai jamais entendu un individu s'addresser à sa *mei êet* par cette dénomination, mais simplement par *mei*. De même pour situer la position d'une femme vis à vis de lui-même, un ou une mnong dira toujours "*geh mei*" ("il y a mère"); ce n'est qu'en insistant beaucoup en lui demandant s'il est "sorti" de son ventre qu'il precisera par *mei êet*. Car quant un individu dit d'une femme "*mei any tööm*" ("c'est ma propre mère"), la femme dont il s'agit peut être sa mère tell que nous l'entendons en français, mais aussi la soeur de sa mère, ou ce que nous appellerions une cousine de celle-ci.

3 *baap:* père. Come pour *mei*—et la remarque sur *êet* s'entend ici—lorsqu'il est classificatoire *baap* peut lorsqu'on insiste devenir:

baap êet: frère cadet du père; fils de la soeur aînée du père (le *moon* du père, donc de la génération d'Ego et quel que soit son âge relatif à celui d'Ego); chez les alliés, *baap* (*êet*) désigne également les maris des *mei êet* (soeur cadette de la mère, soeur cadette du père, fille de la soeur aînée du père).

4 *waa:* frères et soeurs aînés de la mère et du père, et plus particulièrement tous les membres du clan maternel de la génération de la mère et plus âgés qu'elle; chez les alliés: le conjoint du père remarié ou de la mère remariée, les conjoints des *waa*, la femme du *kôony*, et les conjoints des *mii*.

waa pii: les *waa* et les *mii* du conjoint.

5 *kôony:* frère cadet de la mère; tout homme du clan et de la génération de la mère et plus jeune qu'elle; le fils du *kôony* à la mort de celui-ci.

kôony pii: le *kôony* du conjoint.

6 *mii:* frère et soeur aînés; tous les individus plus âgés qu'Ego de sa génération et de son clan; les enfants, plus âgés qu'Ego, des frères de son père et de la soeur cadette de son père; les petits-enfants plus âgés qu'Ego de la soeur aînée du père (donc d'une génération audessous de la sienne). En bref, les enfants plus âgés que le sujet de ses *mei, baap,* et *waa* (sauf la soeur aînée de son père).

7 *oh:* frère et soeur cadets; les enfants plus juenes qu'Ego de ses *mei, baap,* et *waa* (sauf la soeur aînée de son père). Cas inverses des *mii* au point de vue de l'âge relatif à celui du sujet.

8 *rôh:* soeur cadette ou aînée (homme parlant); *oh* ou *mii* féminin, Ego étant un homme.

9 *tlau:* frère cadet ou aîné (femme parlant); *oh* ou *mii* masculin, Ego étant une femme. Cf. 13 *uur*.

10 *koon:* enfants (fils ou filles); enfants des *oh* et des *mii* (exception: les *moon*); les arrières-petits-enfants de la soeur aînée du père (appartenant biologiquement à la génération des petits-enfants d'Ego); les enfants du frère cadet de la mère. Du vivant du *kôony*, on appelle le fils de celui-ci *koon*, mais à la mort du *kôony* le fils du *kôony* est lui-même appelé *kôony*.

koon kôony: la cousine croisée matrilatérale (homme parlant), vis à vis de qui tout homme est en situation de mariage préférentiel possible (*têng koon kôony:* suivre l'enfant du frère cadet de la mère). L'expression a été étendue à la fille du frère aîné de la mère. *Têng koon kôony* est employé d'une manière impropre quand le sujet est une femme; *koon kôony* désigne alors le fils de la soeur aîné du père, et par extension le fils de soeur cadette du père. Quand on veut expliquer la situation exacte par rapport aux fils de la soeur cadette du père, on dira qu'il s'agit des *koon kôony*.

koon pii: conjoints des *koon*. Le sujet est en relation de *tam köih* avec eux.

11 *moon:* enfants de la soeur aînée (homme parlant). C'est le terme réciproque de *kôony*; ses *moon* appellent un homme *kôony*. Cependent *moon* est souvent étendu aux enfants de la soeur cadette, mais toujours pour un sujet masculin. En relation d'alliance la *waa*, femme du *kôony*, appelle également *moon* les *moon* de son mari.

moon pii: conjoints des *moon* (en relation de *tam köih*).

12 *soo:* petits-enfants et au-delà; les petits-enfants des *oh* et des *mii* (cela sous-entend les décalages de génération dans les lignées du frère cadet de la mère et de la soeur *aînée* du père). *Soo* (ou *soo see*) désigne la descendance, proche ou loin-

taine, d'un individu; c'est l'opposé de *yoo*. Les *soo* de deux frères, bien qu'appelant *yoo* les grands-pères des uns et des autres, peuvent s'épouser; le lien de parenté est éteint entre eux.

soo pii: conjoints des *soo* (relation d'alliance comportant *tam köih*).

13 *uur:* femme, épouse. Mais ce mot signifie également "femme" au sens large, c'est à dire qu'il est l'opposé d'"homme" (dans le sens du latin *vir*). Soulignons que "homme" dans cette acception se dit *tlau* et que ce mot signifie également "frère" (d'une femme). Les deux mots servant à différencier les sexes expriment donc que ce frère est l'homme par excellence et que c'est l'épouse qui est la femme par excellence.

14 *sae:* mari. Se marier ("échanger des maris"): *tam sae*.

APPENDICE

En suivant le *World Ethnographic Sample* de Murdock (1957), on obtiendra pour la société mnong gar:

Colonne 1: Cl.

Colonne 2: Da. La division du travail entre les sexes n'intervient qu'à certaines époques du cycle agricole (lors du défrichement où les hommes assurent les gros travaux, mais surtout lors des semailles).

Colonne 3: Ib.

Colonne 4: Ib.

Colonne 5: Ia. La chasse est travail d'homme et la cueillette surtout une tâche féminine. Mais c'est principalement dans les techniques artisanales (non représentées dans l'échantillonage de Murdock) que la division du travail entre les sexes est nettement affirmée.

Colonne 6: Vo. Rappelons que le village mnong gar n'est par fixé au sol comme le village viêtnamien ou européen, mais change d'emplacement au moins deux fois par décade. C'est la raison pour laquelle j'ai souvent qualifié ce groupe de "semi-nomades."

Colonne 7: In. En fait on est passé de E à I; on peut supposer que chaque longue-maison était autrefois occupée par les familles restreintes de soeurs de clan.

Colonne 8: Mm.

Colonne 9: Tg.

Colonne 10: Of.

Colonne 11: Ss.

Colonne 12: Mm.

Colonne 13: Cn. Il faut rappeler cependant que ce n'est qu'en insistant beaucoup que l'on obtiendra *baap êet* ("petit père"), la frère du père étant toujours *baap*.

Colonne 14: Wi. Bien que le fils d'une esclave devienne esclave, celui-ci a toujours la possibilité de se racheter par son travail. Un esclave n'a pas dans la société mnong le statut d'un esclave d'une société techniquement plus évoluée; il est "adopté" (*roong*) et fait d'ailleurs souvent partie du clan de ses maitres (on cherche toujours à racheter les membres du clan en esclavage chez des "étrangers" pour grossir la main d'oeuvre de la "maison-grenier").

Colonne 15: Oo.

CHAPTER 3

THE SAGADA IGOROTS OF NORTHERN LUZON

FRED EGGAN
University of Chicago

In his pioneer study of Philippine society, Kroeber reviewed the scanty data then available for pagan, Christian, and Moro (Moslem) groups and came to the conclusion that the Bontok, Ifugao, and adjacent tribes in the Mountain Province of northern Luzon "represent the original type of political society that once prevailed over all the Philippines."[1] With regard to the terminological systems, he believed that "the pagan Igorot systems are perhaps somewhat nearest to the original scheme," and that "the extremely simple systems, as represented by Ifugao, may be partly the result of a progressive and extreme process of reduction."[2] The divergences of the Christian and Moro groups he ascribes to European and Moslem influences. These conclusions are currently being tested against the data from recent field studies on Christian and Moslem communities carried out under the auspices of the Philippine Studies Program at the University of Chicago.[3]

The Philippines, along with other regions of Oceania, also offers an opportunity to study bilateral social organization in a variety of forms. We tend to take bilateral systems for granted, as if they were somehow "natural" and did not need explanation. Nevertheless they face the same problems that unilineal systems do, and must solve them if the society is to persist. Indeed, Radcliffe-Brown (1935, pp. 301–302), after formulating the essential conditions for the existence of a society in terms of "the need for a formulation of rights over persons and things sufficiently precise in their general recognition as to avoid as far as possible unresolved conflicts" and "the need for continuity of the social structure as a system of relations between persons," finds unilineal institutions in some form as almost a necessity in any ordered social system, and poses the question of how to explain societies in which persons acquire similar and equal rights through both parents. As suggested in an earlier survey (Eggan, 1941), the bilaterally organized peoples of the Mountain Province illustrate a number of solutions to these and other problems at a relatively elementary level.

The present paper[4] is concerned primarily with the social structure of the Sagada Igorots. As such it forms part of a forthcoming study of the social and ceremonial organization of Sagada,[5] as well as the basis for a comparative study of Mountain Province social systems, which it is hoped will throw further light on the nature and development of Philippine society.

Sagada has a central location in the Mountain Province, both geographically and culturally. It is situated about 5,000 feet above sea level on the eastern shoulder of the Cordillera Central in western Bontoc subprovince (see Map 2), where a dozen communities making up the municipality occupy a series of partly eroded limestone basins drained by the headwaters of a tributary of the Chico River. The municipality has a total population of around 10,000 Igorots, of whom some 3,000 reside in Sagada proper.

The Mountain Province, according to the Keesings (1934), contains some ten major ethnic groups with a total population today of around 250,000 and an average density of about 50 persons per square mile. In broad perspective this province might be considered a culture area, but there are important differences in agriculture, settlement patterns, and social institutions which cut across geographical lines and dialect groupings. The basic cultural unit is the village, or group of related villages, and an individual will identify himself as from such-and-such a village. As one goes from one local group to another, changes occur in both dialect and custom without any sharp linguistic breaks. The larger ethno-linguistic units recognized by the ethnologist are useful for descriptive and administrative purposes but have little basis in native society. The differences in social institutions and cultural practices have generally been explained in terms of separate migrations, but I have argued elsewhere (Eggan, 1941 and 1954) that much of the differentiation in the Mountain Province has taken place locally as the result of adjustments to new ecological conditions and increased population.

The Sagada people represent the northernmost extension of the Northern Kankanay Igorots, who occupied the former province of Lepanto to the west and south of Bontok. To the northwest, in Abra, are the Tinguian; to the northeast are the Bontok villages; to the southeast, over a mountain range, are the Ifugao; to the south, in Benguet, are the Southern Kankanay and the Nabaloy; to the far north are the Kalinga and Apayao; and along the coastal plain to the west are the Christian Ilocano, who have gradually expanded around the Mountain Province and infiltrated its larger communities.

The Sagada Igorots today subsist on irrigated rice grown in stone-walled terraces, supplemented by sweet potatoes and other root crops grown on hillside farms and in village gardens. They raise chickens, pigs, dogs, and carabao, which provide sacrifices for ceremonial occasions. There is clear evidence (cf. Scott, 1957) that their ancestors practiced shifting cultivation and depended primarily on taro and other root crops, to which sweet potatoes (*camotes*) were added during the early Spanish period.

Sagada itself was probably founded some two centuries ago. In the process of interaction with the Bontok villages to the north and east, the Sagadans borrowed and adapted much of central Bontok culture, including the growing of terraced and irrigated rice, portions of the Bontok social system, and a good deal of cere-

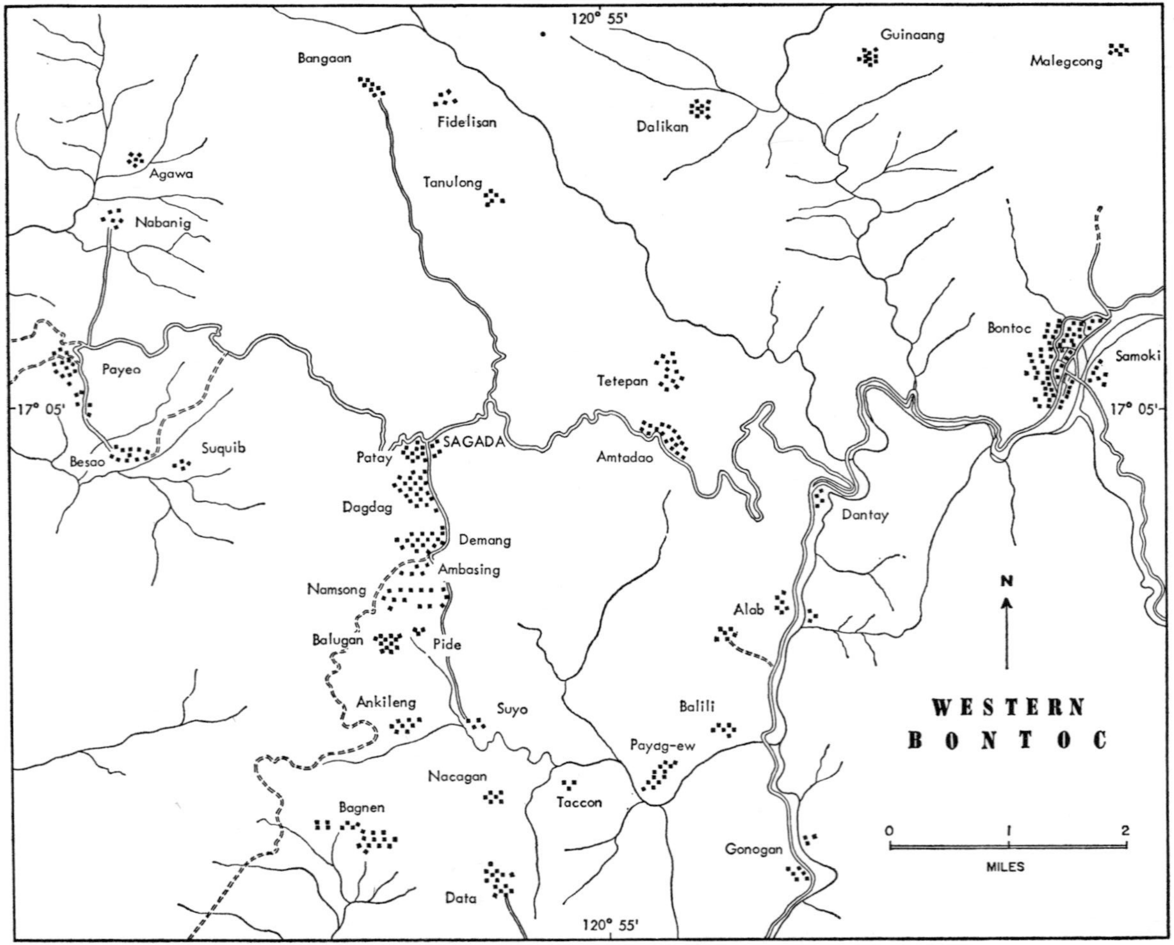
120° 55'
Guinaang
Malegcong
Bangaan
Fidelisan
Dalikan
Agawa
Tanulong
Nabanig
Bontoc
Samoki
Payeo
Tetepan
17° 05'
17° 05'
Besao
Suquib
Patay
SAGADA
Amtadao
Dagdag
Dantay
Demang
Ambasing
Namsong
N
Alab
Balugan
Pide
Ankileng
Suyo
Balili
WESTERN
BONTOC
Payag-ew
Nacagan
Taccon
Bagnen
0
1
2
MILES
Gonogan
Data
120° 55'

MAP 2

monialism and mythology. Much borrowing is apparent in the social and ceremonial calendar which controls the agricultural and ritual activities, one of the interesting features of life in the Bontok-Lepanto region. Sagada also early established trading relations with the Ilocos coastal settlements, and was one of the first communities east of the Cordillera Central to come under the jurisdiction of the Spanish military government in the nineteenth century. "By the end of the century," notes Scott (1957), "Spanish visitors called Sagada the most prosperous settlement in the vicinity, and missionaries arrived in the belief that it was the most promising spot for the introduction of western Christian culture."

Contacts were intensified after the Spanish-American War with the establishment of American government, the Episcopal Church mission, and schools. Despite strong acculturation, however, the pagan portion of the population has managed to maintain a considerable amount of their old culture, including most of the ceremonial cycle. The annual round of community activities—including the agricultural cycle and its rituals, marriage celebrations, and the *begnas* ceremony, the old headhunting ritual transformed for community welfare—is still carried out in unison, directed by the "old men" of the village.

Early writers have given us excellent accounts of Bontok and neighboring communities, although Jenks (1905) overemphasized the significance of the ward and thought of the village as a mere assemblage of politically independent units. Keesing (1949, p. 583) has corrected this view and has called attention to "the vital ties of kinship which criss-cross *ato* groupings, common ceremonial activities, ideological links, and needs of public safety, which bind the village together into a larger whole." Our own researches in Sagada have confirmed Keesing's conclusions and, we hope, have extended and deepened them.

TERRITORIAL DIVISIONS

Sagada proper is composed of two geographical divisions, Dagdag and Demang, which are separated by the streams used jointly for the irrigation of their rice fields. Each division has its own sacred grove (*patpatayan*) with its guardian spirits (*pinading*), and each has its own sacred spring. It is probable that at one time they considered themselves as separate villages, for the inhabitants generally refer to themselves as belonging to one or the other, but for a considerable time they have been integrated into a single community.

In certain respects these geographical units act as "dual divisions," though they do not control marriage in any important way. They are ceremonial rivals to an extent, alternating in the performance of certain rituals for village welfare; and the two sides are opponents in the annual "rock fight" of the boys of the village. More important, there is recent evidence that they formerly buried each other's dead, the people of Dagdag bringing their dead to Demang, whose residents carried the coffins to the southern burial caves, and *vice versa*.

Each of these major divisions is further divided into a series of wards (*dap-ay*), which correspond to the *ato* of the Bontok region. Sagada has twelve such wards, five in Dagdag and seven in Demang. For the pagan portion of the village they average 27 households each, with a range of 15 to 60.[6] Each ward is a geographical unit and possesses a paved ceremonial platform (or platforms) with an attached men's sleeping hut (*abong*). Formerly each also had one or more girls' sleeping dormitories (*ebgan*)—or widows' houses—used for courtship purposes.

The households comprising a ward form a social unit (*obon*), which cooperates for certain purposes but is not a kinship unit. Keesing (1949, p. 587) believes the Bontok ward in earlier times was based on patrilocal residence, in keeping with the conception of the ward as a headhunting and revenge unit, and some informants have suggested a similar pattern for Sagada. But today there are no fixed rules of residence in Sagada; one or the other set of parents usually give their house to the new couple and themselves move into a vacant one. Statistically there is a greater tendency to matrilocality in the postwar period, though informants do not phrase such a rule.

The ward is a political and ceremonial unit. Its older male members make up an informal council (*amam-a*), which settles disputes within its jurisdiction and organizes and carries out the rituals and ceremonies essential for ward and village welfare. Several generations ago, in the days of active raiding and head-taking, the ward was apparently also a unit in guarding and protection, and possibly in revenge. Today these activities are no longer needed, and there has been a corresponding shift in organization and function. Membership is more easily transferred from one ward to another, though genealogies show that this was also possible in the past. And the rituals once essential to head-taking have been remodeled into ceremonies for community welfare.

Wards are grouped today into *sa-il*, for purposes of group work on behalf of the village, or for the collection of financial contributions for the Red Cross and other projects.

The ward also provides a "school" in which boys are informally trained for participation in ward and village activities. Boys leave their households at an early age and sleep in the ward center with their agemates. Here they learn local history from their elders, go courting with other boys, and participate in communal and ceremonial activities as they grow older. Girls secure much of their training from their mothers and other female relatives in the home and fields, as well as through participation in *ebgan* activities.

The household is the smallest social unit that has a territorial base. Each dwelling is occupied by an elementary family, plus perhaps a widowed parent or other relative; these latter and the children over six or seven take their meals with the family but normally spend their evenings in the *dap-ay* or *ebgan*. The pagan population reveals no instances of multi-family households, and the average size of the household group in Sagada in 1952 was 4.4 persons. The house itself is a wooden box-like structure on posts, with a high thatched roof and an enclosed area underneath. Here the cooking and other household activities are carried out, and here the husband, wife, and small children sleep in front of the fire. The second story is called a "granary" and is used primarily for storage purposes. Surrounding each house is a rectangular field devoted to sweet potatoes, and close by is one or more pens in which pigs are housed and fed.

DESCENT GROUPS

In addition to the territorial divisions which divide Sagada into discrete groups, there is a series of bilateral descent groups,[7] which have certain corporate features and act to a degree like unilateral descent groups, and also a series of personal kindreds or "kinship circles" which surround each individual and comprise the kinship system. Beyer, in a joint account with Barton,[8] early noted the presence of bilateral descent groups in northern Luzon, but he did not elaborate further, and his use of the term "clan" for such groups has led later students to neglect his observations. Barton, in his writings on the Ifugao (1919, 1930, 1938, 1946) and Kalinga (1949), emphasized the kinship groupings surrounding each individual, though in his manuscript on Sagada (1940) he mentioned the "main families." Kirchhoff, in an article written about 1935 but only recently published (1955), correctly characterized what he called Igorot "conical clans" but devoted most of his effort to putting them in evolutionary perspective. Lambrecht (1953 and 1954) has presented genealogical evidence for bilateral descent groups among both the Mayawyaw and the Kiangan and has indicated something of their significance in Ifugao life.

In Sagada, the bilateral descent groups are composed of all the descendants of certain prominent ancestors, founding fathers, and important living individuals, regardless of the line of descent. In theory anybody can be the head of such a descent group, but in practice there is a selection in terms of actual or potential benefits to be derived. In Sagada there are some six major "families" or descent groups, plus a number of lesser ones within each. Genealogies collected for several major families show that they range back some eight to ten generations in time. The founders are early migrants, founders of wards, or famous individuals.

These bilateral descent groups are roughly comparable to maximal, major, and minor lineages in unilaterally organized societies. They are usually named after the founder or ancestor, who is always male, e.g., *ap-on Ganga*, "the descendants of Ganga." (An enlarged group, the *men Ganga*, includes the spouses as well.) They do not regulate marriage directly, but they do conduct certain ceremonial activities. They have rights to cultivate certain hillsides first cleared and planted by a particular ancestor, and stands of pine trees are similarly owned and exploited by the direct descendants, who appoint a "warden" to regulate the gathering and use of wood. Moreover, today the major families make up the political factions and largely control elections.

It is significant that neither rice fields nor irrigation sources are associated with these bilateral descent groups. This suggests that they may have been more important in the earlier period of the shifting cultivation of root crops. With smaller populations and more dispersed settlements, the descent groups of a particular region would have exhibited less overlapping and a closer correlation with geographical units. It is perhaps significant in this connection that Beyer thinks the Ifugao "clans were once wholly exogamic,"[9] though he presents no evidence for this assertion. With the increase in population resulting from the adoption of irrigated rice cultivation, the bilateral descent groups presumably became less efficient as corporate groups, partly because of greater overlapping and the consequent difficulty of handling multiple rights and partly because of the differential investment involved in the construction and maintenance of the terrace system and the control of water. Though the bilateral descendants of any ancestral pair may constitute a discrete group with continuity over time, any individual is potentially a member of a large number of such groups. In recent Sagada society these descent groups seem to be marginal survivals, despite the fact that the political system introduced during the American period has given them a new lease on life.

PERSONAL KINDREDS

The personal kindred is the bilateral group of relatives which surrounds each individual or kinship group. It needs to be clearly distinguished from the descent group, for while Ego is the actual or potential founder of a descent group, as well as a member of several, his "kinship circle" embraces all the descendants of his great-great-grandparents or of even remoter ancestors. In Ifugao and Kalinga, the kinship circle that is formally recognized includes the descendants of the eight pairs of great-great-grandparents, and thus extends laterally to include all third cousins. These are the relatives responsible for revenge and wergild, and they also constitute the proper exogamic range. The boundaries of the personal kindred are not so sharply defined in Sagada, possibly because the cessation of war and headhunting has reduced the major obligations of the kindred. Marriages occur today outside the range of second cousins, but marriage between third cousins is common, and kinship ties may be recognized with even more remote collaterals. The extension of the kindred to third cousins possibly derives from the fact that Ego normally acquires much of his kinship knowledge from his grandparents, who in turn were taught by their grandparents.

Personal kindreds overlap to a much greater extent than do the descent groups, since every sibling group has a different kinship circle. These are called into action only in crises which affect particular individuals. In cases of conflict they can act effectively to the extent that the opposing individuals have separate kinship circles; where they overlap, the relatives concerned will have divided loyalties and will be concerned with compromise and arbitration. Marriage is one means of uniting two kinship groups, but is effective only if there are children. Once a child is born, he is equally related to both parental groups, and his welfare becomes theirs. If his parents belong to different descent groups, he likewise belongs to both, though he may choose to consider himself primarily a member of the "family" which offers the greatest advantage or prestige. Intervillage marriages extend the range of kinship to neighboring villages. Approximately 10 per cent of all marriages in certain genealogies are outside Sagada proper. While the percentage has increased in recent years, intermarriage with nearby villages is an old pattern.

CLASS SYSTEM

Though the range of wealth differences has not been great in the Sagada region, a division into "rich" (*kadangyan*) and "poor" (*kodo*) cuts across the village and region. A *kadangyan* is generally defined as one who can eat rice at every meal. However, he must validate his position by elaborate marriage celebrations at periodic intervals. Certain aspects of *kadangyan* status, moreover, depend upon belonging to certain descent groups whose ancestor-founders introduced particular burial practices or special obligations in connection with funeral sacrifices or other rituals. The individual must follow these whether he is actually rich or not. Poor Sagadans today complain about having to follow *kadangyan* customs, but these are nevertheless a source of pride.

KINSHIP TERMINOLOGY

The Sagada kinship system[10] is composed of a set of kinship terms, or rather of several related sets, and of a series of behavior patterns between relatives which concern rights and obligations in daily life or on special occasions. It relates primarily to the personal kindred and their relations after marriage, and thus constitutes a central feature of the social system.

We have not hitherto had any detailed account of kinship for any Mountain Province community, although Barton's Ifugao and Kalinga studies, Keesing's account of Bontok social organization, and the latter's unpublished survey of Lepanto society reveal the general principles. The Ifugao kinship system is generationally oriented and Hawaiian in type; it extends sibling terms to all cousins, as far as third cousin and even beyond, and also exhibits a wide extension of parent and child terms, though there are alternative terms in use for uncle and aunt. The Kalinga pattern is closer to our own, with lineal and collateral relatives separated in the parental generation, special terms for cousins, and modified child terms for nephews and nieces. The Sagada system partakes of both these patterns, so that its analysis helps to clarify problems regarding their variations.

The kinship system, as represented in the terminology, is bilateral in character, is organized on the basis of generation, and has a wide but indefinite range. In the referential terminology for consanguineal relatives the nuclear family is set off from collateral relatives, as is our own, and collateral relatives are not distinguished according to descent (see Fig. 2). There is a considerable variety of sibling terms. Cousins, both cross and parallel, are grouped together in a fashion

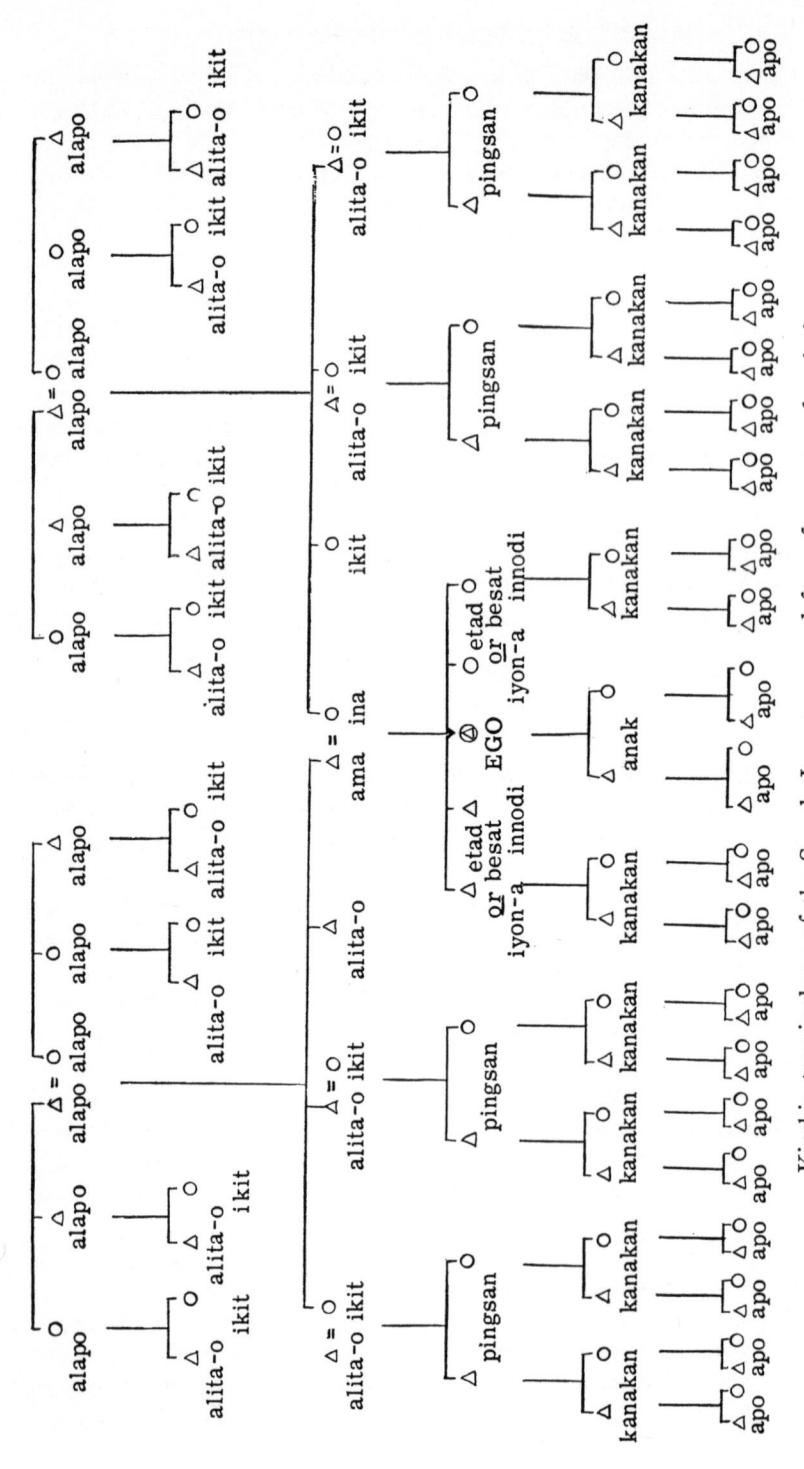

Kinship terminology of the Sagada Igorots as used for reference or description.
EGO = male or female.

FIGURE 2
SAGADA KINSHIP TERMINOLOGY: REFERENCE SYSTEM

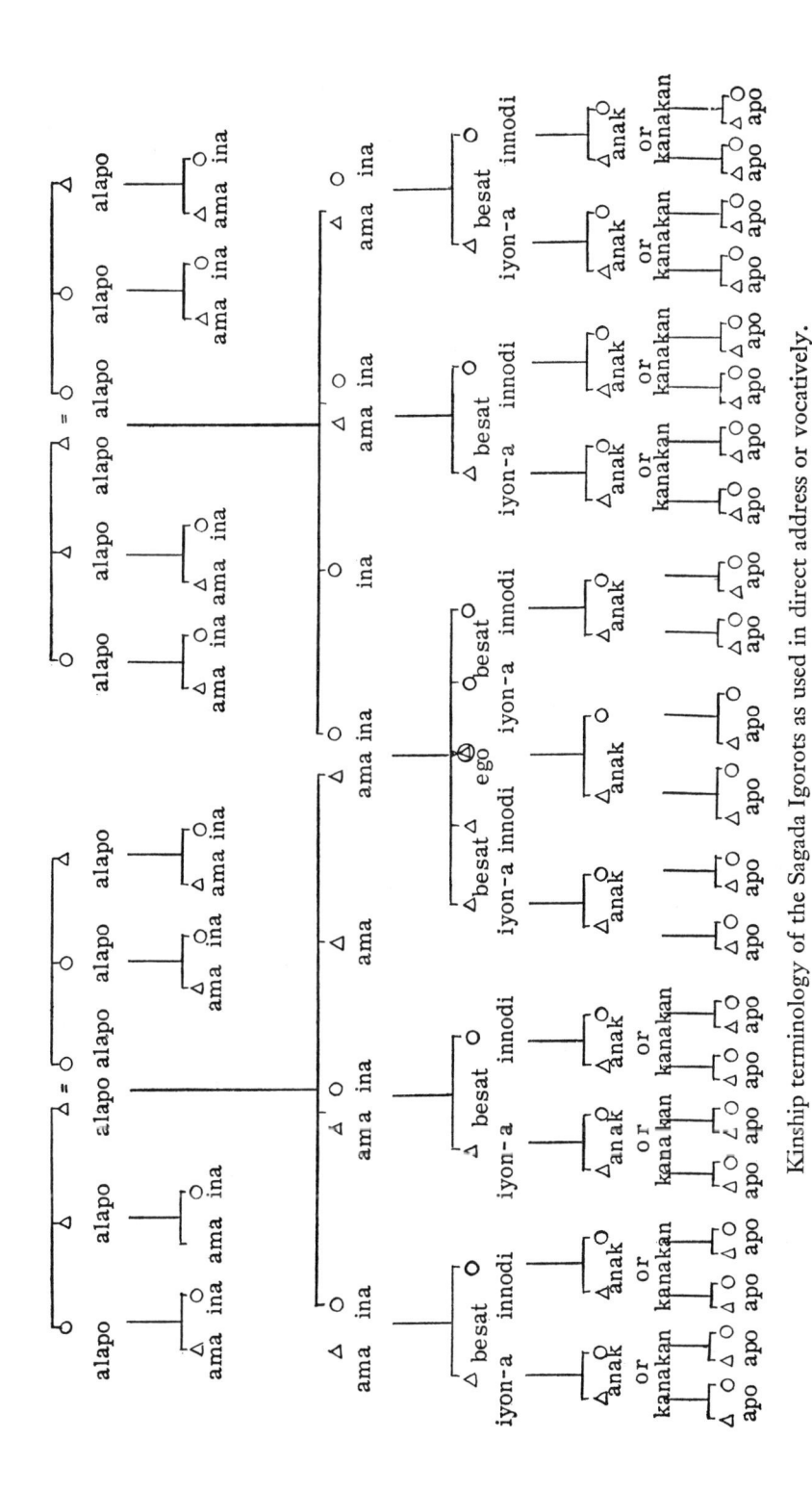

FIGURE 3
SAGADA KINSHIP TERMINOLOGY: VOCATIVE SYSTEM

Kinship terminology of the Sagada Igorots as used in direct address or vocatively.
EGO = male or female.

corresponding to the "Eskimo" types of Spier (1925) and Murdock (1949), though more distant cousins are distinguishable by numerical terms.

The vocative terminology is simpler in its organization and more flexible in its application (see Fig. 3). In address, parental terms are usually extended to parents' siblings and cousins, and certain sibling terms are extended widely to cousins, while nephews and nieces are addressed as "children." Affinal relatives may similarly be addressed by consanguineal terms, though there is a special set of affinal terms (see Fig. 4). Marriage creates important potential bonds between the personal kindreds of the spouses, and these are reflected in the terminology, particularly after children are born.

In the grandparental generation there is a single term for grandparent, *alapo*, which is widely extended to the siblings and cousins of grandparents on both sides. Sex is distinguished where necessary by adding *lalaki* ("male") or *baba-i* ("female"). For ascendants in general, *apo*, the general term for grandparent in the Mountain Province, is used; it is also a term of deference and respect for any old person.

In the parental generation father is *ama* and mother is *ina*. In reference these terms are commonly used with the personal article *si*, e.g., *si ama* ("my father"). The father's brother and mother's brother are classed together as uncle (*alita-o*), the mother's sister and father's sister are aunts (*ikit*), and these terms are extended to their cousins and to their spouses. In direct address all of these relatives may be called "father" or "mother." Such terms as *ka-ama-an* ("like a father") and *ka-ina-an* ("like a mother") may be used in reference where it is desired to indicate greater closeness of relationship than *alita-o* or *ikit* normally convey.

In Ego's own generation there is a variety of sibling terms with different extensions and shades of meaning. These have differing distributions in the Mountain Province, and comparative study will ultimately tell us something of their history. The most general term for sibling is *etad* (meaning "one-half"); it is said to refer to having the same umbilical cord and is restricted to actual siblings. An alternative term for sibling, and one more generally used, is *besat*, which is extended vocatively as far as third cousins. Another set of sibling terms in general use distinguish relative age but not sex: *ion-a* or *oni-a* for older sibling and *innodi* for younger sibling, both extended vocatively to older and younger cousins, respectively, and also to siblings-in-law, if they are congenial. It is also possible to distinguish sex, both of the relative and of the speaker: *kalallakiyan* is used by a woman in reference to a brother; *kababbiyan* by a man for his sister; and *kayong*, a word meaning "friend" in neighboring communities, by a man for his brother. The first two of these terms, built respectively on the word bases for "male" and "female," are used in song debates, and all three may be extended to strangers as a sign of friendship.

In contrast to the complexities of the sibling terminology, the terms for cousins are relatively simple. Cousins are thought of as descending in generations, the terms for them incorporating the numerals one to five. First cousins are referred

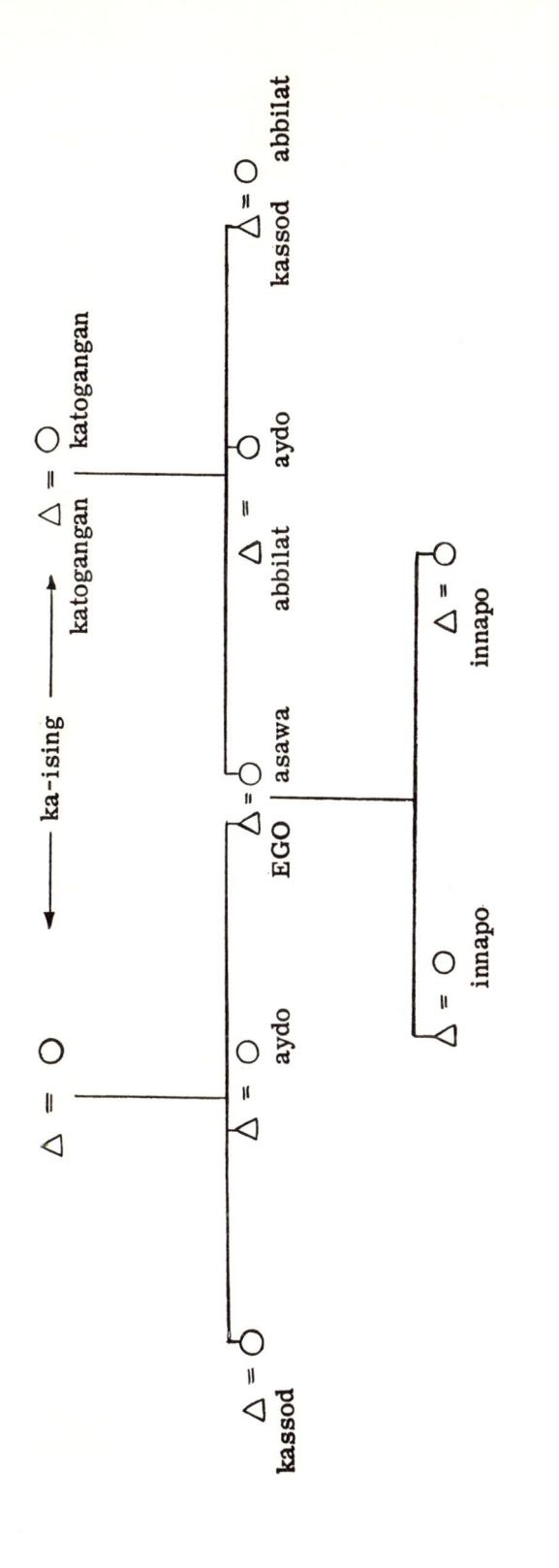

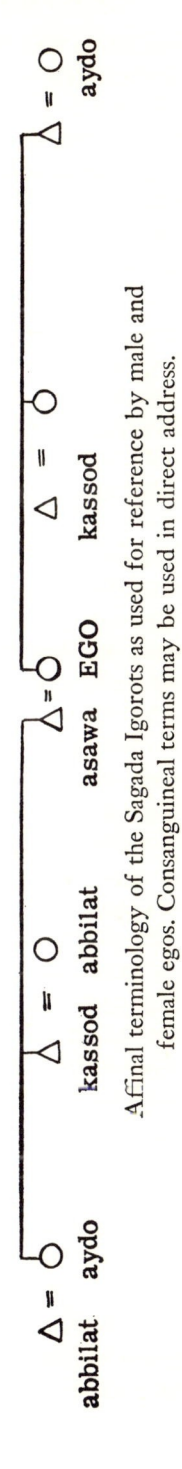

FIGURE 4
Sagada Kinship Terminology: Affinal System

A final terminology of the Sagada Igorots as used for reference by male and female egos. Consanguineal terms may be used in direct address.

to as *pingsan;* second cousins (the children of two *pingsan*) as *pidwa* or *kapidwa;* third cousins as *pitlo* or *kapitlo;* fourth cousins as *pip-at;* and fifth cousins as *kalima*. In practice, however, the cousin relationship seldom extends this far, though certain individuals who are genealogical experts control such data. Instead, the members of a bilateral descent group keep track of distant relationships through the name of the founder, e.g., *men Ganga* or *men Iya-ab*, much as clan relationships may be used in the absence of lineage ties in a unilateral society. The general term for "relative," *agi*, may also be used for cousins. Elsewhere in the Philippines this is a sibling term, and in Sagada it is used for a collectivity of siblings (*sin-agi*). As noted above, however, sibling terms are generally extended to cousins in direct address, and it is possible that the numerical differentiation may be due to recent contacts with Ilocanos and Europeans.

In the first descending generation the term for child, *anak*, is restricted in reference to one's own children, sex being distinguished when necessary by the proper qualifiers, but it is extended vocatively to brother's child and sister's child. The term *kanakan* ("like a child"), widespread in the Mountain Province, is more characteristically used in reference for nephews and nieces.

In the second descending generation the general term for grandchild, *apo*, is widely extended. In most Mountain Province groups this term is used for both grandparents and grandchildren, but there is some tendency to differentiate them by accent or by linguistic modifiers, as is the case in Sagada.

Affinal terminology, in general, utilizes a separate set of terms. There are terms for parent-in-law (*katogangan*); child-in-law (*inappo*); sister-in-law (*aydo*), either wife's sister or brother's wife; and brother-in-law (*kassod*), either wife's brother or sister's husband. In addition, a special term, *abbilat* ("co-sibling-in-law") is used by the spouses of two siblings, and *ka-ising* ("co-parent-in-law") is used by the parents of a married couple for one another. For all relatives by marriage, except the last two, consanguineal terms are frequently employed in direct address, particularly if the respective relatives are congenial.

In addition to these kinship terms, Sagada has a series of generalizing or group terms which reflect the importance of various sets or recurring combinations of relatives in daily life, e.g., *ag-i* ("relatives"), *ap-apo* ("ascendants"), *ap-on Cabayo* ("all the descendants in both lines of Cabayo"), and *sinpang apo* ("all the relatives"). The immediate family is called *sin ba-ey* ("those of one house"), which includes parents and children and possibly a widowed grandparent living in the house. The husband or wife is referred to as *sinpangabong* ("the one with whom I live"), referring to the *abong*, a type of house built on the ground. Important relationships are also grouped in pairs: *sin-agi*, two siblings; *sin-ag-i*, more than two siblings; *sin ama*, father and child; *sin ina*, mother and child; *sin alapo*, grandparent and grandchild; *sin gisan*, two agemates (derived from *gisan*, "born at the same time").

There are likewise terms denoting various stages of life, from infancy to old age, the oldest and the youngest of the sibling group, and sex differences. In addition, the head of the ward or *dap-ay*, who is usually the oldest man, is referred to as *am-ama* (derived from *ama*, "father"), and the old men who make up the ward council and act as priests are collectively known as *amam-a* ("the fathers").

BEHAVIOR PATTERNS

The behavior patterns expectable between relatives and manifest in special or crisis situations as well as in day-by-day conduct correspond rather closely to the terminological patterns sketched above. Together they make up the kinship system. Relatives are usually addressed by kin terms; to use personal names is considered rude, and even strangers are addressed by kin terms if there is a desire to be friendly. The bilateral descent groups and the personal kindreds on which an individual may call for assistance and protection, and to which he owes aid and support on all occasions, have already been noted. With the partial cessation of headhunting a few generations ago, under Spanish and later American occupation, one of the major activities involving the kindred was sharply modified, with resultant effects on the whole social system. The ward system, through taking over certain of the functions of kin groups, has affected their solidarity, particularly with respect to distant kin. The bilateral descent groups, in conjunction with a limited amount of intermarriage with neighboring villages, extended kinship ties rather widely and facilitated trade and intercommunity unity. Today the Sagada say: "We are envious of a man who can trace his relationships; he will never go hungry on a trip because he knows his relatives." In these respects Sagada and her neighbors differ from Ifugao, where kinship ties are more sharply defined and territorial factors and marriage relations are less significant, and from portions of Kalinga where village groups tend to be endogamous (Barton, 1938 and 1949).

In behavioral terms the grandparent-grandchild relationship is one of close affection and aid. Grandparents spend much of their time looking after their grandchildren while the parents work in the fields or elsewhere. They carry the children on their backs in a blanket sling—a symbol of security in myths. Grandparents often give their names to their grandchildren, and the latter are thought to inherit similar qualities of wisdom and strength, though there is no specific belief in reincarnation. Grandchildren in turn have an obligation to look after their grandparents when the latter are old. Within the relationship there is much mild joking and a sharing of meat and other tidbits on special occasions.

When a grandparent is ill, the grandchildren should come to participate in the rituals of curing, and at the death of the former the latter have special roles to play. However, a deceased grandparent may want his grandchild to come and live with him in the caves of the dead, and may offer him food in a dream and entice his soul. When small children die for this presumed reason, the parents may curse the grandparents or ancestors for taking them: *natoto-ok*, "they are crazy."

While the grandparent-grandchild terminology is widely extended, the basic relationship is with one's own grandparents, the degree of actual interaction depending upon residence and other factors. In general the relationship of grandparents and grandchildren is symmetrical, though Sagada has slightly modified the symmetrical terminology usual in the Mountain Province. The relations with higher generations—*apo* or *ap-o*—are an extension of the relations with grandparents; the dead "remind" the living of the obligation to provide them with offerings of food and drink or clothing through dreams or through causing illness by taking their souls. Dead ancestors have more power than living ones, and important ascendants apparently go through a process of semi-deification, becoming major or minor culture heroes and figuring in myths and prayers.

The parent-child relationship is a central one in Sagada society, the elementary family being set off in referential terminology and in the household unit, and a child being essential to the creation and permanence of the family. Children are greatly desired, but a high infant mortality rate, or low fertility, keeps the family relatively small. Parents seldom punish their children by whipping, and after the age of six or seven they usually discipline them only by scolding. Indeed, if a child gets sick after being scolded or otherwise punished, the first reaction of the parent is to promise that he will not punish or scold the child again.

Parents are primarily responsible for training children in economic tasks. Mothers take their small daughters to the *camote* fields, and boys help their father in getting wood, preparing fields, and caring for the carabao. Children are also usually responsible for gathering food for the pigs and chickens, which are kept in pens or cages near the house. A boy receives much of his education, however, from the old men in the *dap-ay*. Here he learns the traditional history of the village and the ward, the ceremonies and prayers, and the songs and legends that enliven the annual round of work and ceremony. Here too, in the past, the boys were disciplined by their peers under the watchful eyes of the old men and developed patterns of loyalty to the village and ward, as well as to their kin.

Children usually receive their portions of inherited property when they marry; the parents retain only a small amount of land to provide food for themselves. Children have an obligation to care for their parents and to provide animals for sacrifice if they fall ill, and further important obligations must be fulfilled when they die.

The use of teknonymy reflects the importance of children. After the birth of a child the parents are referred to as "father of so-and-so" and "mother of so-and-so." Sometimes children are similarly referred to as "child of so-and-so." These usages reinforce the strong tie which the society recognizes between parent and child, as do the special collective terms already noted for "father and child" and "mother and child."

The parental relationship is extended in certain contexts to uncles, aunts, and their spouses and to the old men of the *dap-ay* and the village elders who serve as "fathers" and guides. The older women, however, do not have the ritual position of the *amam-a*, "the old men."

Aunts and uncles are considered like second parents, but more sympathetic. If children are scolded, they may go to stay awhile with an uncle or aunt. They are freer in their behavior with aunts than with uncles but show no special preference for the maternal or paternal side. The Sagada practice neither the sororate or levirate nor sororal polygyny. Formerly, however, if the parents died, one of their siblings would adopt and care for the orphaned children and look after them as their own. Myths nevertheless indicate that orphans often had a difficult time and were frequently cheated or neglected.

Sibling relationships are varied, and in certain contexts are widely extended. An older sibling has the responsibility of looking after his or her younger siblings, and an older brother may take over parental responsibility for his younger brothers on occasion. Until about puberty brothers often work and play together, and sisters cooperate with their mother and older female relatives in the fields and in household tasks. Between brothers and sisters there develops a growing separation, reflected in early sleeping arrangements and in the avoidance of sexual discussions and any common courtship activities after puberty. Brothers seldom went courting girls in the *ebgan* together, and they usually avoided an *ebgan* where their sisters slept. In some neighboring communities there is still greater formality in the relations between brothers, especially in regard to sleeping close together in the men's house.

In Mountain Province mythology the population was recreated after a great flood from a surviving brother and sister. Nevertheless the sanctions against brother-sister incest are very severe and explicit. In one of the Sagada orphan myths two brothers see their sister naked; in her shame she runs away, but she decides to change into an omen bird so that she can aid her brothers in regaining the family inheritance and avenging their wrongs (see Eggan, 1956).

The oldest sibling, male or female, normally marries first and usually has the first choice of the inherited rice lands. The youngest sibling is often the parents' pet and may receive most of their acquired property, particularly, if he looks after them in their old age. The oldest brother, in particular, is a focus for his immediate kin group; he is responsible for helping to provide for his younger brothers and sisters and for looking after their children in case of accident or death. In earlier times the sibling bond was particularly concerned with protection and revenge. A brother was expected to lead the revenge party of kin and *dap-ay* mates and never to give up the effort to obtain vengeance. The reduction of this basic obligation under modern conditions has affected the sibling tie without modifying its character. Siblings consult one another on all important occasions and are expected to present a united front, looking after one another's interests and helping to educate each other's children.

The variety of sibling terms in Sagada is unusual, though Mountain Province groups frequently have alternate sets of terms for clarity in reference. Sagada seems to have assimilated a greater number of sibling terms through intermarriage, occasional immigration, and perhaps by borrowing from Ilocano and other sources, but the various terms for the most part are not mere alternatives; they express differing degrees of closeness and affection, as well as different ranges of extension and indications of age and sex.

Cousins, both parallel and cross, are considered as similar to siblings but less close. In disputes, one helps a cousin "because he is a relative and you don't want to see him or her defeated, but if you are related to both sides you have an obligation to help settle the dispute so that there is no violence." The range to which recognition extends is variable. Informants speak of fifth cousins as the extreme range, but in fact few know those farther removed than third cousins, and the effective range of exogamy stops with second cousins. The reduction in vengeance and wergild obligations through the decline of feuding and warfare and the presence of local groups with their obligations, as previously suggested, make the more precise formulation of a kinship circle less necessary.

The terminology applied to cousins varies considerably in the Mountain Province. Ifugao extends sibling terms to cousins, as do Bontok and Sagada in direct address, but other groups use separate cousin terms. The coastal Ilocano differentiate cousins by numerical terms, a practice which has spread inland through the medium of trade Ilocano as a *lingua franca*.

AFFINAL KIN

In Ifugao consanguineal bonds are the only ones that count, and this was probably once true of many groups in the Mountain Province. In Sagada today it is difficult to get any help, particularly financial, from anyone who is not a relative. In all groups, of course, there exists a potential conflict of sibling and other consanguineal ties with the husband-wife bond, but these have varying relative strengths and are supported by differential acculturative factors, and there is a general tendency to treat affinal relatives to some extent like consanguineal relatives and to draw them partially into the circle of kindred.

The term for a spouse of either sex is *asawa*, but this is never used in address. Married couples generally refer to one another by teknonymy and call one another *gayyem* ("friend") or by some similar term. Since most boys choose their partners freely through the courtship activities in connection with the *ebgan*, there are not the initial difficulties of personal and sexual adjustment that often characterize arranged marriages, such as the Tinguian and Kalinga practice. Many of the "song debates" on social occasions involve detailed recitations of the activities and duties of husband and wife. As in most Mountain Province groups, couples in Sagada are given their inheritances on marriage. They thus assume an independent status, in contrast to the Tinguian and Ilocano practice of keeping them dependent—a difference with important consequences for character building.

Marriage creates a union between two kin groups, though children are essential to make this union permanent. The public and periodic marriage rituals carried out by the families concerned are one of the central features of Sagada life. If no children are born, a series of rituals is performed, and if these fail the marriage usually breaks up. But if there are children, divorce or separation is difficult and rare. Monogamy is the rule, and adultery is a serious crime with sanctions involving the possible death of children, community and kin ostracism, and rituals of repentance. The sharp break between premarital sexual freedom and postmarital strictness has effects on adult personality that need further study; Barton (1938) has commented on its possible consequences with reference to the Ifugao.

Parents-in-law are treated with respect and obedience, but without avoidance or special restrictive patterns. No great difference prevails in the treatment of father-in-law and mother-in-law, or of the husband's and wife's parents. The latter normally reside in separate households, though possibly in the same ward. When children are born, relationships become much closer; parents-in-law are now also grandparents, and they "have to like their children-in-law." Though referred to as *katogangan*, parents-in-law are usually addressed as "father" and "mother" unless they are not congenial. Children-in-law are treated in correlative fashion, and have responsibilities to their parents-in-law, particularly in old age. In funeral ceremonies there is a special ritual for sons-in-law and daughters-in-law to protect them from possible malice.

Once a marriage is concluded, the two sets of parents are brought into a new relationship, and they are required thenceforth to use the term *ka-ising* ("co-parent-in-law"). This relationship is one of respect and of pride in one another's accomplishments. The persons involved cooperate on various occasions, and they are ultimately brought closer together through their mutual concern for their grandchildren. Ideally they should behave toward one another like siblings and take pride in the unity of the two families; even if involved through close kindred, they must not attempt to break up the marriage.

Marriage establishes a variety of sibling-in-law relationships, marked by a number of special terms of reference but by a general extension of sibling terms in address. They are not associated with joking or avoidance behavior, nor are siblings-in-law potential sororate or levirate spouses. Siblings-in-law are expected to cooperate in work groups and on other occasions, but the relationship is not normally close. The spouses of two siblings, on the other hand, compete with one another for family favor. If siblings-in-law establish close and friendly relationships they are brought terminologically into the kinship circle; if they are negligent, they may be reprimanded, though ordinarily only by their own close relatives.

Relations of friendship and companionship between non-relatives as a result of common activities in the ward find expression in terms for "friend," "companion," and "age-mate," which are of some importance in Sagada. A few generations ago, when it was dangerous to travel in regions where one had no known relatives, trading relationships were established with distant communities on the basis of friendship and economic consideration. The institution of the "peace-pact," with accompanying intermarriage, has apparently reached Sagada only in recent years.

THE LIFE CYCLE

The major social groupings and the rights and duties of kinsmen are exemplified during the annual social and ceremonial round and throughout the life cycle of the individual. The interaction of household, ward, and village, and of descent groups and personal kindreds, becomes especially clear in the events and activities centering around birth, marriage, sickness, and death.[11]

Children are both essential and highly desired. There are ceremonies to facilitate pregnancy, and both husband and wife observe numerous restrictions on their behavior before and after the birth of a child. After a child is born the household assembles to eat together. The mother eats from a separate dish, and continues to do so until the navel string falls off. After the first meal the father takes tabacco, goes to his ward center, and says: "Here is what has been caught by the men's (women's, if the child is a girl) fishing." On returning home he puts up two sticks of *runo* reed in front of the house to indicate that visitors are taboo.

Later the families of both parents assemble in the house, bringing gifts, and eat together—an act that symbolizes unity everywhere in the Mountain Province. The naming ceremony, usually held on the fourth day or when the navel string drops off, asks for health and long life for the new individual and calls on the ancestors and the "co-parents-in-law" for aid and protection. The name given the child is usually that of a grandparent or a grandparent's sibling; important ancestors thus have their names, and something of their personality, perpetuated. Small children are looked after by their parents, but during the busy portions of the year the grandfather frequently takes over. Weaning and toilet training are gradual procedures.[12]

At about the age of six or seven, children begin to be "ashamed" to sleep at home. They enter a new phase of life, frequenting the *dap-ay* or *ebgan* but returning to the household for meals and other activities. In the *dap-ay* the younger boys are supervised by the older group and begin to learn the traditional history and ceremonial procedures, as well as the techniques of courtship. Young girls spend much of their time with their mothers and other female relatives working in the fields, but in the evening they repair to the girls' sleeping houses, where visiting and courtship take place.

Marriage is the most important social event in Sagada and is the focus of a great variety of ceremonies designed to cement relationships and induce prosperity. Most marriages were formerly arranged in the *ebgan*, generally after a period of experimental mating, though wealthier families often attempted to arrange marriages by betrothing their children at an early age.

After a union is decided on, a preliminary marriage ritual (*pasya*) is held at which the close relatives of the couple exchange gifts of food and the girl's father recites the *pasya* prayer; this tells how Lomawig, the culture hero, performed a similar ritual and prospered. The couple eat rice and meat together, but each from his own dish. Thereafter they sleep in the house of one of the sets of parents, where they are *na-idnang* ("separated") from their companions, but they must wait until the *bayas* ceremony to get their own house and inheritance. During this interval omens are carefully observed.

The *bayas* ceremony is a public wedding feast. It is celebrated simultaneously throughout the village by engaged couples on dates determined by the old men of the various wards. For this ceremony the relatives of each couple from neighboring communities are invited. A large number of rituals are performed on behalf of the couples, accompanied by dancing, feasting, and "song debates." The principals themselves play a passive role, and are usually bored by the proceedings, but they are under restrictions with regard to continence and must abstain from food and drink.

The rituals of the *bayas* ceremony emphasize the social aspects of marriage and aid in integrating the new family group into the larger social and religious structure of village and region. During their course the couple occupies the house set aside for them, and their inheritance in rice and *camote* fields is transferred to them, along with other inherited property such as gongs, Chinese jars, and beads.

The *bayas* rituals also bring prestige, and wealthy families may go through two or three series during their lifetime as part of the obligations toward maintaining their *kadangyan* status. The rituals contribute not only to the welfare of the new household and family but also to that of the entire community, and the distribution of meat to invited guests and relatives is an important means of strengthening kin solidarity.

Once children are born to them, a couple is not supposed to separate, and adultery is strongly condemned, being thought to bring about the illness or death of the children. An adulterer was formerly shunned and had to eat separately; he could repent and be restored to a normal position only by performing a special ceremony which cleansed him of his action. In case of the death of one of a couple, the survivor normally remarries, often taking a widow or widower as a new spouse. The full marriage celebration is not held for such a second marriage; there is merely a ceremony "to join the property of the couple" in the presence of the immediate relatives.

Sickness is believed to be caused by *anitos*, the spirits of deceased individuals, or by non-human spirits. The living soul can leave the body temporarily, and may be enticed away by deceased relatives or taken by enemy spirits intent on revenge. When a person falls ill, his relatives, friends, and neighbors come to comfort him; it is especially important for children and grandchildren to do so. On such occasions the *awid* is sung, in which the children and grandchildren are represented as visiting the burial caves in the vicinity in search of the soul of the sick person, or in which animals bring medicine for curing (see Pacyaya and Eggan, 1953).

When death comes to an adult, the relatives are notified, and close relatives, particularly the children, should return at all costs. The body is prepared for the death chair by the old men, and is dressed according to customs inherited in the major descent groups. The chief mourners—father, mother, and spouse—may not look at the body and must fast for the period before burial. The bereaved spouse sits inside the house in a corner, shielded from the corpse by a winnowing tray, and the parents, if living, do likewise. The children wear old clothes and barkcloth bands around their wrists.

The social significance of death is indicated by the large number of sacrifices that must be offered by the survivors. Some of these may be performed before death in an effort to comfort the dying or to ward off the approaching end. Dirges sung during the day yield considerable insight into Sagada beliefs as to life after death, and the children and children-in-law "talk" to the deceased in song form, recalling events of their life together and asking the departed for continued assistance (see Pacyaya, 1953). After the corpse has been wrapped in a blanket, preparatory to its final disposal, the sons-in-law and daughters-in-law sit for the last time at the feet of their parent-in-law. If there have been quarrels and hard feelings during the lifetime of the deceased, this rite establishes good relations for the future.

The sons and grandsons carry the body to the burial cave, where it is deposited in a pine-log coffin. It is considered a great honor to be the first to carry the corpse, which is done on the run. Relatives (except brothers) and non-relatives scramble for the privilege of assisting, since the body juices are believed to confer the abilities of the deceased in raising animals and crops. There is some indication that the dead are buried in caves with their ancestors, particularly with their grandparents. However, husband and wife should not be buried in the same cave, nor should siblings or parents and children be buried together. We have not as yet made an accurate census of the remains in the coffins, which are stacked to the ceiling in some caves, but such a census should clarify many points.

The end of the mourning period for members of the immediate family of the deceased—parents, children, and spouse—is gradually achieved through a series of sacrifices, after which they may don normal clothing and eat ordinary food. Sacrifices for the dead (*danglis*) are essential to the future welfare of the soul in the "house of the *anitos*," and inherited property must be sold if the required animals are not otherwise obtainable. The sacrifices must be eaten in the house of the deceased. Parents, spouses, siblings, and first cousins may not partake of them, but grandparents, children, and grandchildren may do so. Children and grandchildren, in fact, are especially obligated to participate since it is they for whom the deceased inherited and accumulated property.

These elaborate rituals are carried out only for adults who are married and have children. Infants are buried in a clay jar beside the house, without prayer or special ceremony. Unmarried youths may be buried similarly, or in a nearby *camote* field, with a sacrifice of one pig, which the surviving brothers and sisters must refrain from eating.

These practices reflect the increased social status which comes with advancing age. The old are revered as the keepers of custom and performers of rituals essential to the maintenance of Sagada society, and consequently hold the highest positions. When they die they assume an even higher status, that of *anito* ancestor, in which they continue to look after the welfare of their descendants and to protest against neglect by sending illness and other disasters. All these rituals betray a general fear of the dead. This may reflect the considerable number of disasters that actually occur, and are attributed to deceased relatives or enemies, and may also involve the projection of guilt arising from transgressions.

SUMMARY AND CONCLUSIONS

The above brief survey of the Sagada social system indicates a considerable degree of complexity, but within a bilateral and symmetrical framework. The kinship terminology corresponds rather closely to behavioral patterns and social usages. The system is organized on a generational basis with reciprocal relations between more distant relatives and a discrimination of the nuclear family and its members. Consanguineal kinship is paramount, and marriage, from the point of view of the community, is essentially an alliance between kindreds. The child has a central position in the family, being essential to the permanence of marriage and to the weaving of kindreds together. Affinal relatives are brought within the consanguineal framework in face-to-face relations but are sharply separated in cases of conflict or inheritance. Cooperation amongst consanguineal kin is assumed as "natural"; with others it is voluntary and must be earned.

The role of kinship takes on an additional dimension in terms of society as a whole. It is the main social network holding the village together, sharing this function with the ceremonial cycle and its rituals. Through the overlapping of personal kindreds, with their distribution in the village and in neighboring communities, and through membership in the various bilateral descent groups, each individual and sibling group is tied by kinship bonds to a considerable number of his fellows over a considerable territory. Marriage provides an additional group of potential kin with equivalent loyalties to the child. The Sagada data fully support Keesing (1949) in his above-cited criticism of Jenks's account of Bontok.

We have noted that the ward or *dap-ay* organization is not a kinship unit, though its original core may well have been a bilateral descent group. From a structural standpoint the ward represents an alternative means of achieving a corporate group, one having greater stability and permanence and depending less on the accidents of survival in particular family lines. With the ward are associated not only a geographical territory for house and garden sites and the public buildings and ceremonial platforms mentioned above but also ceremonial duties and positions, a traditional history, and rights and obligations for residents of the *obon*. If a house needs repairing one's ward neighbors will come and help; if a house catches fire the whole village will pitch in. Ward neighbors are treated in part as if they were kin. In former days of headhunting and feuds the ward was also a unit for defense and war, though the responsibility for vengeance continued to reside within the kinship group.

A great virtue of the ward as a corporate group is that it is clearly definable at any one time. As compared with kinship groups there are fewer conflicting loyalties. In recent years, and probably also in the past, it has been possible to change ward affiliations by obtaining consent and performing a ritual. If a ward grows too large, it may build a second platform and sleeping house, or it can divide and establish a new ward on the edge of the community. If a ward is reduced in numbers, it can recruit new members through offering houses, or it can disperse its remaining members among neighboring units and go out of existence.

In this context the ward organization of the central Mountain Province is intelligible as an innovation designed to solve the problems inherent in balancing kinship and territorial obligations. I have elsewhere (Eggan, 1954) presented the evidence which indicates the probable local development and elaboration of the ward or *ato* system and its associated institutions among the ethno-linguistic groups of the Mountain Province. The two territorial divisions, Dagdag and Demang, also have certain corporate features in terms of sacred groves and guardian spirits, but it is probable that they were once more independent than they are now.

The bilateral kindreds may have worked reasonably well as kinship and corporate groups at an earlier period, when population was less dense and group cooperation for clearing and burning hillside farms was more important. With the acquisition of irrigated rice culture, however, the ancestors of the Sagada Igorots apparently gave up communal ownership and operation on a larger scale, and at the same time increased population and headhunting activities made protection and revenge more essential. A lineage type of organization might have been one solution to the problem; in the mountains of Formosa under apparently similar conditions both matrilineal and patrilineal clans are found, along with bilateral systems. But nowhere in the Philippines were unilineal institutions developed. Instead, a territorial ward organization in compact villages, or centers with outlying barrios, or aggregations of hamlets were the means by which Mountain Province groups attempted to secure continuity, stability, and a structure transcending the kinship level. Here a comparison of the Sagada system with that of Kalinga, as described by Barton (1949), is illuminating.

Why the shift to irrigated rice agriculture involved changes in patterns of ownership and inheritance is a problem which only a comparative study of

Mountain Province communities can solve. As yet we have no adequate studies of shifting agriculture and associated institutions among marginal populations in Apayao, northern Kalinga, or eastern Bontok and Ifugao. But wherever irrigated rice has been introduced, rice lands are treated for purposes of inheritance as though they were movable property comparable to beads, Chinese jars, and gongs. Nowhere in the Mountain Province have rice terraces or irrigation systems become the corporate property of a group larger than the family, though close relatives have certain claims on inherited rice lands in different regions. However the situation developed, it is clear that the introduction of permanent rice agriculture and the new inheritance practices brought about increased differentiation within the kindred and further increased the wealth differentiation underlying the social classes. The varying rules of inheritance—primogeniture, homoparental transmission, and differential inheritance according to relative age—and the distinctions between inherited property and that acquired after marriage suggest that no wholly adequate solution has been developed for handling the new resources.

As regards kinship terminology, the Sagada data do not seriously modify the conclusions reached by Kroeber in his earlier survey of Philippine kinship. After reconstructing the "ancient system" he says:

> The simplicity and adaptability of this system are obvious. It operates with its meager resources by merging most collateral with lineal kin; by mostly treating connections by marriage as if they were blood kin, with the lexical implication that spouses are one person; by not distinguishing sex, except in parents, perhaps uncles and aunts, and possibly siblings-in-law; and by nowhere bifurcating, that is, discriminating the line of descent, the sex through which relationship exists. The primary consideration is generation; this is slightly elaborated by hesitating and inconsistent introduction of the factors of collaterality, sex, marriage, and absolute age. Reciprocity is of moment. Self-reciprocal terms occur in every language, and in the Philippines as a whole are found in every class of relationships except the parent-child group. (Kroeber, 1919, p. 81).

He finds it remarkable that the differences in the kinship systems of the pagan, Mohammedan, and Christian groups are rather slight in view of the differences in civilization and in cultural influences:

> But there have been fairly profound variations of general civilization; and theoretically these seem as capable of modifying a scheme of kinship reckoning as are social institutions in their narrower sense. That these variations of general civilization have affected the scheme so little, except in superficial details, shows that a method of thought involved in dealing with blood relationship may sometimes possess a surprising historical tenacity. It is tempting in the present case to attribute this tenacity in part to the simplicity of the principles on which the system is based and the comparatively strict consistency with which they can consequently be adhered to. (Kroeber, 1919, p. 82).

It is now apparent that the differences in the kinship systems of pagan, Moro, and Christian Filipino populations are more considerable than Kroeber realized, and data now in the process of analysis may ultimately reveal several distinct types or subtypes. Hence his reconstruction of the "ancient system" is perhaps premature. Moreover, Dempwolff (1938), who supports Kroeber on a number of terms, gives three proto-Malayo-Polynesian forms for "father" and three or four for "mother," and some of these have quite different distributions in the Philippines.

It is not yet possible, from the data presented above, to test Kroeber's conclusion that "the pagan Igorot systems are perhaps somewhat nearest to the original scheme." What is clear, though space and data do not allow a full comparative presentation, is that the Sagada Igorot kinship system is reasonably close to Mountain Province norms. With regard to Kroeber's further conclusion that the Ifugao system is probably the result of "a progressive and extreme process of reduction," Murdock (1949, p. 349) has reached the opposite conclusion and considers the Ifugao as one of the societies which has preserved relatively unchanged the original Malayo-Polynesian Hawaiian type of organization. Only a detailed comparative treatment on a wide scale, including linguistic reconstruction, can enable us to decide this important point.

It is likewise not possible, as yet, to characterize the basic structural principles of the Sagada Igorot kinship system with any precision. It is clear that the relationship of siblings is one of great importance in the Mountain Province, and in regions such as Ifugao the sibling bond is central to the kinship structure. But siblings are rarely "equivalent," except from the standpoint of an enemy engaged in revenge. In Sagada, siblings are united against the outside social world but are divided in respect to internal activities, and modern acculturation has favored the latter tendency. The kinship group has unity in feud situations, where any member is equivalent to another, but internal solidarity is reduced through differential inheritance and multiple affiliations. The "lineage principle," even if stretched to cover bilateral descent groups with some corporate features, is only slightly represented, so far as present information goes.

The principle of generation and, to a lesser extent, that of relative age are important in all Mountain Province systems. The position and activities of the sexes are balanced, and sex distinctions in terminology are restricted, for the most part, to the parental generation and the immediate family. Perhaps nowhere in the world is there less discrimination between men and women in matters of customary law. The principle of genealogical connection, as over against affinal alliance, is important everywhere in the Mountain Province and may be related to early settlement patterns. On the other hand, the social significance of primogeniture varies, though it is utilized to a considerable degree in inheritance and in the status systems of all groups. Kirchhoff (1955) argues that systems like the Igorot are more adaptable to the process of social differentiation that accompanies the growing importance and complexity of property relations, and that the early stages of the struggle between developing classes of landlords and landless can be seen among the Igorot tribes.

The meaning of the social system of the Sagada Igorots can be seen more fully by placing it in its ritual and ceremonial context and in its ecological setting. The texts of the ritual prayers recited by the *dap-ay* "priests" on the various ceremonial occasions and the underlying myths often make explicit in direct or symbolic terms the basic values of Sagada social life, as they are formulated by the participants. And the ecological factors of land, wood, and water place limits on population concentration and give direction to developing institutions.

Another avenue to a fuller understanding of Sagada social and ceremonial life is through a detailed comparison with that of its close neighbors in the Mountain Province. By comparing similarities and differences, and by studying their correlates in different groups, we can begin to see the factors responsible for increasing complexity and change. And by looking at these societies as a whole we can see the kinds of problems they have faced and the new forms of social organization they have developed—or borrowed and adapted—to solve them.

In this context the dual division of Sagada into opposing geographical halves, the bilateral descent groups with their corporate functions, the ward organization, and the personal kindreds may be seen in the perspective of increasing population pressures and more complex interaction. The kinship system, wide ranging but capable of narrow definition, serves the tasks both of integrating a wider society and of segregating the nuclear family. In Ifugao it fulfills primarily the former function; in Kalinga and among the Tinguian, the latter. In Sagada, transitional from one type of society to another, it attempts both.

The parallels with unilateral societies are not fortuitous, nor does the Sagada system represent any breakdown or survival from a former unilineal clan system, as some writers assume. As I have remarked elsewhere, "social structures have jobs to do," and bilateral societies, no less than others, must cope with the problems of transmission and continuity without too much confusion. The societies of the Mountain Province demonstrate that these problems can be solved through the creation of a set of social institutions parallel to those of unilateral societies of the same general cultural level.

Some years ago, in a preliminary analysis of culture change in the northern Philippines (Eggan, 1941), I pointed out that the variations in Mountain Province social institutions are not haphazard but have a definite direction. As one proceeds from the Ifugao to the Ilocano coast, village organization becomes more complex; kinship terminology shifts from a Hawaiian type to an approximation of the European or "Eskimo" system, with a gradual narrowing of range and an increasing differentiation of cousins; territorial ties increase in strength relative to kinship bonds; and political centralizaton and class differentiation increase.

Along with these changes occur corresponding variations in marriage customs, parental control, and preferential marriage practices, as well as possibly related shifts in religious beliefs and rituals and prestige activities.

In my initial formulation I characterized this regular series of changes in social and cultural institutions as a "cultural drift," adapting the term from Sapir's concept of linguistic drift. It was clear that the series of changes was in part due to the effects of acculturation, but closer investigation suggested that much of the apparent social change was the result of internal factors rather than of external influences and contacts.

At that time there were few adequate accounts of Mountain Province groups, except for the Ifugao, and our knowledge of social institutions was particularly deficient. We now have a somewhat better historical perspective, and during recent years there have been a number of important published and unpublished studies by Barton, Keesing, Lambrecht, Vanoverbergh, and others which make it possible to see the social systems as units and to compare the components in fuller fashion. Preliminary observations suggest that the north-south series, from Apayao and Kalinga through Bontok and Ifugao, will have an ecological explanation for the gradients observed, though there are still crucial gaps in our knowledge of Apayao and northern Kalinga institutions.

Ultimately we need to see the development of Mountain Province institutions and practices as a whole. When this has been done, the processual and historical components represented by the concept of cultural drift will be clarified, and we can see the directions of social and ceremonial development, and the factors affecting them, in clearer perspective. We should then have a better understanding of bilateral institutions and their methods of solving the problems faced by societies in general, and will be in a position to make comparisons, not only with other regions in the Philippines and Oceania, but also with our own early Celtic and Teutonic ancestors, who had similar social systems, engaged in feuds and headtaking, and paid wergild to satisfy vengeance.

CHAPTER 4

THE EASTERN SUBANUN OF MINDANAO

CHARLES O. FRAKE
Stanford University

THE literature on Subanun social organization dates from the seventeenth century, when these Mindanao pagans prompted Francisco Combés (1667, p. 31), a Spanish Jesuit, to write: "They are a people of little worth . . . living in the hills with scant social life, like beasts, and placing their dwellings a league apart according to the whims of each." Actually, the Subanun live—not "like beasts" but like all human beings—in social groups. Though often informally organized and lacking obvious boundaries, these groups sustain a social life which, characterized by drinking, feasting, religious ceremonies, and almost constant litigation, is by no means scant. Nevertheless, a grain of truth underlies Combés's description. Small, non-continuous, two-generation family groups, living in dispersed households, maintain an unusual degree of corporate independence.

The present paper discusses the structure of the Subanun family and the kinship relations generated by its formation and dissolution. Other publications (Frake, 1957a and 1957b) have dealt with the nature of wider social groups and the means by which a complex network of litigation flourishes within them without the benefit of formal political authority or the sanctioned use of force.

The Subanun, who number some 70,000, inhabit the interior of Zamboanga,[1] a mountainous peninsula, 17,673 square kilometers in area, connected to central Mindanao by a narrow neck of land. Here the majority derive their livelihood by alternately clearing, cultivating, and fallowing forested hillsides on which they grow rice and a variety of other grain, root, and tree crops. In recent years, population pressure and deforestation caused by the immigration of Christian Filipinos have forced the Subanun in a number of areas to supplement or replace swidden[2] farming by permanent-field agriculture.

Effectively isolated by geography and the activities of warlike Moslem neighbors, the Subanun have no knowledge of culturally or linguistically distinct mountain-dwelling pagans. To them, all mountain people are *subanen* ("upstream people"), who share a similar culture, social organization, and linguistic affiliation in contrast to known categories of outsiders who visit or inhabit the lowlands: the Moslem *glenaun* (Maranaw) and *samal*, the Christian *bisaya'* (Bisayan) and *kasila'* (Spanish mestizos), and the mercantile *ginsik* (Chinese).

Relations with Subanun of the same or other groups are invariably devoid of warfare and class distinctions. External relations, on the other hand, have been marked by coercive exploitation and social inequality.

The peaceable and anarchic Subanun have long been prey to more strongly organized neighbors. Beginning before the Spanish conquest of the Philippines and continuing intermittently until the twentieth century, Moslems from Sulu and Lanao raided the Subanun for slaves, collected tribute, and established a system of forced trade.[3] In some coastal areas, to better enforce their control, they instated a hierarchy of titled Subanun officials (*begelal*) with the responsibility of collecting tribute and implementing trade. These individuals became the foci of indigenous political and judicial authority, deriving their power from their position as trade intermediaries and from the physical might of their backers. Moslem exploitation and hegemony in Zamboanga ceased with the American occupation. With the removal of the foundations of the incipient Subanun political organization, the titled offices rapidly disappeared or lost their political significance.

In recent decades Christian settlers from the Bisayan islands to the north, encouraged by the weakening of Moslem power, by roadbuilding, and by the tractability of the native population, have invaded Zamboanga. Through markets, schools, tax collection, and land laws, Christian settlement has meant the gradual extension of a new political and economic system over the Subanun. While effective political control, heralded by the bestowal of the new titles of *tininti* (barrio lieutenant) and *kunsyal* (councilor), has been established only in the coastal and foothill areas of permanent cultivation, the threat of land appropriation, "tax" assessment, and police interference reaches the interior shifting cultivators.

Linguistically, Subanun constitutes a subgroup of the Central Philippine languages and embraces two closely related languages, Eastern and Western Subanun. These are separated by a boundary across the low, narrow, middle portion of the peninsula, a division which was perhaps effected by Moslem penetration (Frake, 1957c). The present study[4] concerns only the Eastern Subanun, who include some 55,000 people dispersed across the wider eastern sections of Zamboanga Peninsula.

The Eastern Subanun exhibit no overall formal organization or conscious unity; the social world of any one Subanun includes only a small fraction of the total population. Moreover, despite both dialect diversity and the restriction of individual social spheres, it is impossible to draw clearly defined linguistic or sociological boundaries between any adjacent groups. There is, rather, an overlapping network of small socio-linguistic communities, whose boundaries can be defined only from the point of view of each of the minimal discrete units of which Subanun society is built.

The distinction between discrete and non-discrete groups[5] is basic to Eastern Subanun social organization. The maximal social group—the total society from the point of view of one individual—is non-discrete. Of Subanun social groups, only the family, the household, and the settlement are discrete. The first two of these groups tend to be equivalent in membership and form the fundamental socio-economic unit. A family's social relationships extend outward along ties of propinquity and bilateral kinship. Maximally they encompass a politically unorganized circle of neighbors and kin whose membership overlaps with, but never precisely corresponds to, those of other families.

Whether cultivated by swidden farming or by permanent agriculture, areas of Subanun settlement always present much the same pattern: isolated small dwellings, each within its own fields, usually on a prominence overlooking the crops. What nucleation there is derives from the practice of cultivating adjacent fields in order to reduce the perimeter exposed to faunal enemies. In areas of shifting cultivation, settlements can be better defined as clusters of adjacent or nearly adjacent swiddens than as clusters of households. A Subanun locates, and periodically relocates, his dwelling according to agricultural requirements and, if anything, endeavors to place his house as far from any neighboring dwelling as is consistent with these requirements. The value placed on household isolation is explicit. When I showed an informant photographs of compact house clusters among other shifting cultivators, his response, typically legalistic, was: "Bah, if I were there, I would fine them. Are they so suspicious of each other that they must live where they can always watch one another?"

The settlement is an unnamed, discrete local group generally comprising from three to a dozen dispersed households. Its boundaries, though not always geographically apparent, can at any one time easily be defined with reference to the quantity and quality of social activities among its members (Frake, 1957b). Over time, however, the settlement exhibits little stability or continuity. The unity of its component families is a temporary product of current agricultural opportunities, impermanent kinship obligations, and fluid social ties.

The Subanun house—a rectangular, thatched pile dwelling—has among its physical aspects three characteristics of sociological importance. First, it is small. Floor space averages about twelve square meters and rarely exceeds twenty. This small size reflects single family occupancy, but it has the consequence of limiting the number of persons that can assemble together. With the exception of a few religious ceremonies, all Subanun social functions take place indoors in a dwelling house; there are no outdoor areas or other buildings for such purposes. Although an all-night drinking party, a legal case, a wedding, or a religious ceremony may pack people until there is literally standing room only, attendance at social gatherings can exceed forty or fifty persons only with difficulty. I have never seen as many as one hundred Subanun in one place at one time. Their social life takes place entirely within small groups.

Second, a Subanun house has only one room and one hearth. Household space is defined functionally—the sleeping area, the living area, the cooking area—and finds architectural expression only in slightly different floor levels. Within the household there can be little privacy in working, cooking, eating, or conversation. Darkness alone brings the privacy necessary for licit and illicit sexual activity. (With regard to the latter, the granaries, the only non-dwelling structures in a Subanun settlement, sometimes acquire a sociological function.)

Third, a Subanun house is a temporary construction. A new house is usually built within the annual grain swidden every other year, or at most every third year, as old swiddens are fallowed. Longer occupancy, even if feasible agriculturally, can not contend with increasing vermin infestation and disintegrating thatch. A house, therefore, has no value as permanent real estate, nor, since there are no tenure rights to land *per se*, does an unoccupied house site.

Typically a house is occupied by a single nuclear or polygynous family, the minimal discrete social group of Subanun society and the maximal corporate unit. A *full family* comprises a man and his wife or wives, with or without real or adopted unmarried offspring. Dissolution of a full family through death or divorce produces one or more *partial families*, each consisting of a surviving or divorced spouse with or without unmarried offspring. Completely orphaned children are absorbed by adoption into existing families. Partial families, especially those consisting of a single individual, often join with a full family to form a single household, but by doing so they do not lose their socio-economic independence. Compound households, comprising more than one full family, are rare, and are invariably temporary (and disliked) expedients to facilitate access to new swiddens.

Whether nuclear or polygynous, full or partial, a Subanun family (*senglanan*) is strictly limited to two generations: parents and unmarried offspring. It is not a descent group with continuity beyond the life span of its founders. Its lateral extension by polygyny, occurring in less than 10 per cent of recorded families, increases the family's life expectancy by adding female members to the spouse set, but in no way alters its basic character. A family of any type exhibits a series of characteristics, each distinguishing it from all other Subanun social groups:

1. Its formation, through marriage, and its dissolution, through death or divorce, require legal action.
2. Its members always live together in a single house, sharing a common hearth and a common, unpartitioned living space.
3. It has joint title to all property brought into, created by, or inherited by its members.
4. It has collective legal responsibility.
5. It always jointly cultivates a single annual swidden and/or plowed field. (Male adolescent offspring may, in addition, cultivate individual swiddens for several years prior to their marriage.)
6. It is entirely responsible for its own economic support through its own resources.

Taken together, these characteristics give the family a unique corporate nature. Every Subanun acquires membership in one such corporate family (his family of orientation) through birth or adoption, and normally enters into the formation of a new similar unit (his family of procreation) through marriage Not only does marriage establish a new corporate unit; it terminates in perpetuity the membership of both partners in their families of orientation. Once married, a Subanun, to enjoy the rights of membership in a full family, must remain married—though not necessarily to the same person—throughout his life.

The formation of independent family units is consequently a continual process in Subanun society. The establishment of a new family of procreation through marriage requires the concluding of a legal contract between the families of orientation of the prospective spouses. This contract, guaranteed by the payment of a substantial bride-price, defines the interest of the two sponsoring families in the sponsored family.

Any two families may sponsor a new family by a marriage between their respective offspring, providing only that no member of the parental generation of one sponsoring family is an offspring in the other. Incest taboos exclude marriage with siblings and parents' siblings—persons who have shared membership in one's own or one's parent's family of orientation. This rule does not exclude first-cousin marriage; indeed, this is quite common, even though it violates verbally stated ideals and requires payment of a token fine. The behaviorally manifest preference for cousin marriage reflect's Murdock's (1949, pp. 318–320) "positive gradients of propinquity and kinship" in the absence of correspondingly strong negative gradients, as well as the fact that marriage with a close neighbor and/or kinsman facilitates negotiation of the marital contract and obviates difficulties in the choice of postmarital residence. Furthermore, because of the corporate independence of families, even when closely akin, a marriage between cousins unites fundamentally distinct groups by the ties of joint sponsorship of a new corporate unit.

On the other hand, no social, economic, or political advantages are to be gained by marital alliances between wider social groups—kindreds and settlements. These groups are consequently agamous, i.e., irrelevant in the choice of marital partners.

The complex legal negotiations preliminary to marriage often begin before the prospective couple has reached puberty. The acceptance by the girl's family of a token from that of the boy signals willingness to enter into negotiations and establishes a relationship of *bina'* ("engagement") between the families. It then becomes a legal offense for either party to open negotiations with a different family without formally breaking the engagement by legal action, for which there must be sufficient grounds. Go-betweens conduct all negotiations, draw up the final agreement, and serve as witnesses to the terms of the unwritten contract in the event of subsequent dispute. To qualify as a go-between a man cannot be a member of either sponsoring family, but he must be a close kinsman of the family he is representing. Above all, he must be skilled in legal procedure, for marital alliances emerge only from litigious combat.

When the couple are ready for marriage and the groom's family has raised an acceptable down payment on the bride-price, the wedding can take place. During the ceremony the bride-price must be calculated in terms of traditional, non-exchangeable units of value (*kumpaw*), also used in reckoning fines, that are assigned to each of the items composing it (see Frake, 1957a). These units of value are in turn arbitrarily represented by kernels of maize laid out in patterned groups and rows, the kernels in each of the traditionally named groups having different, and again purely arbitrary, values. The complex procedure of laying out the pattern which properly represents the total value of the bride-price, and then of removing kernels from appropriate rows as items in the down payment are paid, is marked at every step by prolonged debate and often takes most of the night to complete. Upon receipt of the down payment, the bride's family must distribute a large portion of it to kinsmen who have contributed to the wedding expenses, to the attending legal authorities and go-betweens, and to others who, by figuring significantly in the girl's life history, have established a claim to a share in her bride-price.

Following the maize-kernel computations the participants must agree on the details of payment of the future instalments on the bride-price by the new family and on the duration of bride-service. The latter obligation, usually lasting three or four years, functions as security on the unpaid portion of the bride-price. A couple cannot ordinarily leave bride-service until these payments have been completed. It is possible, through clever legal argument and an impressive, or even total, payment on the bride-price, to eliminate bride-service altogether, but this rarely occurs except in cases of secondary or polygynous marriages. In primary marriages the total bride-price, including down payment and later instalments, generally has a cash value ranging from 50 to 100 Philippine pesos, an amount several times the annual cash income of an average family.

The newly married couple sets up a household of their own as soon as feasible. Since both partners have married out of their natal families to form a new and independent corporate unit, marriage is neolocal in terms of corporate-group affiliation. In terms of the geographical location of their initial residence, the only requirement is that it be sufficiently close to the household and fields of the girl's family of orientation to make bride-service possible, so that in this sense initial residence is matrilocal. Bride-service constitutes a demand-right held by the girl's family of orientation entitling it to periodic agricultural labor from the family it sponsored. The latter family, however, from the moment it is instituted by marriage, is an independent economic unit responsible for its own support through the cultivation of its own fields. Its obligation to contribute a certain amount of labor to another family is simply a corporate liability and in no way infringes on its fundamental independence.

After fulfillment of its bride-service obligations a family can make its periodic residence changes without necessary regard for the location of the woman's family of orientation. Nevertheless, couples normally continue to live near the parents of one spouse or the other, often alternating between the two. Ultimately, especially after the dissolution of their parents' families, residence becomes in every sense neolocal. Unlike a corporation in the Western legal sense, a Subanun family does not have continuous existence irrespective of that of its members. It resembles a partnership in that its continuity as an economic unit depends upon the existence of a legal bond (marriage) between a man and one or more women. It may augment its personnel by procreating new members but is deprived of these members as soon as they marry. Termination of the relationship between marital partners dissolves the family corporation and requires settlement of its estate. The non-recognition of property rights in land by the Subanun shifting cultivators simplifies the division of property (Frake, 1956). An estate consists principally of movable property such as Chinese jars, gongs, jewelry, and currency; of perishable goods such as stored grain and planted crops; and of intangible assets such as credits and outstanding legal claims. Rules of estate settlement are simple in principle but complex in details of application to specific cases. The dissolution of a Subanun family involves litigation often as intricate as that which attended its formation.

In cases of divorce the problem is twofold: to settle any obligations the broken family may have to its sponsoring families and to divide the remaining estate between the two resulting partial families. Sponsoring families are in part responsible for underpaid and overpaid portions of the bride-price. The complexities enter when attempting to determine in a given case the respective rights of each of the four families involved (the two sponsors and the two divorced partial families). These rights depend primarily upon the establishment of legal responsibility for the failure of the marriage.

Procedures following the death of a spouse are somewhat simpler, for the question of responsibility does not arise. Malevolent supernaturals cause most deaths, and these beings enjoy immunity from legal prosecution.

Rights to the estate of a family terminated by the death of a parental member follow from the basic principle of inheritance, according to which the ultimate title rests with the offspring of that family, among whom the estate is divided regardless of sex or relative age. Problems arise over the allotment of specific items, over the rights of offspring who were members of their family of orientation at the time of a parent's death as opposed to the rights of offspring who had already married out, and over the rights of the surviving spouse and his (or her) subsequent offspring after he marries again. The resolution of these problems in particular cases depends upon a variety of factors related to the life histories of the individuals concerned, to the kinds of property at stake, and—not the least important—to the respective legal skills of the opposing claimants.

The principles of estate settlement, despite their litigation-engendering complexities, clearly point up a fundamental fact of Subanun social organization: a full family broken by death or divorce ceases to exist as a corporate group. Partial families are not surviving members of a full family corporation; they are new corporations. A partial family can become a full family in only one way: by the remarriage of a surviving spouse, which, in turn, establishes a new and different corporate unit.

Being independent corporate entities, partial families, whether or not they establish independent households, are responsible for their own support by the only means open to any Subanun family, namely, agriculture. This is as true for an elderly widow as for a young divorcee. In order to clear and cultivate its annual grain swidden, a partial family, especially when lacking an adult male member, must ordinarily recruit additional labor. This it can do by drawing upon kinship obligations such as that of bride-service, by providing an equivalent amount of labor in exchange, by offering a feast, or by paying wages in crops or cash. However, a family cannot long depend upon labor recruitment without seriously depleting its resources. The insistence on the independence of partial families makes their lot a hard one and puts a premium on remarriage.

Several factors facilitate secondary marriage. Foremost amongst these is the institution of levirate and sororate marriage, whereby a sponsoring family has the legal obligation to provide a new spouse from its membership as a replacement if this is at all possible. A second is polygyny, which enables a married man to absorb a widow and her children into his existing family unit. A third is the relative legal simplicity of secondary marriage for a woman, especially one whose parents are deceased, since in such cases the bride-price is minimal and bride-service is not ordinarily required.

Subanun definitions of family and marriage assure that the population will at all times be divided into a maximum number of independent full-family units—social groups which are not only large enough to be economically self-sufficient but which can also procreate the personnel to produce new families. By way of summarizing Subanun family organization, these definitive factors can be listed as follows:

1. A family, full or partial, is an independent corporate unit.
2. A family is strictly limited to two generations.
3. Once married, a person can never rejoin his family of orientation.
4. A new family is bound by an intricate legal contract to two sponsoring families.
5. Every full family must eventually dissolve into one or more partial families.
6. A partial family can resolve its subsistence difficulties only by becoming a full family through the remarriage of its parental member.
7. Remarriage is facilitated by levirate and sororate obligations, by polygyny, and by simplified legal procedure.

The continual process of family formation by sponsorship engenders a set of important relationships among the parental members of the sponsoring and sponsored families. These fundamental relationships receive distinctive linguistic designation in the basic kinship terminology. Any discussion of Subanun kinship terminology, however, must begin by delimiting the particular linguistic material involved.

In the Eastern Subanun language there is a vast corpus of words and phrases, often with overlapping referents, which have kinship meaning. The traditional dichotomy between terms of reference and terms of address does not suffice to segregate this terminology into meaningful contrastive sets. There are, for example, at least sixteen alternative single-word designations applicable in reference to any cousin. In addition, there are a large number of possible multiverbal constructions specifying attributes such as sex or describing the relationship more precisely in terms of other relationships. All this is apart from the fact that a Subanun Ego must also make choices among the several ways he may be related to many of his kinsmen.

The Subanun are not unique in possessing co-existing sets of relationship terms. A similar situation prevails in other Philippine languages, in English, in German, and in Javanese.[6] It is doubtless common elsewhere, but reliance on the genealogical method alone to elicit terms will not document it. Kinship terms must be recorded in use in a variety of cultural situations. It is no accident that existing descriptions of multiple alternatives in kinship designation have come from investigators who are native speakers (e.g., Schneider and Homans, Koentjaraningrat) or unusually fluent speakers of the languages concerned.

Our primary concern here is with terms that function to define kinship relations, in contrast to terms used to name individuals as subjects of discourse in address or reference. The latter terms in Subanun are morphologically and syntactically distinct. The choice of alternatives among them reflects social distance much as does our own alternative use of the proper nouns "Joe," "Uncle Joe," or "Uncle" in reference or address to a kinsman designated by the common noun "my uncle" (Schneider and Homans, 1955). Terms used as names, here called *nominals*, do not designate classes of kin; they merely identify single individuals. *Designative terms*, on the other hand, denote an individual as a member of a class of kinsmen whose distinctive features are signified by the term (Lounsbury, 1956, pp. 167-8).

A Subanun chooses among alternative designative terms according to the degree of specification required in a particular cultural context. Some contexts require only a distinction between kin and non-kin; others, such precise distinctions as that between mother's brother's elder daughter and mother's brother's younger daughter. At different levels of contrast the Subanun kinship system exhibits different fundamental distinctions. At one level cousin terminology is of the Hawaiian type; at another, of the Eskimo type. At one level siblings-in-law are differentiated by sex; at another, by the sequence of affinal and collateral links; at still another level, appearing only in special types of discourse, they are not differentiated at all.

Although the kinds of distinctions that the Subanun are capable of making at various levels in their hierarchy of kinship taxonomy is a subject of considerable interest, we are at present concerned with the maximal, obligatory distinctions that they must make in response to the query: *mekendun 'amu run ni X?* ("How are you related to X?"). If we change our query to *meguseba 'amu run ni X?* ("Are you a consanguineal of X?"), or to *kandun mekpated 'amu rua' ni X?* ("How are you a sibling-cousin of X?"), we will obtain responses at different levels of specification. Obligatory responses to the query "How are you related to X?" yield a set of single-word terms which designate sixteen mutually exclusive classes of kinsmen at a single level of contrast. These classes are the basic kinship categories. Eliminating dialect synonyms and terms reserved for drinking songs and other special types of discourse, we are left with a corpus of sixteen distinct *basic kinship terms*. These terms are listed and defined at the end of the paper.

The criteria by which the sixteen basic kinship categories are differentiated have significant cultural correlates in the processes of family formation. The importance of marriage, the institution through which new families are formed, is reflected in the kinship terminology by the observance of the criterion of affinity throughout the system. This criterion segregates all kin in Ego's generation who are connected to Ego by one or more marriage links, as well as kinsmen in different generations who are connected to Ego by at least one marriage link in the first descending generation. A consistent analysis of Subanun kinship criteria requires this special definition of affinity, for the Subanun classify parent's sibling's spouse with parent's sibling and spouse's sibling's child with sibling's child. They differentiate these consanguineals from such affinal categories as spouse's parent's sibling and sibling's child's spouse.

The kinship terminology further segregates the pivotal, i.e., parental, members of each of the five families with which an individual normally relates during his lifetime in the process of family formation and sponsorship. These families are listed below, the term designating each kin type being indicated in parentheses:

1. Ego's family of orientation, in which his father (*gama'*) and mother (*gina'*) are the pivotal members.
2. Ego's family of procreation, in which he and his spouse (*sawa*) are the pivotal members.
3. Ego's spouse's family of orientation, in which Ego's spouse's parents (*penuganan*) are the pivotal members.
4. Ego's child's family of procreation, in which Ego's child (*bata'*) and Ego's child's spouse (*minuganan*) are the pivotal members.
5. Ego' child's spouse's family of orientation, in which Ego's child's spouse's parents (*bela'i*) are the pivotal members.

These are the families which Ego forms by marriage (2), which sponsor his marriage (1 and 3), which Ego sponsors (4), and which act as co-sponsors with Ego (5).

The five pairs of pivotal kinsmen fall into three generations: Ego's, the first ascending, and the first descending generations. The basic kinship terminology distinguishes these three generations throughout the system and lumps all consanguineals in other generations into one category (*gapu'*) signifying "consanguineal kin more than one generation removed." Affinal kinship is not extended beyond the first ascending and descending generations.

These five kin pairs, finally, are all connected to Ego by lineal, affinal, or a combination of lineal and affinal links. Unlike other basic kinship categories, all of which include collateral kin, the designata of the terms for these categories are not infinitely extendable; the terms can denote only these kin types and no others. We shall label as lineal categories those classes of kin with finite designata, and define a *lineal* as any kinsman not connected to Ego by any collateral links. Thus defined, the distinction between lineals and collaterals pertains only in the three crucial generations: Ego's and the two generations adjacent to his.

The three basic criteria of Subanun kinship classification—affinity, generation, and lineality—intersect, in short, in such a manner as to distinguish the five pivotal pairs of kinsmen from each other and as a group (lineals) from all other kin (collaterals). Among consanguineals, all kin not included in the five pivotal pairs are segregated only by generation and, in the first ascending generation, by sex. Degree of collaterality is nowhere recognized in basic terminology beyond the distinguishing of lineals (zero-degree collaterals) from collaterals (see Lounsbury, 1956, p. 168). The "uncle" and "aunt" terms (*kia'*, *dara'*) extend to all collaterals in the first ascending generation; the "sibling-cousin" term (*pated*) to all collaterals in Ego's generation; and the "nephew-niece" term (*manak*) to all collaterals of the first descending generation.

That a society which attaches such marked importance to the independence of nuclear families should fail to distinguish siblings from cousins in basic terminology may seem paradoxical, since siblings but not cousins share family membership with Ego. However, both Ego and his siblings ultimately marry out of their common family of orientation, establishing independent families of their own, and it is only the parental members of a family, upon whom its existence depends, who receive distinctive kinship designation. Siblings become parental members of independent families collateral to Ego's, and Ego's patterned relationships with families founded by siblings is not significantly different from those with families founded by cousins. In situations where a greater degree of specification is required, e.g., in designating marriageable kin, a special derivative term, *gagunapu'*, may be employed to distinguish those consanguineals of Ego's generation who are not siblings.

Among affinals, complex types of linkage with Ego must be distinguished from simple types in both lineal and collateral sets. A complex lineal affinal is connected to Ego by two lineal links, one down and one up in this order. A complex collateral affinal is connected to Ego by two affinal links and one indefinitely extendable collateral link. Observance of this criterion in Ego's generation segregates child's spouse's parents from spouse and spouse's sibling's or cousin's spouse from spouse's sibling or cousin. Complex collateral affinals are further distinguished by the criterion of whether the relationship is between males or not between males, the latter covering cases where Ego, or the relative, or both are female. In these categories only male speakers differentiate sex of relative, and the terminology remains reciprocal.

Figure 5 diagrams the intersection of all criteria to form the basic kinship categories. The consanguineal categories can be extended indefinitely in both vertical and lateral directions to embrace all persons with whom Ego can or cares to trace genealogical ties. The affinal categories are infinitely extendable along collateral links, but cannot be extended, in designative nomenclature, by the addition of further affinal links. Affinals not included in the basic categories can be designated only by special derivative or descriptive terms, which are not part of the basic terminology.

FIGURE 5
Subanun Basic Kinship Categories

Generation and Complexity	Consanguineal				Affinal		
	Collateral		Lineal		Lineal	Collateral	
	Female	Male	Female	Male		Between Males	Not Between Males
+2, +3, etc.	gapu'						
+1	dara'	kia	gina'	gama'	penugaŋan	kayug	
0 Simple	pated		EGO		sawa	bati'	gipag
Complex					bela'i	bilas	
−1	manak		bata'		minugaŋan	kayug	
−2, −3, etc.	gapu'						

Pivotal kin stand out not only in the linguistic designation of basic categories but also in the behavioral correlates of kinship classification. Patterned kinship behavior among the Subanun falls along a continuum from intimacy to formality or reserve. Varying possibilities in the use of nominal kinship terms to name individuals, which are themselves aspects of kinship behavior (Murdock, 1949, p. 97), permit a fivefold division of this continuum. Distinctive behavior patterns characterize each division. In the table below, these behavior patterns are roughly identified in English, the included kin are noted for each pattern, and the definitive nominal usage in reference or address is indicated by means of the following symbols: N—personal name, nickname, or reciprocal nickname; K—nominal kinship term (these terms are distinct from the designative terms discussed above); O—no nominal usage possible (personal names can not be mentioned).

Within the relationships of informality and mutual respect, Subanun kinsmen can express a wide latitude of social distance by means of alternative kinship terms and types of nicknames, alone or in combination with personal names. Non-kin can be brought into the framework of these relationships and named by a kinship term appropriate to an existing or desired social relationship. On the other hand, the extreme relationships of intimacy, obedience, and reserve are more circumscribed in permissible behavior and in nominal usage. These patterns prevail only between lineals and include all the pivotal kin pairs except child's spouse's parents (who are usually treated with mutual respect and are named with one of the terms applied to collateral affinals). The appearance of lineals at both extremes of the scale of patterned kinship behavior provides further illustration of the distinctive importance of these kin in Ego's life history.

SCALE OF PATTERNED KINSHIP BEHAVIOR

Patterned Behavior	Included Kin	Nominal Usage
Intimacy	Spouse, Child	N
Informality	Collateral Consanguineals	K,N
Mutual Respect	Collateral Affinals	K ± N
Obedience	Mother, Father	K
Reserve	Parent-in-law, Child-in-law	O

Subanun kinship terminology and behavior reflect the fundamental significance of the relationships generated by the establishment of new families. There are, of course, many other kinds of relationships linking independent families, for example, those fostered by economic, religious, festive, and legal activities. Nevertheless, despite this network of formal and informal social ties among families, there have emerged no large, stable, discrete socio-political units. The Subanun family remains, like that of the Iban, largely a "sovereign nation" (Freeman, 1958, p. 8).[7] But unlike the Iban *bilek* or the Gilbertese *oo* (Goodenough, 1955), the Subanun family is not a descent group. Its corporate unity endures only as long as does the marriage tie of its founders. The continuity of Subanun society must be sought in the continuous process of corporate group formation and dissolution rather than in the permanency of the groups themselves.

The kinship terms listed below are the basic designative terms of the Gulu Disakan dialect of the Eastern Subanun language. Other dialects exhibit different forms at several points, but the system is much the same throughout the Eastern Subanun area. The category *kayug*, however, is absent in southern dialects. Several synonyms of dialectical origin may be common in any one region, e.g., *gyaya'* for *dara'* and *giras* for *bilas* in the Gulu Disakan region. It might be noted here that the writer has found no evidence of the bifurcate collateral terminology reported by Christie (1909, p. 116) and discussed by Kroeber (1919, p. 79) in any dialect of Eastern or Western Subanun for which he has recorded the kinship terminology.

LIST OF KINSHIP TERMS

1 *gapu'*: grandparents; ascendants of grandparents; siblings, cousins, and siblings' (and cousins') spouses of the foregoing; grandchildren; grandchildren of siblings

and cousins and of spouse's siblings and cousins; descendants of the foregoing. Distinctive criteria: consanguineal; more than one generation removed.
2. *gama'*: father. Distinctive criteria: consanguineal; first ascending generation; lineal; male.
3. *gina'*: mother. Distinctive criteria: consanguineal; first ascending generation; lineal; female.
4. *kia'*: parents' brothers and male cousins; husbands of parents' sisters and female cousins. Distinctive criteria: consanguineal; first ascending generation; collateral; male.
5. *dara'*: parents' sisters and female cousins; wives of parents' brothers and male cousins. Distinctive criteria: consanguineal; first ascending generation; collateral; female.
6. *pated*: siblings; cousins (with indefinite lateral extension). Distinctive criteria: consanguineal; Ego's generation.
7. *bata'*: sons and daughters. Distinctive criteria: consanguineal; first descending generation; lineal.
8. *manak*: children of siblings and cousins; children of spouse's siblings and cousins. Distinctive criteria: consanguineal; first descending generation; collateral.
9. *sawa*: spouse (husband or wife). Distinctive criteria: affinal; Ego's generation; lineal; simple.
10. *bela'i*: child's spouse's parents. Distinctive criteria: affinal; Ego's generation; lineal; complex.
11. *bati'*: wife's brothers and male cousins; husbands of sisters and female cousins (male speaking). Distinctive criteria: affinal; Ego's generation; collateral; simple; between men.
12. *gipag*: wife's sisters and female cousins; wives of brothers and male cousins (male speaking); husband's siblings and cousins; spouses of siblings and cousins (female speaking). Distinctive criteria: affinal; Ego's generation; collateral; simple; not between men.
13. *bilas*: spouses of spouse's siblings and cousins. Distinctive criteria: affinal; Ego's generation; collateral; complex.
14. *penuganan*: spouse's parents. Distinctive criteria: affinal; first ascending generation; lineal.
15. *minuganan*: spouses of sons and daughters. Distinctive criteria: affinal; first descending generation; lineal.
16. *kayug*: wife's parents' brothers and male cousins; wife's parents' sisters' (and female cousins') husbands; siblings' (and cousins') spouses' fathers (male speaking); siblings' (and cousins') spouses' parents' brothers, male cousins, and sisters' (and male cousins') husbands (male speaking); siblings' (and cousins') daughters' husbands (male speaking); wife's siblings' (and cousins') daughters' husbands; children's spouses' brothers and male cousins (male speaking); siblings' (and cousins') children's spouses' brothers and male cousins (male speaking); wife's siblings' (and cousins') children's spouses' brothers and male cousins. Distinctive criteria: affinal; one generation removed; collateral; between men.

CHAPTER 5

THE IBAN OF WESTERN BORNEO

J. D. FREEMAN
Australian National University

THE Iban, or Sea Dayaks,[1] are a Proto-Malay people of western Borneo. Today, most of them live in Sarawak, where they are the predominant element in a heterogeneous population. The total population of Sarawak, as computed in the census of 1947, was 546,385, of whom 190,326, or 34.8 per cent, were Iban. Sarawak, like all the countries of Southeast Asia, has a plural society. Along the coast, among the deltaic swamps and in the low-lying country bordering the tidal reaches of the rivers, are the main centers of Malay, Chinese, and Melanua settlement. Farther inland, in broken country covered with tropical rainforest and drained by fast-flowing rivers, live the indigenous hill peoples: the Land Dayaks, the Iban, the Kayan, the Kenyah, the Kajang, and others, all with subsistence economies based on the shifting cultivation of dry rice. Other Iban tribes inhabit tht headwaters of the great Kapuas River of what is now Kalimantan, or Indonesian Borneo, but on these information is scant and reliable population estimates are not available.

The people with whom the present account is primarily concerned are the Ulu Ai Iban of the Baleh River in the Third Division of Sarawak. The Baleh enters the great Rejang River from the west at a point about 170 miles from the sea, and along its banks and those of its many tributaries (the Sut, Mujong, Gat, and Merirai being the most important) are scattered some 130 Iban communities with a total population of about 11,500. Almost all of these people are the descendants of migrants from the interior of the Second Division of Sarawak (particularly the Ulu Ai, or Upper Lupar River) and from parts of the Kanyau, a tributary of the Kapuas. Leaving these areas in the early decades of the nineteenth century, they moved intermittently forward by way of the Katibas and Rejang rivers, cultivating the hillsides in their path, and reached the primeval forests of the Baleh about 1880. During the years that followed the Iban were several times expelled from the Baleh, a number of punitive expeditions being sent against them by the Brooke government because of their recalcitrant addiction to headhunting, and not until 1922 was permanent settlement achieved. Today the Baleh is an exclusively Iban area.

The field work on which my findings are based was carried out during two different periods: the first from February, 1949, to January, 1951, and the second from December, 1957, to March, 1958.[2] During the former period the Iban of the Baleh region were a pagan and preliterate people whose *adat* and way of life had been little influenced by the outside world. Since then governmental and missionary activities have brought about various kinds of cultural change. To date, however, at least within the Baleh, there have been no significant departures from the traditional kinship system described in this paper. Moreover, such comparative data as are available to me (mainly in the form of inquiries which I have made in other parts of the Third Division, and in the Second Division during a two months' survey in 1951) suggest that the system here described is the traditional system of all the Iban tribes of Sarawak.

A more detailed account of the Iban family and the kinds of residence and descent associated with it has been published elsewhere.[3] In the present paper I shall direct attention to the wider cognatic social structure of the Iban and their system of kinship and affinity.

THE *BILEK* FAMILY

The Iban of the Baleh all live in long-houses, each consisting of a series of separate family apartments occupied by small family groups. Later I shall have something to say of the general kinship structure of the long-house community. First, however, because of its relevance to the understanding of the Iban system of kinship terminology, I would like to make brief reference to some of the salient characteristics of the family units of which a long-house is composed—*bilek*[4] families, as the Iban call them.

Every Iban *bilek* family is an autonomous corporate group. This fundamental fact is expressed in several ways. For example, the *bilek* family is always a local group owning and occupying a single long-house apartment. Again, it is always an independent entity economically, its members constituting a single household and providing for their subsistence by the cultivation of hill rice and other crops. Likewise, it is always an allodial unit possessing both land (including tree crops) and valued heirloom property in its own right. Finally, in ritual matters every *bilek* family is a distinct group performing its own rites (*gawai*) and possessing its own magical charms (*pengaroh*), its own special kind of sacred rice (*padi pun*), and its own set of ritual prohibitions (*pemali*).

Typically a *bilek* family contains three generations, consisting of a pair of grandparents, a son or daughter and his or her spouse, and grandchildren. Stem families of this type usually have about six or seven members. Such families are perpetuated as corporate groups by a simple expedient: at least one of the children of the family, when he (or she) reaches maturity and marries, remains permanently in the ancestral *bilek*. All the other children of the family may marry out, and so become members of other units, but one (either a son or a daughter) always stays in the natal *bilek*. In this way an Iban *bilek* family achieves continuity through time as, from one generation to the next, one elementary family grows out of and succeeds another in an unbroken sequence. This means that every *bilek* family is (in theory) a perennial corporation aggregate. In other words, although birth, adoption, marriage, and death result in regular changes in its personnel, a *bilek* persists through time as a jurally defined entity—an estate in land and property which, at any moment, is always held in common ownership by a group of coexisting family members.

To achieve continuity in this way a *bilek* family, generation by generation, must produce the children one of whom will, in due course, succeed his (or her) parents as a manager of the family estate. This requires that the parents in each generation should be joined in a productive and ideally a stable marriage.[5] Further, as the *bilek* family is a strictly exogamous unit, it must in each generation recruit to its membership at least one affinal member. As we have already seen, the individual who remains a resident of the ancestral *bilek* may be either a son or a daughter. In actual fact, sons remain in the parental *bilek* to approximately the same extent as do daughters, and, similarly, sons and daughters marry out of their natal *bilek* to about the same extent. In other words, the in-married affine of a *bilek* is just as likely to be a husband as a wife.

The significance of marriage for the *bilek* is shown in the fact that affines acquire full membership in the family into which they marry, while relinquishing all parcenary rights in their natal *bilek*.[6] Further, affinal members frequently come to play a dominant role in the management of a *bilek* family's affairs. In Iban society, then, the conjugal tie is of great importance; indeed, it can be shown in certain respects and contexts to matter more than does the relationship between siblings.

RESIDENCE AND FILIATION

From the foregoing it will be seen that marriage among the Iban is of a kind that may be called utrolocal,[7] meaning by this term a system of marriage in which either virilocal or uxorilocal residence may be followed and in which rules of kinship and inheritance result in no special preference for either form of domicile. In fact, virilocal and uxorilocal residence occur with nearly equal incidence; for an extensive series of marriages of Baleh Iban, 51 per cent were instances of uxorilocal and 49 per cent of virilocal residence.

Every individual in Iban society is born into one particular *bilek*, and the system of marital residence just described means that this is just as likely, in general, to be the *bilek* of the child's mother as it is to be the *bilek* of the child's father. Further, the *bilek* in which a child is born and grows up is the only *bilek* in which he (or she) jurally possesses parcenary rights, for rights may not be held in more than one *bilek* at a time. These rights over the *bilek* estate are relinquished only by adoption into another *bilek*, by out-marriage, or by death. Filiation among the Iban is thus of a special kind which I have called *utrolateral*,[8] meaning by this term a system of filiation in which an individual can possess membership in either his father's or his mother's corporate birth group (i.e., the *bilek* family among the Iban), but not in both at the same time. In practice, both types of filiation occur to an approximately equal extent.

Among the Iban, then, filiation takes the form of attachment to a local family estate, principles of both descent and residence being involved. In other words, it is filial consanguinity and local residence acting together which establish the jural rights of the natal members of any *bilek* family. In practicing this type of filiation to a local family estate the Iban have solved the problem of establishing a system of corporations without resort to any unilineal reckoning of succession.[9] It is one of the virtues of the Iban system that it defines the rights of *bilek* members without ambiguity, and in this respect it can be said to be just as efficient as a family system based on unilineal descent. The *bilek* family assumes great importance among the Iban, for it is the principal corporate group of their society.

SIBLINGS AND PARTITION

Within a *bilek* family, siblings are parceners; there is no differentiation of rights between older and younger members, between the sexes, or between natural and adopted children. In other words, co-resident siblings hold equal rights jurally over the family estate. This equivalence of siblings in the structure of the *bilek* is one of the basic principles of Iban society. Unmarried siblings, we may say, are joined by a common interest in their family estate. In the course of time, however, when siblings marry, affines enter the *bilek*, and children are born, the situation is changed by the intrusion of rival loyalties. The *bilek* family is now no longer a simple group, for it contains within its boundaries two different elementary families, and when two such families emerge within the confines of the same apartment there is a very strong tendency for their interests to diverge. The recognized course in such circumstances (and here we are dealing with one of the basic values of Iban society) is for one of the siblings to claim his (or her) share of the family estate, secede from the ancestral *bilek*, and set up a separate domestic unit. This process of family partition is, in fact, a common occurrence. It is important to note, however, that partition occurs only when the seceding sibling is already married, or has established an elementary family of his (or her) own, and, moreover, that in about 80 per cent of the cases there are two married siblings and their spouses in the *bilek* immediately prior to partition.

Thus, whereas prior to partition the solidarity of a *bilek* family depends on the sibling tie, after this event the solidarity of each independent section rests primarily on a conjugal tie. These two forms of relationship—the sibling tie and the conjugal tie—are, I would argue, the most important in the kinship structure of Iban society. As already indicated in part, the two ties assume importance at all the main stages in the developmental cycle of the *bilek* family. They are also of cardinal significance beyond the *bilek*. Immediately before or during partition siblings within a *bilek* frequently quarrel. After partition, however, the siblings concerned stand at the head of autonomous *bilek* families, and in these changed circumstances it is usual for their solidarity to be gradually reestablished, though in more diffuse terms. That is, while no longer possessing a common interest in a family estate, they behave toward one another with the same kind of general affection and helpfulness that normally exist between siblings of the same *bilek*. It should be noted, however, that the same kind of relationship exists between the affinal spouse of a *bilek* and his (or her) siblings, wherever they may be. Indeed this remark may be extended to the general statement that a *bilek* family normally maintains the same kind of friendly relationships with the cognates of both its natal and its affinal members.

THE LONG-HOUSE COMMUNITY

Bilek families are grouped together in long-house communities. These communities vary considerably in size: from as few as 4 to as many as 50 *bilek* families, the average size being about 14. Of a sample of 61 houses in the Baleh region,[10] 25 per cent contained fewer than 10 *bilek* families, only 13 per cent comprised more than 20 *bilek* families, and 62 per cent consisted of from 10 to 20 *bilek* families.

In the Baleh region all Iban long-houses are situated on the banks of rivers or streams navigable by dugout canoes. Their dispersal along the banks of these rivers is irregular, and the distance between houses may vary from a few hundred yards to four or five river miles. Nowhere in the Baleh are there clusters of houses such as occur among the Land Dayaks of the First Division or the Iban of the Rejang delta. The universal rule is that each long-house constitutes a single community; in other words, the village and the long-house coincide. Moreover, traditionally each long-house community is an autonomous entity not subject to the control of any other group.

Every long-house is situated on part of a specified tract of land, and between long-houses there are always recognized boundaries, consisting in the main of easily distinguishable natural features such as streams or ridges. A long-house, then, is the domicile of an independent community of families situated on the bank of a river that runs through a specified territory over which these families have either rights of access or ownership.[11]

Most of the families making up a long-house community are related to one another cognatically. It is important to realize, however, that, despite the high degree of interrelatedness that may exist among its component families, a long-house holds no property of any consequence in common ownership, nor is there collective ownership of swiddens. Again, there is an absence of economic activity by the long-house community as a corporate group. Nonetheless, membership in a long-house does impose upon a *bilek* family many duties and obligations, for it is universally accepted that the well-being of any community is dependent upon its ritual state, and for the maintenance of this all are responsible. Thus, joining a long-house always involves ritual incorporation.

General responsibility for preserving the ritual well-being of a long-house rests with its *tuai burong*, or augur, who also performs the important task of taking auguries for the community as a whole. Every long-house also has a *tuai rumah*, or headman, whose principal duty is the safeguarding and administering of the customary law, the *adat*. Today the *tuai rumah* is accepted as the official intermediary between his community and the British colonial administration, which has conferred upon him limited magisterial powers. Thus, in jural as well as ritual matters the long-house is a conditional corporate group, for all its *bilek* families willingly place themselves under the jurisdiction of their *tuai rumah*. For the offices of neither house augur nor house headman is there any rigid dogma of succession; any male cognate may succeed to either.

THE KINDRED

In Iban society there is no semblance of any sort of unilineal descent groups of the type usually described as a lineage or clan. Instead, Iban social structure is based on purely cognatic principles. Let us begin our analysis of these principles with an examination of the main categories of relationship which the Iban themselves recognize, considering first the term *kaban*. In its widest connotation, this term refers not only to an individual's cognates and affines but also to all of his (or her) friends and acquaintances. In this connotation the term *kaban* refers to the same social category as the Old English phrase "kith and kin."[12] The extension of the term *kaban* to cover this broad field may be seen as an expression of the fact that in Iban society, with full bilateral recognition of all relatives, almost all of those persons with whom an individual associates are, in some degree, either his (or her) cognatic or affinal kin.

There is, moreover, a general assumption that most if not all the members of a tribe are kinsfolk, even though their exact relationships to one another can no longer be traced. This can be discerned in such assertions as *itong se kaban magang kami Iban* ("We Iban, it may be said, are all kin of one kind or another") and *se ribu kaban tu kaban magang magang, enda olih kira* ("One's kin [cognatic and agnatic] run into thousands; all, all are kin, they can not be counted"). The Iban are also well aware, as the second of these assertions implies, that because of the widely ramifying nature of their cognatic system many kinsfolk become forgotten to one another in each generation. Furthermore, this forgetting is frequently erratic and one-sided, so that it is by no means an unusual experience for an Iban to be hailed as a kinsman by a tribesman whom he himself does not recognize. The term of address used within the category of kith and kin, where there is no knowledge of the generational relation of the two persons concerned, is *wai*. This term may be used of and by both sexes and all ages. In its widest sense it is best translated as "friend," but in many contexts it carries the general implication of "to whom I am probably related."

Within the broad category of kith and kin three main distinctions are made, namely:

(a) *kaban mandal:* cognatic kin;
(b) *kaban tampil:* affinal kin;
(c) *orang bukai:* other people.

The adjective *mandal* has the primary meaning of near or close, as in the sentence: *umai aku mandal amat* ("My swidden is very near at hand"). The phrase *kaban mandal* is used to designate an individual's cognates, i.e., all of his (or her) known consanguineal kin, tracing descent through both males and females. The word *tampil* has the primary meaning of joined together, as in the sentence: *iya nampil ka brang kalambi iya* ("She is joining on the sleeves of her jacket"). The phrase *kaban tampil* is used to refer to all of an individual's affinal kin, including both the cognates of his (or her) spouse and the affines of his (or her) cognates. In these phrases the distinction between cognatic and affinal kin is made semantically clear. However, as we shall see, the Iban custom of marriage between close cognates, e.g., between second cousins, results in a frequent overlapping of the two categories.

Those within the pervasive category *kaban* who cannot be shown to be cognates or affines are said to be *orang bukai*, or other people. This does not contradict the assumption mentioned earlier that such people may perhaps be one's relatives; indeed, a common statement among Iban is that if cognates do not intermarry they will eventually become *orang bukai*, or strangers, to one another.

For any individual the category *kaban mandal* is identical with his (or her) personal kindred. In recent years some anthropologists[13] have extended the term "kindred" to include affinal as well as cognatic kin. For my part, I see no justificaton for this tinkering with an ancient and concise term, and in this account I shall continue to employ kindred in its long-established sense of the category which embraces all of an individual's father's kin and all of his (or her) mother's kin, or, to put it more succinctly, all of an individual's cognates.[14]

As has long been recognized by those engaged in the study of Germanic societies, strictly speaking no two individuals have precisely the same kindred.[15] However, if the relationships between themselves are excepted, and assuming they have not produced children of their own, the members of the same sibling group do have the same kindred. Looked at in this way, a kindred is seen as radiating out bilaterally from the children of an elementary family to include all those persons to whom relationship can be traced consanguineally through both male and female links.

The point of reference in a personal kindred is the individual at its center who in reckoning its membership must trace his (or her) relationship to collateral kin through one or more ascending generations. Looked at synoptically, however, a kindred is made up of a series of affinally related cognatic groupings, which, it should be noted, are in no sense corporate groups. A child is directly a member of two cognatic groupings: those of his father and of his mother. Similarly, each parent is directly a member of two cognatic groupings, to all of which the child also belongs, making four in all. The number of cognatic groupings to which an individual belongs thus doubles with each additional ascending generation that is taken into account. It becomes an essential task, therefore, in the analysis of cognatic societies like that of the Iban, to establish the extent to which bilateral relationships are in fact reckoned. As we shall presently see, the average Iban is able genealogically to trace bilateral relationships only as far as the second ascending generation, i.e., to the siblings of his (or her) grandparents and their descendants.

In a kindred of this range four cognatic stocks are represented, namely, those stemming from the sibling groups of father's father, father's mother, mother's father, and mother's mother. While from the point of reference of the individual at the center of the kindred the members of all these four groupings are cognates, a number of them are ordinarily not cognatically related to one another. In other words, at ascending generation levels the cognatic groupings of which a kindred is composed are often linked primarily by a conjugal tie between two of their members.[16] Indeed, in a genetic sense all kindreds are brought into being by a succession of marriages through the generations; thus the four unions of a man's great-grandparents produce the four individuals whose two marriages produce his parents. In short, affinal kin (*kaban tampil*) in one generation become cognatic kin (*kaban mandal*) in the next. It can thus be said that the conjugal tie is of great importance in the general kinship structure of Iban society, just as it is within the *bilek* family.

Let us next consider briefly the average range of an individual's personal kindred, or *kaban mandal*. An obvious criterion to use in attempting to establish the range of the kindred is the extent to which the average Iban adult can bilaterally trace his (or her) genealogical relationships. According to this criterion, it can be said that the normal range of a personal kindred is two generations (alternatively, it can be described as of second-cousin range); that is, it extends as far as an individual's four grandparents, the siblings of these grandparents, and their descendants. Within this range an individual's cognates often number more than a hundred, and further they are commonly dispersed over a wide area. To take an example, the second-cousin-range kindred of Kubu, a man of Rumah Nyala, Sungai Sut, aged about 57 years in 1957, numbered 120 and were living in more than twenty different long-houses scattered over several hundred river miles, mainly in the Baleh and its tributaries, the Rejang and the Katibas.

The plotting of genealogical knowledge is an essential first stage in the exploration of an individual's kindred, but in all the cases I have investigated (and I am confident that this is quite a general phenomenon) an individual recognizes many cognates beyond the second-cousin range which we have just been discussing. While the exact genealogical details of their relationship may be forgotten, cognates commonly know that two or more of their grandparents were cousins. The usual limit to the identification of cognates in this manner is fourth cousinship, i.e., where a pair of individuals know that two of their grandparents were second cousins. Very occasionally the limit may extend to fifth cousinship. A typical Iban utterance on this point runs as follows: *agi empat sarak agi damping itong kaban mandal, ngilah empat sarak enda alah tusut nyau nyadi kaban jauh* ("Up to four generations kin are still close and are reckoned as cognates, but beyond four generations relationships can no longer be established; cognates become lost and turn into distant kin"). Another informant likened the network of cognatic relationships under discussion to an Iban *jala*, or casting-net, which, when finished, is conical in shape and weighted around its circumference by iron rings or small lumps of lead. At the commencement, a casting-net is a very small cone, but as the knotting proceeds and one circle of mesh is succeeded by the next it increases in size until its final circumference is measured not in inches but in fathoms. In the same way, said my informant, cognates grow farther and farther apart, generation by generation, until in the end they no longer know that they are kin.

As these examples indicate, the kindred is an uncircumscribed cognatic category which the Iban think of as extending indefinitely outwards. The total number of cognates which any individual Iban recognizes obviously varies from person to person, depending on such factors as age, memory, and domicile, but they are always numerous. Kubu, the genealogical composition of whose kindred has already been cited, estimated that altogether his *kaban mandal* (i.e., all of his cognates known to him) would number from two to three hundred. And this, I believe, is probably typical of the personal kindreds of elderly and prominent men, of whom Kubu is one.

It will be obvious that an individual's *kaban mandal* do not in any sense constitute a group. But it can also be said that these cognates do make up an important part of the social field within which activity is organized. Indeed, one of the most significant characteristics of bilateral societies like that of the Iban is the broad scope which they offer for the organization of activity among kinfolk. Among the Iban, for example, work groups (for hunting, the gathering of jungle produce, etc.) are largely composed of cognates, who may be drawn from both sides of the leader's kindred. However, such groups also commonly contain affinal kin, or *kaban tampil*, the category next to be discussed.

MARRIAGE AND AFFINES

Iban marriage rules are predominantly concerned with alliances between cognates. There is no objection to marriage with an unrelated individual (*orang bukai*) as long as it is known that he (or she) has no hereditary taint of the evil eye (*tau tepang*) and is not descended from a slave (*ulun*). Such marriages are not favored, however, and are infrequent; instead, it is the marriage of cognates which is the norm, both preferred and actual.

For cognates the rules governing marriage are strictly formulated. In summary, sexual relations are forbidden as incestuous (*jadi mali*) between:

(a) all cognates of the same *bilek* family;
(b) siblings (both full and half), even though they may be members of different *bilek* families;
(c) all close cognates (i.e., within a kindred of second-cousin range) who are not on the same generation level.

The most stringent of these incest prohibitions are those which apply to relationships within the elementary family, and they hold with the same force whether or not the individuals concerned are members of the same *bilek*. In the majority of cases, of course, the members of an elementary family are all members of one *bilek*, but it is significant that the Iban have extended these prohibitions (though with lessened stringency) to all cognates living in the same household, thereby making the natal members of a *bilek* family an exogamous group. Thus the union of first cousins, though normally a permissible form of marriage, is interdicted if they are members of the same *bilek* family on the ground that, having grown up in the same *bilek*, it is as though the cousins concerned were siblings.

Beyond the *bilek* and elementary family, incest prohibitions apply exclusively to relations between cognates on different generation levels. Particular emphasis is placed on the avoidance of sexual relations and marriage between individuals of adjacent generations; *adat* prescribes that within a kindred of second-cousin range individuals in adjacent generations must never marry. Breaches of this rule do sometimes occur at the outer limits, e.g., in the case of a man marrying the daughter of his second cousin, but in all instances known to me severe action was taken, e.g., the infliction of a fine and expulsion from the community where the offense occurred.

It is significant, I think, that it should be the kindred of second-cousin range that marks the generally enforced limit of marital prohibitions among the Iban, for, as already noted, the second-cousin kindred also marks the extent to which the average Iban is able to trace genealogical relationships. Beyond the second-cousin range it is possible, provided certain sacrificial and placatory rites are performed, for cognates on adjacent generation levels to marry; thus, if he first performs the required rites, a man may marry the daughter of his third cousin. By following a similar course it is also possible for a man to marry the granddaughter of his first cousin. Beyond these limits the rites lessen in magnitude as the relationships involved become more attenuated, but the appropriate rites are always insisted upon by the cognates concerned when it is known that those entering upon a marriage belong to different generation levels.[17]

On the other hand, if cognates belong to the same generation level there are no objections to their marrying as long as they are not siblings or do not belong to the same *bilek*. Thus, if they belong to different *bilek* families, it is fully permissible for cousins of the first, second, third, or any other degree to marry if they so desire; and those of the first degree may be either parallel or cross-cousins. Indeed, the marriage of cousins is strongly preferred in Iban society; about 75 per cent of marriages are between individuals who are *kaban mandal*, and of these the majority are *petunggal*, or cousins of some degree.

The Iban, as has presumably become apparent, are a monogamous people. Moreover, marriage is not accompanied by any kind of substantial bride-price or dowry. This, I would argue, is correlated with the absence of any large-scale corporate kin groups and with the fact that marriage among the Iban is very much a matter of personal predilection. Beyond the limits of the prohibited categories mentioned above, Iban men and women please themselves whom they marry. For parents, the main concern is with where the couple are to live. It is a common occurrence for each set of parents to be strongly opposed to losing one of their children in out-marriage, and there is often serious disagreement and quarreling between *bilek* families before a solution, i.e., a decision as between virilocal or uxorilocal residence, is reached. Neolocal residence is never practiced.

The dissolution of a marriage may be achieved without difficulty. According to the *adat* of the Third Division Iban, any married couple is permitted to divorce at any time by mutual consent, and a partner who discards his (or her) spouse is liable to little more than a nominal fine.[18] Under these conditions any husband or wife can easily terminate a marriage if this be desired, and divorce is a common occurrence. There is a marked tendency, however, for divorces to be confined to young men and women under 35 years of age. By the time they have reached the age of 35 years or thereabouts most men have settled down to a stable and lasting marriage. This, it is significant, is the age at which men usually become responsible for managing the *bilek* estate, and there is widespread realization that the successful preservation and advancement of a *bilek* family, as well as the attainment of wealth, prestige, and the other goals valued by the Iban, depend on the successful maintenance of a marriage.

In almost all such settled marriages husband and wife are joined in a relationship which each finds congenial. In the course of time a married couple become linked by intimate ties of both sentiment and material interest, and it is commonly said by the Iban, in discussing marriage and the *bilek*, that the relationship between husband and wife is closer than that which exists between siblings (*laki bini itong damping agi ari menyadi tampong pala*). In a successful marriage, it is pointed out, a husband and wife share equally in the most important undertakings of life: the bringing up of children, the cultivation of rice, and the custody of the *bilek* estate (*ngimpun anak, ngimpun bilek, enggau turun*). The conjugal tie, it may be said, is basic to the structure of the *bilek* family.

This leads back to the category of affinal kin, or *kaban tampil*. A husband and wife, should there be no cognatic relationship between them, possess entirely separate personal kindreds, each of which becomes part of the personal kindred of their children. For the husband and wife, however, the relationship between their personal kindreds is purely affinal, the cognates (*kaban mandal*) of one spouse being the affinal kin (*kaban tampil*) of the other. In practice, however, about 75 per cent of marriages are between cognates, and it is thus usual for the categories of *kaban mandal* and *kaban tampil* to coincide to at least some extent; when close cousins marry the overlap may be considerable.[19] Here we are confronted with one of the most important features of Iban society: the intermarriage of cousins constantly reinforces the network of cognatic ties linking individual Iban, and kin that might otherwise have become dispersed are brought together again.

COMMUNITY STRUCTURE

Having briefly adumbrated the cognatic basis of the Iban kinship system we are now in a position to give a summary account of the social structure of the long-house. Within every long-house community there is a core-group of *bilek* families linked by close ties of cognatic kinship. These families are commonly those of the founders of the community, and their apartments are usually side by side in the center of the long-house. For example, in Rumah Nyala (of the Sungai Sut), which contained 25 apartments in 1950, there was a compact block of eight *bilek* whose families were all joined by relationships which were, for the most part, between siblings, or first or second cousins. Moreover, each of the other 17 *bilek* was related to one or more of this central block of eight families, which therefore constituted a kind of core around which the rest of the long-house was grouped. A similar sort of structure is found in most Iban communities, though occasionally there may be two distinct core-groups. It is important to note, however, that while each family is always related to at least one other family, it seldom if ever occurs (except in small houses of under ten apartments) that there is complete interrelatedness among the families of a community. Again, while the linkage of *bilek* families in a community is chiefly in the form of cognatic ties between the natal members of these families, it does happen in an appreciable number of cases that the linkage of a *bilek* to others in the long-house is traced either predominantly or exclusively through an in-married member.[20] We may say, then, that a long-house community is a local confederation, based on cognatic kinship, of a series of autonomous family corporations.

It should be stressed, however, that an Iban long-house community is an open and not a closed group, for its component *bilek* families are joined in free association from which withdrawal is always possible. Each *bilek* family always possesses cognatic kin in a number of other long-houses, and may join any of these other settlements should its members so desire.[21] There is, indeed, a good deal of movement from one long-house to another. In pioneer regions like the Baleh, where land is still in fairly abundant supply, few long-houses maintain the same combination of *bilek* families for more than a year or two at a time. In general the core-group is stable, but it occasionally happens in cases of serious dispute that a long-house breaks up completely, its component families dispersing to a number of separate and often widely scattered destinations. Such cases of community disintegration offer striking evidence of the conditional nature of group formation at the long-house level.

When a *bilek* family does change its place of abode it always seeks out a long-house in which kinsfolk are already established. Usually there are many different possibilities, for, as we have seen, the basis of long-house organization is cognatic kinship, and it is recognized that all cognatic ties, whether they be traced from natal, adopted, or affinal members of the *bilek* family, are equally available for purposes of affiliation. This means that a family is free to join any long-house in which there are cognates of either husband or wife, or of both.

The kinship network we have been considering was formerly also the basis of the Iban tribe. The tribe was a diffuse territorial grouping of long-house communities dispersed along the banks of a major river and its tributaries. Throughout the entire tribe there extended an intricate network of cognatic and affinal relationships linking its various members, all of whom recognized one another as *kaban*, kith or kin. Although the Iban tribe entirely lacked any sort of overall political organization, it did provide an area within which disputes could usually be settled, i.e., through the mechanisms of kinship. Furthermore, it was endogamous, and its members did not take one another's heads. Today, however, with the establishment of colonial government, the tribe—alway a diffuse and inconsiderable entity—has been almost entirely superseded by a series of administrative districts under officially appointed Iban leaders called *pengulu*.

KINSHIP TERMINOLOGY: COGNATES

Having sketched some of the salient features of Iban society I shall now turn to a brief discussion of the system of kinship terminology. In this discussion I shall be chiefly concerned with an examination of some of the ways in which the kinship terminology of the Iban reflects or is functionally consistent with the more important relationships and distinctions of their social structure. This approach to kinship terminologies is by no means a new one,[22] and its cogency has been amply demonstrated in recent decades by Radcliffe-Brown and others. Most of these studies, however, have been concerned with unilineal societies. The modern literature on kinship in purely cognatic societies is a sparse one, and there is thus some ground for looking at the Iban system from this point of view.

The main terms of reference for cognates are shown in Figure 6. The first point I would like to note is that there are no distinctions in terminology based on the sex of the speaker.[23] This, I would argue, is consistent with the fact that in all matters of property, inheritance, and the like, both within the family and beyond it, males and females have equivalent jural rights.

Next, I would like to direct attention to an important general feature of the

FIGURE 6
IBAN KINSHIP TERMINOLOGY: COGNATES

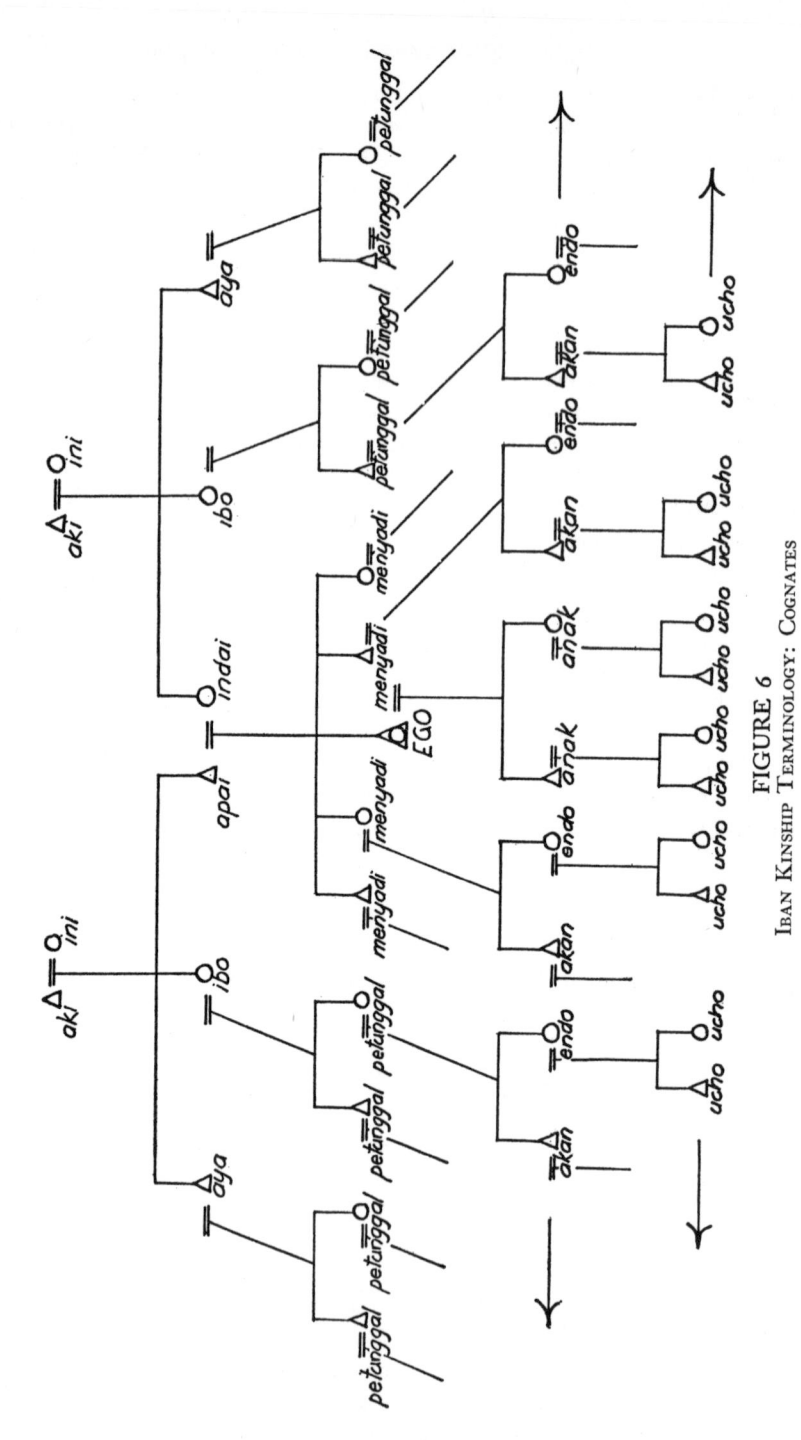

Iban system of kinship terminology. The whole system, it will be observed, is bilaterally symmetrical. In other words, none of the relationships traced through one's mother are distinguished terminologically from homologous relationships traced through one's father. Thus father's sister and mother's sister are both referred to by the term *ibo;* father's brother and mother's brother are both referred to by the term *aya;* and all first cousins (both parallel and cross, and on both sides) are referred to by the term *petunggal*.[24]

In all these instances it can be shown that the relationships referred to by the same term have, in general, the same structural significance. In the absence of any unilineal principle of descent, father's siblings do not assume any differential significance, either jurally or in any other way, as against mother's siblings. Both are equally available to Ego should he wish to seek assistance, and both are equally expected to give such assistance should it be sought. Similarly, at rituals held by Ego (or for him after his death) father's siblings and mother's siblings are equally entitled to shares of property distributed to cognates. The same considerations apply to all of an individual's first cousins (and beyond to second and remoter cousins). All these cousins, moreover, if they are of opposite sex to Ego, are equally available as partners in marriage. It is possible, then, to make the generalization that, beyond the *bilek*, rights and duties within the personal kindred are so balanced as to be bilaterally symmetrical.[25]

The Iban, with an attention to detail that delights the ethnographer, have symbolized this in one of their more important personal rites, the *gawai tusok*, which is concerned with the ritual piercing of a child's ear lobes. This operation is an event of moment in the life of an individual, for it is believed that on its proper performance will depend his (or her) subsequent health and welfare. The rites are elaborate, involving the invocation of tutelary gods and the employment of special charms and magical materials. The culmination of the *gawai* is the actual piercing of the ears with a small steel augur. It is common practice to have the lobe of one ear pierced by a cognate of the father and that of the other by a cognate of the mother, thus symbolizing the child's equal dependence on both sides of his (or her) personal kindred.

An individual's siblings, it will be noted, are all referred to by the same term, *menyadi*. In other words, brothers are not distinguished from sisters, and, furthermore, the term *menyadi* is applied to all brothers and sisters irrespective of seniority within the sibling group. Similarly, no distinction is made by either parent in respect of his (or her) children; both sons and daughters, and whatever their birth order, are referred to by the same term, *anak*. These usages also illustrate the reflection of basic jural rights in kinship terminology, for, as noted earlier, sons and daughters irrespective of age possess full and equal rights over the family estate.[26]

From the facts cited it will be seen that the Iban system of kinship terminology (in its terms of reference) is of the type called Eskimo by Murdock (1949, p. 233). That is, cross-cousins are referred to by the same term (*petunggal*) as parallel cousins, and both are distinguished from siblings, who are referred to as *menyadi*.[27]

Another feature of the Iban system of kinship terminology is the clear demarcation of kin by generation. No term is used in more than one generation level; there are no intergeneration reciprocals. This leads us to a principal regularity in Iban kinship behavior, namely, that all cognates at any generation level stand in a subordinate relationship to all those of the immediate senior generation and in a superordinate relationship to all those of the immediately junior generation. This is expressed most clearly in the relationship between parent and child. It is the duty of parents to care for their children and to instruct them in the traditional ways of the Iban. In these as in other matters they have authority over their children, who are expected to show them deference and respect. For example, there should be no undue levity between child and parent, and a child must not address a parent by his (or her) personal name, nor by the familiar term *wai*.[28]

The terms *apai* (father) and *indai* (mother) as terms of reference apply only to an individual's own parents; as terms of address, however, *apai* and *indai* are extended within the personal kindred to embrace all males and females of the parental generation. It is common practice, for example, to address uncles on both sides of the kindred as *apai*, and aunts as *indai;* and the same practice holds for the cousins of both parents. Similarly, all cognates on the same generation as one's children may be addressed as *anak*. The general superordination-subordination relationship of parent and child is also extended to all of these classificatory categories, though its force diminishes as genealogical distance increases. It can be said, therefore, that the classificatory terms of address *apai, indai,* and *anak* serve as indicators of kinship behavior. This is seen most clearly in the regulation of sexual relations between cognates. The prohibition of such relations between siblings and between members of the same *bilek* is made so obvious as a child grows up as to be taken for granted. The prohibition of sexual relations between cognates who are not on the same generation level is a pervasive rule applying, in theory, to all such cognatic kin. Parents make no attempt to nominate for their children all of the individuals in this prohibited category; instead, as they grow up, children are told that they may not *jadi* (marry) anyone they address as *apai, indai,* or *anak*. In this way the prohibition is unequivocally expressed and in a readily comprehensible way.

In contrast to the authority-respect relationship between members of adjacent generations, that which prevails between members of alternate generations is of the kind usually described as a joking relationship. Although grandparents are expected to help in the education of their grandchildren and to this end may exercise discipline over them, grandchildren are nevertheless treated in general with great affection and indulgence. By custom, moreover, grandchildren are licensed to joke (*tau nundi*) with their grandparents. The terms for grandmother (*ini*) and grandfather (*aki*) are extended both in reference and in address to include all collateral cognates of the same generation; similarly the term *ucho* (grandchild of either sex) is applied to all collateral descendants on the same generation level as one's own grandchildren.[29]

The rationale of the Iban kinship system for cognates will now have become apparent. In the absence of unilineal descent groups of any kind there is no need in Iban society to distinguish, unilaterally, different sets of collateral kin or specific unilateral kinship roles; instead, at each generation level all collaterals are seen as homologous. In its essentials the whole system may be looked on as a simple extension of the relationships existing within the three-generation stem family, which, as we have seen, is a modal form of the *bilek* family. Thus, in respect of general kinship behavior, collateral cognates are viewed in approximately the same way as lineal kin of the stem family. For example, beyond the *bilek*:

(a) all cousins are viewed like siblings, and are addressed by the same classificatory term: *menyadi*;
(b) all collaterals of the first ascending generation are viewed as being like parents, and are addressed by the same classificatory terms: *apai* and *indai*;
(c) all collaterals of the second ascending generation are viewed as grandparents, and are addressed by the same classificatory terms: *aki* and *ini*;
(d) all collaterals of the first descending generation are viewed as children, and are addressed by the same classificatory term: *anak*;
(e) all collaterals of the second descending generation are viewed as grandchildren, and are addressed by the same classificatory term: *ucho*.

KINSHIP TERMINOLOGY: AFFINES

The Iban system of terminology for affines (see Figures 7 and 8) exhibits the same general characteristics as that for cognates. Thus the whole system is bilaterally symmetrical, both for the cognates of Ego's spouse and for the affines of Ego's cognates. For example, both the patrilateral and matrilateral aunts and uncles of Ego's spouse are known as *entua mata ari*, and both parents-in-law as *entua*. Again, all of a spouse's cousins on both sides of his (or her) kindred are called *ipar*, the same term as for spouse's siblings. Similarly, with the affines of Ego's cognates, the wives of both patrilateral and matrilateral uncles are termed *ibo*, and the husbands of both patrilateral and matrilateral aunts are called *aya*. As in the case of cognates, this symmetry in terminology reflects structural equivalence.

Affinal kin are also clearly demarcated on a generational basis. Particularly noteworthy is the avoidance relationship which exists between a *menantu* (child-in-law) and *entua* (parent-in-law). Here, as with parent and child, the *entua* is superordinate and the *menantu* subordinate. Sexual relations between them are severely prohibited, and all familiarity and joking are interdicted. These aspects of the relationship are expressed in a strong prohibition (with supernatural sanctions) against a *menantu* uttering the personal name of his (or her) *entua*.

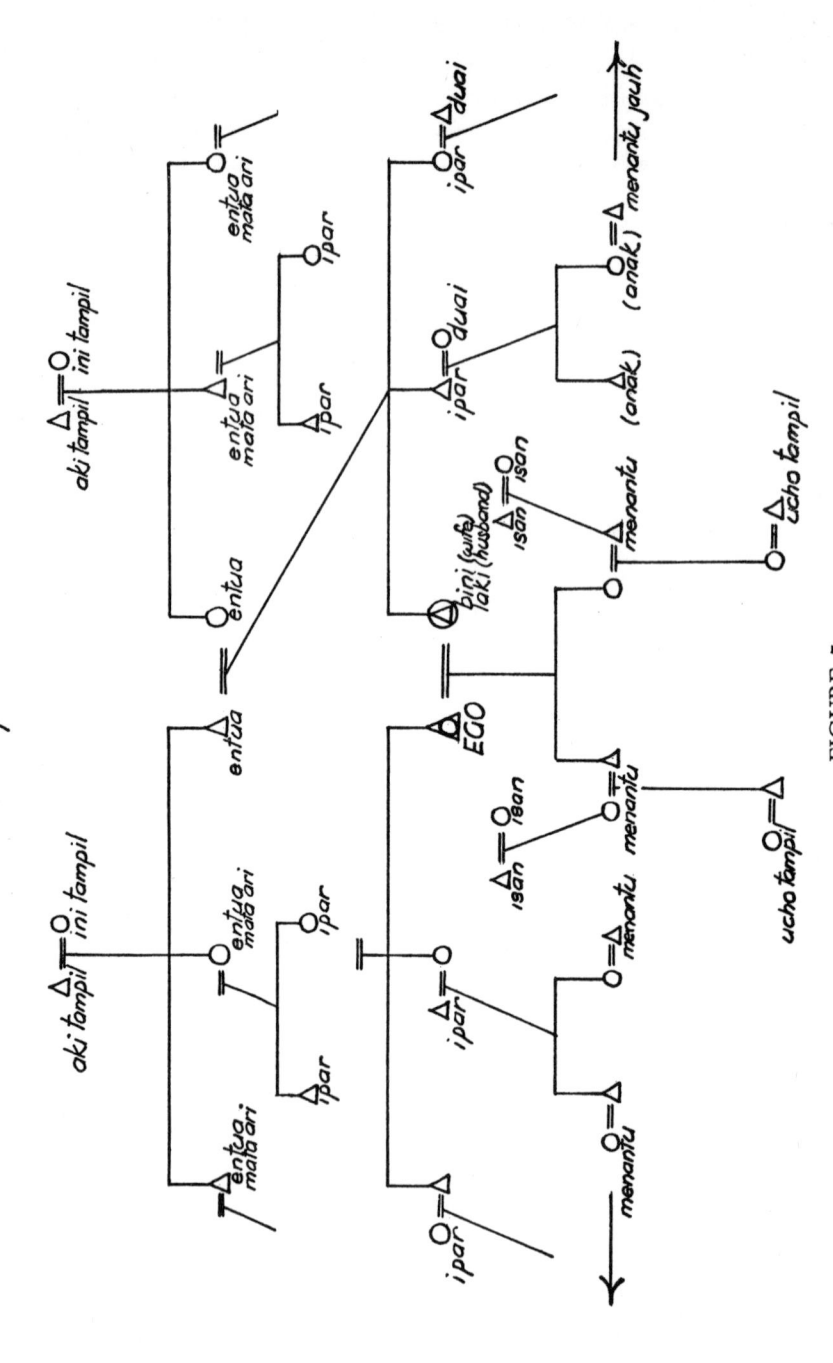

FIGURE 7
IBAN KINSHIP TERMINOLOGY: AFFINES I

These prohibitions also apply to all the siblings of both parents-in-law, i.e., to all of an individual's *entua mata ari*. I would argue that the ritual prohibitions associated with the relationship of *menantu* and *entua* have the primary purpose of precluding the possibility of sexual relations between them. Whereas the moral sentiments which interdict incestuous behavior between child and parent (and parents' siblings) are adequately internalized in the process of socialization, this does not happen for an *entua*, whose identity is not known until a marriage takes place. It is significant to note, for example, that there is no comparably severe attitude of avoidance between a male child and the wives of his uncles, or a female child and the husbands of her aunts, all of whom a child is likely to have known from infancy. These affines are called *aya* or *ibo*, and are not regarded as *entua*. As the survival of a *bilek* depends very largely on the maintenance of proper relations between *entua* and *menantu* it can be seen that the ritual prohibitions associated with this affinal tie serve an important social function.

AFFINES [kaban tampil]

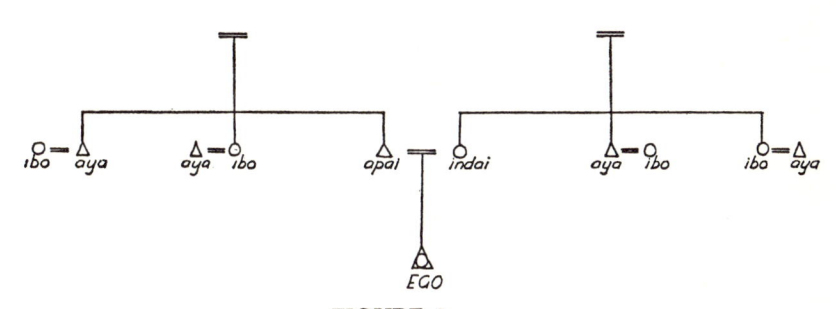

FIGURE 8
IBAN KINSHIP TERMINOLOGY: AFFINES II

The relations between affines of alternate generations also closely resemble those existing between cognatic kin. Thus the spouse of a grandchild is, in general, treated in the same way as a grandchild. Similarly, between affines on the same generation level, i.e., *ipar* and *duai*,[30] there are relations of familiarity and solidarity resembling those which exist between siblings and cousins.

An affinal term which deserves special mention is *isan*, used reciprocally by parents whose children marry one another. At the time a marriage is contracted there is almost always disagreement between the two sets of parents over the selection of the place of marital residence, but after the resolution of this difficulty resentments are usually forgotten, and where marriages are stable and productive the relationship between *isan* becomes one of mutual helpfulness and friendliness. It will be noted that when children are born of a marriage, both sets of *isan* become members of the personal kindreds of these children. Again, because the *bilek* is an exogamous group the *isan* relationship never occurs within the same *bilek* family; instead, it is always a link between *bilek* and is, therefore, of importance in the wider social structure.

As indicated previously, affinal kin are of great consequence in the kinship structure of Iban society. In the *bilek*, for example, affinal ties have an importance fully comparable to that of ties between natal members. Furthermore, it can be shown that all affinal relationships (with the exception of that linking *isan*) closely resemble in their social functions the homologous cognatic ties. This point is well appreciated by the Iban themselves, who when asked to explain the significance of affinal relationships commonly compare them directly to relationships existing between cognates. For example, it is said that the relationship between *ipar* (siblings-in-law, etc.) is like that between *menyadi* (siblings) and *petunggal* (cousins). Again, *entua* are often described as being virtually equivalent to father and mother (*itong apai indai*), and *menantu* as nearly the same as sons and daughters (*runding anak*). As noted earlier, a *menantu* acquires full membership in the *bilek* into which he (or she) marries. This jural incorporation, moreover, is accompanied by a gradual psychological absorption until a *menantu* does become virtually "a child of the family." This process is nicely illustrated in the Iban custom whereby a *menantu* who has become a widow or widower may be ritually transformed into a son or daughter (*anak*). In such cases there is an adjustment of kinship terms, and the new son or daughter is free to marry again, although it is usually insisted that such an adopted affine should remain resident in the *bilek* of his (or her) adoption. In general terms, then, affinal relationships may be said to reduplicate in their significance the basic cognatic relationships of Iban society.[31]

Finally, we may comment briefly on the most important affinal relationship of all, that of husband and wife. The conjugal tie, as already noted, is basic to the structure of the *bilek* family and is of crucial significance to the kinship system as a whole. Monogamy is reflected in the fact that the terms *laki* (husband) and *bini* (wife) can be applied to only one person at a time. Between husband and wife there is no clearly structured pattern of superordination-subordination; although there is a sharply demarcated sexual division of labor, and a differentiation of ritual and other roles, a husband and wife, in their family life, are equals. Again, marriage among the Iban rests not on status, class, clan membership, or any other kind of prescriptive structural consideration but on the affection and regard which a husband and wife have for one another. It is understandable, therefore, that the bond between husband and wife is ideally, in the opinion of the Iban, closer than that between siblings.

A husband and wife always live together as members of the same household; indeed, the conjugal tie is the only relationship, affinal or cognatic, which invariably occurs within the confines of the *bilek* family. The conjugal tie may be looked on, then, as the keystone of the *bilek* family. In particular, it is important to realize that a *bilek* family in the arrangement of its affairs has available to it the cognates and affines of all its members. From the point of view of the senior natal members of a *bilek*, the cognates of an in-married member are *kaban tampil*, or affines, but to the children of the marriage they are part of these children's personal kindreds, or *kaban mandal*. In this way, as generation succeeds generation, affinal relationships become cognatic relationships and part of the network that forms the wider kinship structure of Iban society.

CONCLUDING REMARKS

Social structure theory, as it has been developed over recent years, has been predominantly concerned with societies having unilineal descent groups, and in this field valuable results have been attained. In comparison, our understanding of cognatic or bilateral societies, which are not very much less numerous,[32] is lamentable. Preoccupation with unilineal descent systems can lead to dangerously lopsided views of social structure in general, as, for example, in the assertion by Radcliffe-Brown (1952, p. 8) that "unilineal institutions in some form are almost, if not entirely, a necessity in any ordered social system." Although thorough studies may still be sparse, we do know enough about some of the hundreds of bilateral societies still in existence to be able to demonstrate that there are a number of solutions alternative to unilineal descent all of which result in ordered social systems. The Iban solution, in which family corporations are perpetuated by a system of utrolateral filiation, is one of them. This type of family, supported as it is by the ramifying cognatic kinship structure of the Iban, does result, beyond any question, in an ordered social system. Furthermore, if the expansion of the Iban people during the past 150 years of their history be any criterion, it is also an efficient system.

It would be of the greatest interest for social anthropological theory if a detailed comparative study of the morphology of bilateral kinship systems could be undertaken. Unfortunately, the dearth of modern structural analyses prevents this. Many of the world's bilateral societies are to be found in Southeast Asia and the Insular Pacific. It is to be hoped that research in these regions during the coming years will provide the materials for a comparative analysis of bilateral social structures of the kind already achieved for the unilineal systems of Africa.[33]

APPENDIX: LIST OF KINSHIP TERMS

The terms listed below are to be understood as used in both reference and address except where particular referents are followed by the letters R or A in parentheses indicating that for these referents the term is used, respectively, only in reference or in address.

1 *aki:* grandfather, either maternal or paternal; grandfather's brother or male cousin; spouse's grandfather (A); parent-in-law's uncle (A).
   aki tampil: spouse's grandfather (R); parent-in-law's uncle (R).
2 *ini:* grandmother, either maternal or paternal; grandmother's sister or female cousin; spouse's grandmother (A); parent-in-law's aunt (A).
   ini tampil: spouse's grandmother (R); parent-in-law's aunt (R).
3 *apai:* father; parent's brother or male cousin (A); spouse's father (A); spouse's parent's brother or male cousin (A); father's sister's husband (A); mother's sister's husband (A).
4 *indai:* mother; parent's sister or female cousin (A); spouse's mother (A); spouse's parent's sister or female cousin (A); father's brother's wife (A); mother's brother's wife (A).
5 *aya:* father's brother or male cousin; mother's brother or male cousin; father's sister's husband; mother's sister's husband; spouse's father (A); spouse's parent's brother or male cousin (A).
6 *ibo:* father's sister or female cousin; mother's sister or female cousin; father's brother's wife; mother's brother's wife; spouse's mother (A); spouse's parent's sister or female cousin (A).
7 *menyadi:* sibling, either brother or sister; cousin of any degree and of either sex on the same generation level as Ego (A).
8 *aka:* elder brother or sister (A); cousin of any degree and of either sex older than Ego but on the same generation level (A).
9 *adi:* younger brother or sister (A); cousin of any degree and of either sex younger than Ego but on the same generation level (A); spouse's younger sibling or younger cousin (A); sibling's spouse if younger than Ego (A); spouse's sibling's spouse if older than spouse (A).
10 *petunggal:* cousin of any degree and of either sex on the same generation level as Ego.
11 *anak:* child, either son or daughter; sibling's child (A); cousin's child (A); son's wife (A); daughter's husband (A); nephew's wife (A); niece's husband (A).
12 *akan:* nephew, i.e., sibling's son; cousin's son.
13 *endo:* niece, i.e., sibling's daughter; cousin's daughter; son's wife (A); nephew's wife (A).
14 *ucho:* grandchild of either sex; sibling's grandchild; cousin's grandchild; grandchild's spouse (A); sibling's grandchild's spouse (A); great-grandchild (A); sibling's great-grandchild (A); cousin's great-grandchild (A).
   ucho tampil: grandchild's spouse (R); sibling's grandchild's spouse (R).
15 *ichit:* great-grandchild (R); sibling's great-grandchild (R); cousin's great-grandchild (R).
16 *entua:* spouse's parent of either sex (R).
   entua mata ari: spouse's parent's sibling or cousin (R).
17 *laki:* husband (R). In address, a spouse is called *wai*, or by his (or her) personal name, or by a teknonym.
18 *bini:* wife (R). For usage in address, see above under *laki*.
19 *ipar:* spouse's sibling or cousin of either sex; sibling's spouse; cousin's spouse.
20 *ika:* spouse's elder sibling or cousin (A); sibling's spouse if older than Ego (A); spouse's sibling's spouse if older than spouse (A).

21 *duai:* spouse's sibling's spouse.
22 *isan:* child's spouse's parent; child's spouse's uncle or aunt.
23 *menantu:* son's wife (R); daughter's husband (R); nephew's wife (R); niece's husband (R).
24 *igat:* daughter's husband (A); niece's husband (A).
25 *wai:* relative (A). This term may be used in addressing a kinsman of unknown generational level, of Ego's own generation, or of the second ascending or descending generations, but not one of an adjacent generation.

CHAPTER 6

THE JAVANESE OF SOUTH CENTRAL JAVA

R. M. KOENTJARANINGRAT
University of Indonesia

THE published literature on Javanese culture, though vast, contains little information on kinship beyond a brief description by Ukun Surjaman (1955) and scattered data in a compilation of *adat* law by Djojodigoeno and Tirtawinata (1940). There is, however, an important unpublished study by Hildreth Geertz (1955), and Subandrio (1951) has devoted a chapter to the subject in her unpublished dissertation on Javanese peasant life. The present paper is based in part on the author's personal knowledge of urban areas in south central Java, where he has spent a large part of his life as a participant in the culture, and in part on recent field work in two rural villages[1] in the same general area. If the data presented herewith differ on a number of points from those recorded in the sources cited above, this is scarcely surprising in respect to a people who number about 35 million (Reed, 1956, Vol. 1, p. 85), who are spread over geographically distinct regions, and who exhibit marked differentiation of social levels.

The Javanese occupy the central and eastern parts of the island of Java. They are distinguished from other ethnic groups in Indonesia by a separate historical background, which has given rise to a distinct language and culture. The majority are poor sedentary farmers on an overcrowded island,[2] working very small plots of irrigated rice land, which they cultivate with a plow and simple tools.[3] In addition to these lowland rice cultivators, a large population inhabits the mountainous interior of Java, which stretches across the center of the island from the west to the extreme east. In this area the people practice agriculture mainly on dry fields with manioc, rather than rice, as their principal crop (Pelzer, 1954, pp. 66–78). Most of Java is rural, its inhabitants living in villages characterized by strong solidarity and loyalties. Usually, though not always, each nuclear family in a village has its own small bamboo or wooden house, with a garden, a small granary, and an adjacent stable where a water buffalo, goats, and chickens are kept. The garden is planted to coconut trees and a variety of crops which supplement the predominantly rice or manioc diet.

Except for Surabaja and Semarang, which are seaports and centers of commerce and industry, and Djakarta, which is not primarily a Javanese city, urban development in Java is confined largely to administrative centers and reflects the hierarchy of governmental organization. District and subdistrict centers, to be sure, are small towns, and the capitals of regencies have populations usually well below 20,000, but the capitals of residencies and provinces are large enough to be called cities, having populations ranging usually from 20,000 to 100,000 but in a few instances even in excess of this.[4] Here live most of the old administrative elite, the merchants, and the new social levels which social mobility has produced since World War II. Two court cities in south central Java, Djokjakarta and Surakarta, the capitals of former principalities, are the centers of Javanese classical culture, art, and literature.

SOCIAL STRATIFICATION

The Javanese themselves distinguish two primary social levels: (1) the *wong tjiliq* ("little people"), comprising the great mass of the peasants and the lower strata of the urban population, and (2) the *prijaji*, including members of the administrative bureaucracy and the academically trained intellectuals. In addition to these they recognize a third level, relatively small in size but prestigeful: the *ndara* or nobility. Distinct from this horizontal stratification there exists a vertical classification of Javanese society based on the degree of participation in Islam, distinguishing (1) the *wong abangan*, who do not regulate their lives according to the basic principles of Islam, from (2) the *santri*, who follow these principles seriously. At least some of the latter form a culturally distinct group, which is assigned a level in the horizontal stratification somewhat below that of the *prijaji*.

The *wong tjiliq* are for the most part farmers (*tani*), who live in villages (*ndesa*) that are small worlds in themselves. However, there are also *wong tjiliq* in the towns and cities. Here they form the lower levels of the population and follow occupations ranging from laborers to petty traders, including artisans, barbers, pedicab drivers (*betjaq*), automobile and truck drivers, servants, and other groups engaged in manual labor.

The *prijaji* do not engage in manual labor. The majority hold government positions and are stratified according to the bureaucratic hierarchy. At the lowest level they comprise government clerks, schoolteachers, and local postoffice, telegraph, and railway officials in the small towns. Higher levels include officials of superior rank in the larger towns and the cities. The traditional administrative personnel, formerly called *Pangreh Pradja*, constitute the core of the *prijaji*. The majority are probably descended from the bureaucratic administrators of the pre-colonial Javanese states, since the Dutch government preserved the exclusiveness of the group by admitting to the training schools for administrative officials, for the most part, only applicants who could show kinship ties with members of the administrative service. The *prijaji* enjoyed great prestige, especially in rural communities where most of them lived, and they sought to enhance this prestige by marrying into the nobility and by imitating court culture and tradition in their homes. The higher administrative posts, such as the heads of residencies and provinces, were filled almost exclusively by Dutchmen until after World War II.

Another important subgroup of the *prijaji* consists of those who have received advanced academic training. In the colonial period up to 1940 there were only three schools of university level. The first graduates of the oldest of these, the Medical School, came into Javanese society in the period before World War I. Not until after 1939, when the Netherlands was cut off from its colonies, were the academically trained intellectuals able to gain promotion quickly and easily in the government service, but they gradually came to occupy high positions. Although the system of social stratification was still based primarily on the pattern of a bureaucratic hierarchy, medical doctors and lawyers who did not go into government service, but rather into private practice, also enjoyed high social prestige because of the association of an academic title with the upper ranks in the government service. It was mainly the *prijaji* intellectuals, especially those not in government employment, who became active in nationalistic movements before World War I.

The *ndara* or nobility live mainly in the four court centers of central Java—Djokjakarta, Surakarta, Mangkunegaran, and Paku Alaman—into which the old Javanese state of Mataram split after 1743.[5] Its members comprise persons who can trace their descent, in either the male or the female line, from rulers of the four principalities, and they are divided into different ranks, with distinctive titles, according to the degree of their relationship to one or another of the four princely families. As noted above, many members of the administrative *prijaji* have become related to the nobility through intermarriage and the transmission of noble status to the descendants of such unions. The *wong tjiliq* subjects of a prince regard him as a divine king, the center of magical power in the state (according to Berg, 1938), who embodies in his personality every aspect of the universe. The court culture, widely imitated by the *prijaji* even outside the principalities, includes a strong artistic and literary tradition and a complex of religious customs of pre-Islamic as well as Islamic origin—all centering on and derived from the concept of the sacred king.

During and since World War II numerous changes have occurred in the horizontal stratification of Javanese society. The bureaucratic hierarchy still plays a dominant role, but the academically trained *prijaji* moved upward in the hierarchy when the Dutch were interned by the Japanese, and the leaders of the nationalistic movements, released from exile, assumed political leadership under the Japanese military government. Since the establishment of the Indonesian state the academically trained intellectuals have filled the highest positions in the government, and today they surpass the nobility in status except in the environs of the four court centers in Central Java. The *prijaji* of lower rank have moved upward and occupied the middle positions. Younger members of the *wong tjiliq* with a junior-high-school education have entered the lower ranks of the government service, especially in rural areas, and have thereby become *prijaji*. The varied occupational possibilities in the cities have blurred the distinction between *wong tijiliq* and *prijaji*, which is still striking in the smaller towns with fewer opportunities for advancement. The structure of the *Pangreh Pradja* has changed little until very recently, when some of its members, aware of the enhanced status of other occupations, have begun to leave the lower administrative ranks. The prestige of the nobility has receded markedly, and many have dropped their titles, which today have little significance except in the immediate vicinity of the four court centers. The Javanese have changed greatly their attitude toward these courts, which they no longer regard as models for behavior and as the chief repository of social values. Only the court of Djokjakarta still enjoys a measure of general, as well as local, prestige because of the pro-national attitude and activities of its prince, the Sultan of Djokjakarta, during the revolution. In addition to the shift in the bureaucratic structure, the extension of educational facilities and growing urbanization have contributed to the drive for upward mobility on all levels of Javanese society.

To the people themselves, with their sharp sense for social differences, the horizontal stratification described above is only one way of looking at Javanese society. They also recognize another way of dividing their society, namely, into two vertical groups: the *wong abangan* and the *santri*. The former are those who do not live according to the basic principles of Islam as understood by the Javanese, i.e., who do not perform the *śalât* five times a day, who do not fast in the month of *pasa* (Ramadan), who have no desire to make the pilgrimage to Mecca, and who eat pork. The *santri* are people who follow Islamic principles seriously and hence differ sharply in all these respects. Although the criterion of differentiation is the degree of participation in Islam, the two groups can certainly be regarded as two subcultures with contrasting world views, values, and orientations within Javanese culture as a whole.

The greater part of the Javanese are *wong abangan*, but *santri* are found in all social strata. In certain places there are localized *santri* communities with a distinctive social status. These consist of merchants and, more recently, a few entrepreneurs. In the region of the princely courts they do business in gold and silver work, batik, and other handicrafts—occupations which do not harmonize with the values of Javanese culture, which, being basically a court culture, has little interest in economic gain and a positive dislike for commerce and entrepreneurship. Because of their wealth, these *santri* occupy a level higher than the *wong tjiliq* in the eyes of the Javanese but one inferior to the average *prijaji*. They live mainly in towns and cities, where they usually occupy a separate quarter called the *kauman*, lead an exclusive social life, and distinguish themselves by a special style of dress. Differences in wealth divide the *kauman santri* into several distinct levels. The highest among them are the *kadji* (from Arabic *hadj*). These are people who have made the pilgrimage to Mecca—an act of piety which only a person of considerable wealth can afford—and have thus achieved extremely high social prestige.

There are also *santri* among the peasants, but in the villages they do not segregate themselves in separate quarters. Other than that they adhere to the Islamic values and world view, the average Javanese has no conception of how these rural *santri* live. Nor does the author know in what respects they differ from the *kauman santri*. They clearly deserve special study. There are likewise numerous *santri* among the lower-ranking officials, the intellectuals, and the nobility but very few in the higher administrative ranks (though many are called *santri* out of courtesy). Intellectual *santri* played important roles in the nationalistic movements prior to the war and have since become leaders in the powerful Moslem political parties, Masjumi and Nahdatul Ulama. In recent years many *kauman santri* have expanded their mercantile activities from the local to the international level.

In discussing Javanese social stratification we have avoided the term "social class." If this term be applied to the *wong tjiliq* and *prijaji* categories, we should have to regard them as open classes, since the borderline between them is easily crossed—especially since the war, when education has facilitated rising from the *wong tjiliq* to the *prijaji*. Theoretically, too, a government official can lose his position and become a pauper, thereby falling from the higher to the lower stratum. The *kauman santri* and the nobility, on the other hand, cannot be regarded as open classes—the former because of their strong in-group feeling and preference for endogamy, the latter because admission to membership is possible only by birth and because the right to a title becomes extinguished at the sixth descending generation from the ancestral prince.

Income is not a crucial differentiating criterion. To be sure, differences in wealth play an important part in separating the *prijaji* from the *wong tjiliq*. Nevertheless, through private enterprise and petty trade *wong tjiliq* people in urban centers can achieve incomes greater than those of the average lower-ranking government officials. The *kauman santri* usually have larger incomes than most *prijaji*, and even than many members of the nobility, yet they are assigned to a lower status than either. The four principal stratified groups— *wong tjiliq, kauman santri, prijaji,* and *ndara*—are differentiated more sharply by cultural differences than by wealth distinctions. In rural areas all four are readily distinguishable by superficial differences in styles of dress and in behavior, as well as by more subtle cultural contrasts more visible to the inhabitants than to the outside observer. Except in some rural areas where a localized nobility is unknown, every Javanese is aware of the major strata of his society. Though few comprehend the entire range of Javanese stratification, everyone knows the levels above and below his own and is able to adjust his behavior, speech, and gestures appropriately in all relationships with those of higher, equivalent, and lower status. This fact has peculiar relevance to the understanding of the Javanese kinship system.

THE COMMUNITY

Though its associations and meanings are many and subtle, the term community in this paper will denote a group of individuals brought together by the fusion of certain integrative forces such as shared locality and shared interests (Ruopp, 1953, p. 4). For central and perhaps also for eastern Java the most concrete example of such a group is the self-sustaining village or *ndesa*, a corporate local group of strong solidarity which is predominantly engaged in agriculture and which forms the agrarian base of the Javanese population.

Javanese villages commonly fall into two main types. In the hilly and mountainous interior of the island most villages consist of clusters of separated and often dispersed hamlets with cultivated fields in between. In the lowland areas, however, settlements tend to assume the form of compact nucleated villages comprising three or four rows of houses strung along a river or a road, with only outlying homesteads or small satellite hamlets revealing a dispersed pattern. Villages vary in size in correlation with many regional factors. Small villages have a minimum of about 100 to 150 households, while larger ones may contain up to 400 or 500 households. In the densely populated lowland areas, where villages are situated in a much more crowded pattern, their average size does not differ very much from that of mountain villages.

Full participation in village affairs is exercised by persons having the status of *kuli*, i.e., those who hold the titles to undistributed family lands (see below under Property). In addition to their administrative powers with respect to the land rights of their siblings and other kinsmen who do not have this status, the *kuli* exert a major influence in decisions reached at village assemblies. On the other hand, they have numerous obligations toward the community and government; they pay the land tax, contribute toward the support of the village officials, and participate actively in public enterprises of various kinds. In compensation for these responsibilities, villages in many parts of Central Java allot to each *kuli* a special plot of land, called *siti pekulèn*. The status of *kuli* is hereditary. It normally descends, together with the *siti pekulèn*, to the eldest son of the previous occupant. Not infrequently, however, a younger son is selected, and in default of sons a daughter may succeed to the position, so that not all *kuli* are males.

The local headman (*lurah*) has for centuries been elected by the villagers who have the status of *kuli*. He is assisted by a staff of ten to twenty officials (*prabot*), who are sometimes also elected but more commonly appointed. The headman and his officials receive no salaries from the government but are supported in part by the usufruct from plots of land (*siti bengkoq*) that are allotted to them during their periods in office and in part by a variety of traditional duties and services owed to them by the *kuli*.

Once elected, the headman continues in office without reelection as long as he retains the confidence and respect of the villagers—oftentimes until his death. If, however, he loses this confidence, the villagers can petition the district head (*wedana*), who has the power to dismiss the incumbent and to call a meeting of the *kuli* of the village to elect a new headman. An incumbent who retires voluntarily usually nominates one or two candidates from among the more respected men of the village—often one of the local officials or a relative who has served without pay as the headman's assistant (*magang*)— and the villagers choose the successor by vote.

The headman symbolizes the village as a whole, and his relationship to the villagers can be compared to that of a father of a family to the other members of his household. Though the office is always elective, there is in actuality a tendency to fill the position with a relative of the previous headman, so that a trend toward hereditary succession is observable. In the past, village headmen of great prestige and influence have often sought to consolidate their positions by marrying into the families of the heads of adjacent villages. The resulting affinal relationships have given rise in certain areas to large bilateral extended families whose members form an upper social level in the villages. Often these have achieved for themselves a religio-magical status through genealogies and mythical stories relating them to heroic figures in Javanese epics or folk-history[6] whose sacred graves are allegedly located in the forest or on a mountain top in the vicinity of the village. Many families keep as treasured heirlooms the manuscripts on which such genealogies have been recorded in poetic form.

Social relationships within the village community are largely based on mutual aid (*gotong rojong*), of which various forms are clearly distinguished by separate terms. Though not restricted by kinship ties, mutual aid rests in the main on extended kin relationships, which exert a powerful force in the total pattern of interpersonal interaction. In addition to mutual aid, of course, labor and services are also obtainable by ordinary payment.

CHILDBIRTH AND INFANCY

Basic to the religious beliefs of the Javanese, though they are formally Muslims, is the conception of a cosmic and social order that is determined in all its aspects. The individual human being plays but a very small part in this structural whole. The principal points of his life and status are fixed, his fate is foreordained, and within this framework he must patiently bear the hardships of life. This conception is closely related to the belief in the supernatural guidance and support of idealized ancestral spirits who, as well as Allah or God, generate religious emotion and provide a sense of security.

Deeply concerned with the well-being of the family, the Javanese strive to create within it a state of emotional calm or *slamet*, a state in which events will run their fixed course smoothly and nothing untoward will happen to anyone. Emotional upsets and other disturbing experiences expose the family to supernatural dangers which find expression in accidents, sickness, and death. Of the several ways of obviating anxiety over such dangers, the most important is to achieve a spiritual state of *préhatin*, the essence of which is that every member of the family is aware of the range of possible disturbing events and strives to adapt his behavior to this awareness. Though not expressed in particular concrete ways, this spiritual state must be reinforced by the observance of various taboos and by the performance of socio-religious rituals, called *slametan*, which are designed to promote a state of *slamet*.

The *slametan* is, as Geertz (1956, p. 238) has correctly observed, a "central ceremony" in Javanese life.[7] Its essential feature is the distribution of sanctified food to neighbors living on the same street who are invited, along with a few friends and relatives, to partake in a sacred meal. A large *slametan* requires elaborate preparations and a great variety of food items. It is opened by the host, the father of the house, who explains its purpose. Then a Muslim religious official, who plays a central role in the ceremony, recites several verses of the Qur'ân, after which the guests are invited to eat and drink. As a rule, only the closest neighbors actually attend the celebration, and servants carry the food to the homes of the other invited guests. *Slametan* rituals are performed at birth, circumcision, marriage, and various other points in the life cycle of the individual.

In anticipation of childbirth the entire family enters the state of *préhatin* during the fourth or fifth month of pregnancy. The prospective mother now begins to observe a series of food and other taboos, although she continues to carry on her ordinary duties until her actual confinement. The *slametan* ceremonies begin during the seventh month of pregnancy, when the elaborate *slametan mitoni* is performed. This ceremony is supposed to assure a successful delivery and to bring security and *slamet* to the unborn child and to the family, but it serves in addition as an anticipatory announcement of the coming birth.[8] Another *slametan* for the security of the unborn child is held during the ninth month of pregnancy; it is given ostensibly in honor of the prospective child's symbolic siblings, the amniotic fluid and the placenta, which are supposed to be his intimate guides throughout life.

Childbirth (*babaran*) is the climax of a period of crisis in the household which has lasted from the fourth month of pregnancy. It usually takes place in the home; only recently have mothers begun to go to a hospital for confinement. For assistance in delivery many families today call in a *bidan*—a nurse who has received special training and a license in obstetrics—or a doctor if available. In rural communities, however, most people still obtain the services of a *dukun*, a midwife who is also a specialist in magical or shamanistic practices. Mayer (1897, Vol. 1, pp. 279-285) has described in detail many of the charms, spells, and other symbolic acts formerly performed by a *dukun* to ward off supernatural dangers from mother and child. Though these have now been largely abandoned, most of the traditional medicines and practices like massage used by the *dukun* in treating mother and child, as well as most of her equipment, e.g., the bamboo knife for cutting the umbilical cord, are still in use.

Special care is taken of the placenta because of its peculiar significance to the Javanese (cf. Subandrio, 1951, pp. 126-127). In the case of a boy the placenta is deposited in an earthenware jar and thrown into a river. In the case of a girl, however, it is always buried in the back yard of the home along with certain objects having symbolic meanings—batik equipment, a needle, a piece of paper inscribed with letters of the Javanese alphabet, etc. A series of *slametan* are also held: one in connection with the naming ceremony; one, usually on the seventh day, in connection with the ritual cutting of the child's hair; one on the day when the umbilical cord falls off; and one on the thirty-fifth day of life. The number 35 is arrived at by combining the five-day and seven-day weeks. Every 35 days there recurs the same combination of days as those on which an individual was born. This is called his *weton* (the day he came out), and is important in scheduling magical practices and ceremonies throughout his life cycle.

According to Islamic religious law, a mother is unclean and subject to a series of ritual taboos for a period of forty days after childbirth.[9] Sexual intercourse is prohibited, and mother and child are supposed to remain under the care of the *dukun* although in practice this responsibility is usually assumed by the mother's own mother. The postparturient woman stays in the house for two or three weeks, and when she leaves, the baby is placed under the care of a female servant if available.

In normal circumstances the infant is breast-fed for fourteen to eighteen months, sometimes even longer. The author has seen children still at the breast after two years of age. In many *prijaji* families the infant is given a bottle at an early age, but only as a supplement to the breast. Among *wong tjiliq* families, especially in peasant communities, babies are given supplementary solid food, such as soft cooked rice, mashed bananas, or maize pudding, after the first or second week. Feeding usually follows a self-demand schedule; the infant gets food or the breast whenever it cries. Weaning in the sense of achieving emotional independence from the mother does not usually occur until long after breast-feeding has ceased.

An infant is bathed at least twice a day according to a very regular schedule. When it sleeps at night it is usually swaddled tightly in a piece of cloth (*digedong*). A tiny baby spends most of its waking hours in someone's arms—the mother's, the grandmother's, or a servant's—where it is fondled tenderly, or else is carried in a sling (*slendang*) securely fastened to the body of its carrier as the latter goes about her daily activities or visits a market, often two or three hours' walking distance from the village. Mothers frequently entrust an infant to the care of its elder sisters, who are usually not more than five or six years of age. In the cities, where most families do not have servants, mothers commonly leave their infants alone in baby pens while they busy themselves with their household duties.

Slametan ceremonies similar to that on the thirty-fifth day are also held on the infant's third *weton* day (105th day) and on its fifth *weton* day (the 175th), but on the seventh *weton* day occurs an especially important ceremony called *tedaq sitèn* (going down on the earth). On this occasion, with a definite ritual, the baby is brought for the first time into contact with the earth. In addition to an elaborate *slametan*, wealthy families celebrate this event with the performance of a *wajang* or puppet play.[11] Besides establishing contact of the new individual with the earth, the most important factor in the life of millions of Javanese, the *tedaq sitèn* marks the end of the crisis period following childbirth and symbolizes the capacity of the child to stay alive on its own.

In rural areas small children go naked and are toilet-trained gradually with a minimum of punishment. The popular belief of foreigners that Javanese children are rarely punished, which is considered identical with spoiling,[12] has, however, no basis in reality. Up to the age of two, indeed, the Javanese child is petted and appeased, but thereafter he is expected gradually to adjust to his social environment. The usual methods of inculcation and discipline include snarling (scolding is highly unusual), corporal punishment, and invidious comparisons with the superior behavior of siblings and others in order to encourage pride. Another very common method is to threaten the child with external sanctioning agents, e.g., ghosts, evil spirits, bogeymen, or strangers. This has serious drawbacks; one result is that most Javanese children are shy, afraid of strangers, and slow to make acquaintanceships outside the family.

CHILDHOOD AND ADOLESCENCE

As the child grows up, he gradually extends the range of his social relations to embrace neighbors and their children and relatives beyond his family of orientation. In doing so he must learn to adjust himself to social realities and to shape his behavior according to the prevailing social standards. In particular, he must learn to curb open expressions of his emotions, for self-control is highly valued in Javanese culture. He develops more respectful modes of behavior, expressed concretely in the adoption of formal styles of speech, in his relations with his father, other senior relatives, and all older people. Respectful behavior toward elders and persons superior in rank plays an important role in Javanese social relations.

During the pre-adolescent period the range of social contacts for boys expands beyond the limits of the household, but this is much less true for girls. In rural areas, where both sexes attend school at a walking distance of an hour or two from their homes, the boys, after school is out or during holidays, hire themselves out as buffalo, cattle, or goat herders[13] or join neighborhood play groups, whereas girls are given increasing responsibilities in the home in such matters as cooking, threshing paddy, and tending younger siblings.

One occasion on which children have an opportunity to meet a wider circle of relatives comes during the *lebaran* holiday at the end of the fasting month of *pasa* (Ramadan). At this time the family pays annual visits at the homes of its older relatives, beginning with the senior relative of the oldest living generation who happens to live in the same community. On these occasions it is customary for a person to ask forgiveness for his mistakes from his older relatives. In *prijaji* and noble families there is an additional custom, called *sungkem*, which consists in kneeling before the elder relative, kissing his knees, and asking his blessing.

The onset of adolescence for girls is marked by a *slametan* at the first menstruation, but in general the transition to adult status is a gradual one. For boys, however, circumcision, which occurs between the ages of ten and fifteen, is an important event, dramatizing a sharp transition from childhood to adolescence. The circumcision ceremony, called *tetaq* or *sunat*, is regarded by most Javanese, even in remote mountain villages where the notion of Islam is very superficial, as an initiation rite whereby the boy becomes a Muslim.[14] The operation is performed by a professional circumciser (*bong*), who has the requisite skill and also knows how to treat wounds, especially in emergency cases when serious bleeding occurs. There are several good descriptions of Javanese circumcision rituals (e.g., Inggeris, 1921), and regional variations in their details are reported by Schrieke (1921). In urban *prijaji* families the celebration of circumcision is becoming less and less important, and no feasts or *slametan* are given. Sometimes the boy is simply sent to a doctor, and formalities are dispensed with except that someone capable of reciting the circumcision formula is invited to attend the operation.

The transition at puberty does not necessarily involve the imparting of sexual knowledge. Parents avoid mentioning matters of sexual significance in the presence of their children, and, despite the fact that the village family sleeps in a single room, husband and wife are careful to wait until the children are asleep before engaging in sexual intercourse. These adult attitudes do not, of course, prevent the acquisition of sexual knowledge through indirect observation, the overhearing of adult conversations, or the imparting of information by older people such as grandparents.

Premarital sexual relations are prohibited in Javanese society, especially among the rural *wong tjiliq* and among the *prijaji*, and the methods of controlling the sexual behavior of adolescents involve a certain amount of segregation of the sexes and chaperonage of girls. Boys are less carefully watched, so that clandestine meetings between the sexes and sexual intercourse before marriage do occur. The author has the impression—not acquired, however, by careful social investigation—that the adult attitude toward premarital affairs during adolescence is less serious among the lower levels of the urban population and that many cases of sexual experimentation take place without incurring severe punishment. Generally, however, Javanese girls are expected to be chaste until marriage. An unmarried girl who becomes pregnant brings shame upon her family. Abortion, however, is not practiced in such cases because it is considered an even greater sin. The only practical solution to the problem is to compel the boy to marry the girl before her condition becomes public knowledge.

MARRIAGE AND THE FAMILY

Although many marriages, especially in rural communities, are still arranged by the parents without the consent of the girl or the boy, Javanese youth in general do their own courting and make their own choice of a mate. Young people get to know each other at school and through youth activities, and in the villages, after finishing elementary school at about the age of fifteen, they meet each other in other work groups at planting and harvesting and at parties and festivals. In the towns and cities, boys generally begin to date when they reach senior high-school age. Dating is strictly controlled by the girl's mother; a girl never accepts an invitation before asking her mother's permission, and many mothers even require the boy to come himself and ask in a formal manner. Boys and girls are not supposed to make appointments to meet at places outside the home; the boy must call for the girl and escort her home again.

Contact between the sexes in school does not normally result in early marriage. Boys who go to college or other institutions of higher learning usually do not marry until late in their thirties. The author has the impression that only a very small percentage of the graduate students at universities are married. Boys who get a job after high school, or who go into professional schools on the high-school level, marry younger, namely, as soon as they obtain a position and are settled in it. They commonly marry girls whom they meet in their work or who come from the neighborhood where they reside.

Because of the fact that marriage always requires parental consent, the cultural definitions of prohibited, disapproved, and permitted marriages play an important role in marital choices. Prohibited marriages (*sirikan djedjodoan*) are those which are considered really incestuous. They include unions between siblings or other members of the same nuclear family. There is no conception of supernatural punishments for unions of this type; they are merely considered so absurd that nobody even thinks of the possibility. Javanese mythology, however, includes several accounts of incestuous unions between siblings or between mother and son; the offspring are always magically potent heroes. There are two other types of prohibited marriages, both of which are sanctioned by supernatural punishments. These are unions between a grandparent and grandchild and those with a *misanan* (second cousin). The latter prohibition, though apparently unknown among the higher *prijaji*, is very strong among peasants and in rural families. The Javanese are not able to give an explanation for this prohibition, but a Dutch scholar, Bertling (1936), has attempted a structural interpretation.

Disapproved marriages are those which, though theoretically prohibited and also sanctioned by supernatural punishments, can nevertheless be arranged by performing a variety of preventive rituals designed to protect the couple against the supernatural dangers. Unions of the disapproved category include: (1) those between consanguineal relatives where the groom belongs to a younger generation than the bride (e.g., between nephew and aunt); (2) marriages between paternal parallel cousins (*pantjer wali*);[15] (3) sororate unions and in general any marriage with a relative of a deceased spouse.

Marriage is permitted between adopted children in a nuclear family and between maternal parallel cousins. In general, the Javanese do not have the notion of approved or preferred marriages. In several areas, to be sure, unions with a cross-cousin are regarded with positive favor, but in other regions cross-cousin marriage is simply a frequent form of permitted marriage. In the area where the author did his field work there exists a special type of approved marriage, namely, between *mindoan* (i.e., third cousins).

Although Javanese youth usually choose their own mates, they may not neglect parental approval. It is firmly believed that a marriage without the parents' blessing will be unhappy. When a boy wishes to marry a girl and is sure of her consent and her parents' approval, he informs his own parents. If they likewise approve, they pay a ceremonial visit (*nglamar*) to request the girl's hand. The girl's parents, when they have given their formal consent, accept a betrothal gift (*paningset*), after which an engagement period of several months or longer ensues.

Among orthodox families in urban areas, and even more frequently in rural areas, many marriages are arranged by the parents without the consent of the children, or at least of the girl. In such cases the boy's parents informally send an intermediary to the girl's family to ask their approval of the proposed match. When this is secured, a formal visit, called *nontoni*, is made and is then followed by the ceremonial *nglamar* visit. When the girl's family has accepted the *paningset*, and this has been confirmed by a *slametan* ceremony, the couple is considered engaged.

The date of the wedding is decided by the girl's family. Its determination involves a complicated series of calculations in which the girl's and the boy's *weton* days play an important role. The wedding is the most important and elaborate ceremony in the entire life cycle. In urban families, where the circumcision celebration is being increasingly abandoned, it even becomes the only major festivity in a person's life.

Several days before the date of the wedding the groom's parents select a delegation, consisting of both paternal and maternal relatives, who walk in procession to the bride's home to offer her family the bridal gift (*sasrahan*). In the case of a prosperous villager this may consist of cattle, foodstuffs, textiles, and some money. In urban areas, however, this custom has been completely abandoned, and the traditional *sasrahan* is replaced by a sum of money "to buy the salt which will flavor the food for the wedding feast." On the day before the wedding several senior male relatives of the bride are selected to visit the ancestral graves and to ask the blessing of the ancestors, a custom which is called *reresik* and is concluded by a *slametan* at the bride's home. On the night of the same day the bride's kindred remain awake until after midnight to receive the blessings of the good spirits, the *widadari*.

The next morning the groom—without the bride—goes to the mosque for a ceremony, called *idjab*, in which he declares his intention to marry the bride and pronounces the Muslim confession of faith before a Muslim religious official, the bride's guardian (*wali*), and two witnesses. At this ceremony the groom presents a money gift of at least five rupiah to the bride's guardian; this is considered to satisfy the bride-price requirement in Muslim religious law. After the participants in this ceremony have signed the marriage document the groom is considered lawfully married to his bride. After the *idjab* ceremony the groom and his escort go to the bride's house. Here she awaits him at the entrance of the house, surrounded by her oldest female relatives. Several ritual acts which symbolize the unity of the couple and the acceptance of the new son-in-law bring the wedding ceremony proper to an end, and the couple are considered socially as well as legally married. An elaborate party, at which the guests are entertained with food, drinks, and classical dances or a puppet play, concludes the festivities.

Many people drop their childhood name and adopt a new adult name at their wedding. This is usually confirmed by a special *slametan*, but in urban families people commonly start using their adult name after marriage without any formalities, although their relatives and close friends may continue to use the childhood name. In rural communities, however, the childhood name tends to be dropped completely after the adoption of an adult name, and the author knows many cases where a man has forgotten his wife's childhood name.

In the villages where he did his field work the author observed a peculiar form of almost potlatch-like gift exchange, which takes place several days after the wedding. According to this custom, called *ngaturi pundjungan pengantèn*, the bride's relatives serve each of the groom's maternal and paternal relatives a complete rice dish with a chicken as its main item. When one of the groom's relatives receives such a dish, he is expected to pay for it with a sum of money greater than its actual value. According to convention, moreover, the size of the chicken determines the amount of money he is supposed to pay. To refuse the gift is considered very shameful and would expose the relative to unfavorable public gossip. Hence a poor man who can not actually afford the payment will usually borrow money or sell some of his property rather than refuse the gift.

There is no fixed rule of residence determining where a married couple should live. The ideal is to set up an independent household, but in the villages studied by the author he observed a definite pattern of initial uxorilocality. In this region, with an early marriage age of 15 to 18 for girls and 17 to 20 for boys, a young couple is not considered capable of standing on their own economically, and consequently reside in the home of one set of parents until they are considered fully adult, usually for a period of three to five years. The choice is nearly always the home of the bride's parents since a young wife prefers to stay with her own mother rather than live in a strange house with her mother-in-law, whereas the young husband, who spends most of his daytime hours working on dispersed rice fields, is usually more indifferent as to where he lives.

After the initial period, a new house is built for the couple, usually by the wife's parents, who also assign the couple the use of a garden plot and a few fruit trees. Permanent residence in such cases is uxorilocal, especially when, as not infrequently happens, the new dwelling is built immediately adjacent to that of the wife's parents, sometimes even sharing the same roof though with a separate kitchen. In the village of Tjelapar the author observed 130 large houses, each occupied by a uxorilocal extended family of three or four nuclear families. In any event, one married daughter always continues to reside permanently with her parents in rural communities, caring for them in their old age and eventually inheriting the house from them.

Permanent uxorilocal residence is nevertheless by no means invariable. A shift to virilocal residence may occur after the termination of the initial uxorilocal period, and this is particularly likely to happen if the husband has prospects of inheriting a larger amount of land from his own parents. Neolocal residence is the norm in urban *prijaji* families, as is comprehensible from the fact that most *prijaji* are government officials whose duties normally require them to remove to localities other than those where they and their wives were reared. It is nevertheless customary in such cases for a young couple to spend the first five days after their wedding in the home of the bride's parents in symbolic initial uxorilocal residence. Because of the acute housing shortage in the cities and towns of Indonesia since World War II, young couples tend to reside after marriage in the home of either the bride's or the groom's family, depending upon convenience, and hence in ambilocal residence.

The household (*somah*), as the primary unit of consumption, production, child rearing, ritual performance, and social activity, is the most basic kin group in Javanese society. A man who establishes an independent household becomes its head (*kepala somah*). A household is not always characterized by a separate dwelling, but invariably by a separate kitchen, for each Javanese household cooks its own meals. Among urban *prijaji* families the average household consists of the *kepala somah*, his wife, five to ten children, the widowed mother of either the husband or the wife, and from three to five servants. In rural villages the household lacks servants and has fewer children because of the higher infant mortality rate, but it is augmented by the families of a married daughter or two living in initial uxorilocal residence.

Most Javanese desire a large family because of the general belief that many children are a blessing and contribute to *slamet* within the household. There is, in addition, the very practical consideration that children can take care of their parents in old age. A couple without children usually consult a physician or, in rural areas, a *dukun*, who is a specialist in supernatural methods of inducing impregnation as well as in midwifery. Birth control is absolutely unknown in rural areas, and the urban population, though usually possessing some knowledge of contraceptive devices, rarely utilizes them.

A Javanese household may include one or more pre-adolescent or adolescent relatives in the status of *ngèngèr*, a term meaning "taking a child to serve in the house." According to this custom, which should not be confused with adoption, a pre-adolescent child (nearly always a girl) may be placed in the home of an older married sibling, an uncle or aunt, or a grandmother, who provides for her maintenance, her education, and sometimes even her marriage. This may be done for several reasons: the family may have few children, or it may need additional household help, or it may be prosperous and thus in a position to render a service to relatives in less fortunate circumstances. A child in this status does not sever her ties with her own parents; she visits them from time to time and may eventually return to them. Moreover, she acquires no inheritance rights in her foster home.

Genuine adoption has quite a different basis, being confined almost exclusively to families lacking children of their own. It requires little formality, either social or religious. In urban areas the adoptive parent merely registers the new member of his household as his own child, and in rural regions reports the event to the village headman. An adopted child is equated legally, socially, and emotionally with an own child, and the relationship with him is supposed to rest on the same principle of "unconditional love" (*trisna*). He receives identical treatment from the community and has equal rights of inheritance. The sole difference is that the adoptive father may not act as *wali* (bride's guardian) for an adopted daughter.[10] This role must be taken by one of her own close male relatives or, in default of such, by a Muslim religious official.

Polygyny is rare in Javanese society. According to the census of 1930, only 2 per cent of all marriages in Java were polygynous. Widjojo Nitisastro (1956, p. 6) reports an incidence of 6 to 7 per cent in the village of Djabres in Central Java. The author found only three out of 36 households to be polygynous (each with two wives) in a random 10 per cent sample of the 364 households in the village of Tjelapar. It is also his impression that polygyny is unusual among the urban *prijaji*, somewhat more common in the lower levels of the urban population, and quite general in the more orthodox families among the nobility.

Although the husband is the head of the household, the wife does not have an inferior status. According to the Javanese point of view, husband and wife are expected to work together for the maintenance of the family. This holds true particularly in rural areas and among the lower levels of the urban population. In the country, husband and wife cooperate in agriculture. Preparation of the soil for tillage, plowing, harrowing, and the repair of irrigation works fall primarily within the masculine sphere of activities, whereas women do most of the planting, weeding, harvesting, threshing, and storage, as well as the further processing and preservation of food. Both sexes transport crops from the field to the home and products from the home to market. In many market centers, rural as well as urban, however, one notices a preponderance of female buyers and sellers. Among the lower levels of the urban population the wives hold jobs, e.g., in domestic service, or peddle foodstuffs and other wares on the streets.

Among the *prijaji* the support of the family depends more exclusively on the husband's income, but the wife, as in the case of her rural counterpart, plays a dominant role in household affairs. Having given his wife the money to run the household, the husband rarely interferes. One difference between urban and rural housewives is that the former always receives formal guests along with her husband whereas the latter retires to the rear of the house when formal guests arrive. This difference is striking to the foreigner and has often given the latter the erroneous impression that the Javanese wife holds an inferior status in the household.

In regard to divorce (*pegatan*), the Javanese follow the rules and procedures laid down by Muslim law. Consequently divorce may be granted upon request of the husband without the consent of his wife. There seems to be no definite rule determining which of the divorced parents the children should follow, but infants who still require maternal care always follow the mother. No matter with whom the children reside, however, both divorced parents have the obligation to provide for their maintenance until they reach adulthood. When a divorce occurs, each spouse retains the property which he or she brought into the marriage, but the property which they acquired together during the marriage (called *banda srajan*) is divided according to the principle of *sagendong-sepikul*, which allocates two thirds to the husband and one third to the wife.[17]

The incidence of divorce appears to be quite high in Java, especially in rural areas but also among the lower strata of the urban population. One reason is probably the high frequency of traditional arranged marriages, without the consent of the young people themselves, and the consequent lack of deep emotional ties in the early years of married life. Other factors include the haphazard methods of choosing a mate prevalent among the lower urban class and the absence of a conception among the Javanese that divorce is morally wrong.

OLD AGE AND DEATH

There is no clearly defined point of transition to old age in the Javanese life cycle. In rural areas, when a man feels his strength waning and his capacity to farm diminishing, he retires and turns over his responsibilities to his sons, to his sons-in-law, or occasionally to his tenants and hired laborers. He may also decide to resign his position as head of the household, in which case this responsibility is assumed by the son-in-law or the son who has resided permanently in his house. He derives his support from a special plot of land (*siti gantungan*) and from contributions from his children according to their abilities.

Javanese funerals are not elaborate. The corpse normally remains in the house for only one day, during which preparations for its interment are made. The immediate neighbors and relatives assist in these preparations and contribute collectively to the costs of the funeral. After being bathed, the body is wrapped in white cotton (white is the Javanese color of mourning), and religious officials recite verses of the Qur'ân. Relatives, neighbors, and friends escort the body to the cemetery.

Slametan are held on the third, seventh, fortieth, hundredth, and thousandth days after death. During this period the deceased becomes transformed into one of the idealized and sacred ancestors who provide guidance to their surviving relatives. The grave is visited on important occasions. Its care devolves, in rural communities, upon all the bilateral descendants of the deceased, who are known collectively as the *alur waris*. The members of this group who live in the village where the grave is located are responsible for keeping it clean and for performing *slametan* ceremonies at fixed intervals. Those who reside in other villages or have migrated to another region are expected to make money contributions whenever the grave requires major repairs.

PROPERTY AND INHERITANCE

Property becomes inheritance (*warisan*) at the moment of the owner's death. The mode of inheritance differs with the kind of property, necessitating a division of the latter into the following categories: (1) house and garden, (2) agricultural land, (3) fruit trees, (4) domestic animals, (5) heirlooms, and (6) the separate and joint property of husband and wife.

The dwelling, its furniture, utensils, and other contents, and the surrounding garden (but not its fruit trees) are regarded as a single inseparable complex. As previously noted, one married daughter is normally chosen to reside permanently in the parental home with her husband and children, being charged with the obligation of caring for her aging father and mother after his retirement. Her husband succeeds to the responsibilities of head of the household and automatically inherits the house and garden of his father-in-law when the old man dies.

Cultivable land is inherited by the children of both sexes. When a young couple set up an independent household at the conclusion of the initial period of uxorilocal residence, they are given, as we have seen, a new house and garden plot by the bride's parents, together with the use of a few fruit trees. At the same time the husband is allotted the use of a plot of land (*siti garapan*) by his father. What he receives, however, is only a usufruct right, not a property title with the power to sell or lease. In assigning land to a son, or to a married daughter and her husband, a man takes into account the number of children he has, and if his wife later gives birth to another child he has the right to reduce the amounts assigned to his married children to provide a proportional share for their new sibling.

When a man reaches the age when he expects no more children he normally makes a definitive division of his land among his children, because no Javanese likes the idea of dying before his property has been divided. The division is into plots of equal area, of which one is permanently allocated to each child and one, called *siti gantungan*, is retained for his own support in his old age. Though comparable in area, the plots are not equal in quality, for the Javanese prefer to allocate their best irrigated rice fields (*sawah loh*) to their daughters and to allot dry fields (*tegalan*) and paddy land of inferior quality (*sawah tjengkar*) to their sons. Such allocated land (*siti dunungan*) is not yet the property of the children. It becomes such only with the death of the father, when it becomes inherited land (*siti jasan*). To confirm these property rights they must be reported to the village headman and registered with the village clerk, so that these officials can later serve as witnesses in the event of disputes.

The heirs do not, however, report their inherited property to the headman individually. Only one of them, usually the eldest son, has the responsibility for doing so. Moreover, he registers, not the separate pieces of land to which his siblings are individually entitled, but rather the entire landed estate of his father as a single unit with himself as the holder of the collective title or *petuq*. With it is included the *siti gantungan*, the plot reserved by his father for his own support when he allocated the rest of his land to his children. The *petuq*-holder uses this for the support of his widowed mother until her death, when he distributes it equally among his *pondoq* or dependants. An individual who holds a *petuq*, with its collective responsibility for the landed property of an entire sibling group, enjoys in the community the status of a *kuli*, with the duties and privileges previously described.

Whenever an individual feels capable of assuming the status of *kuli* he has the right to separate his own land holdings from the collective estate and to acquire his own *petuq* or title to them. People are reluctant to do so, however, until they are firmly established economically and socially, since the status of *kuli* involves heavy community responsibilities. It is therefore usual to preserve the collective title to the estate of an ancestor more or less intact for three or four generations, even though individual descendants gradually withdraw from the collectivity to become independent *petuq*-holders.

A man can acquire land in other ways than by inheritance from his father or his father-in-law, e.g., by purchase or by inheritance from an uncle, aunt, or other relative. His holdings thus tend gradually to accumulate. Because of the varied modes of acquisition a man commonly has to work on three, four, or more plots of land which lie at a distance from each other, sometimes in different villages. The system of mutual aid (*gotong rojong*) facilitates the simultaneous cultivation of such dispersed fields.

Fruit trees, including coconut palms, are inherited separately from the garden plots on which they grow, and are divided equally among the children. Domestic animals, notably carabaos, cattle, sheep, goats, and fowl, are likewise inherited by the children with an equal division. When there are not enough animals to go around, as frequently happens with larger animals like carabao and cattle, they are shared equally by the entire sibling group, and their division is deferred until they have produced offspring. Heirlooms (*pusaka*), consisting of sacred weapons (e.g., a *kris*) and other small or valued objects, are given to one of the sons, usually the eldest.

As regards the possessions of husband and wife, a distinction is drawn between *banda gawan*, the personal property brought into marriage by either the husband or the wife, and *banda srajan*, their joint property accumulated during their married life. In contrast to the situation in the case of divorce, both kinds of property are pooled for the purpose of inheritance and are divided equally among the children. When a couple die childless, however, the *banda gawan* of the wife is inherited by her kinsmen and that of the husband by his, while the *banda srajan* is distributed between the two groups of kin in the ratio of one to two.

KINSHIP TERMINOLOGY

The Javanese language incorporates in its structure certain obligatory distinctions in regard to the social relationships between addresser and addressee. The consideration of differences in status or rank, in relative age, and in degree of acquaintance between addresser and addressee gives rise to a number of styles in speech. In terms of linguistic analysis, the elements producing these styles fall into two categories:

1) morphological alterations of affixes in relation to the radical elements;
2) syntactic alterations in the choice of alternative words, particles, personal pronouns, and demonstrative pronouns.

There are at least seven styles that relate to seven distinctive social-status relationships. Among these, two may be considered the most basic, namely, those called *ngoko* and *krama*.

In addition to the seven styles, there are in Javanese about 300 alternative references, called *krama inggil*, which are obligatory in reference to the possessions, body parts, actions, and qualities of the addressee and to those of a third person who is higher in status or older than the speaker. *Krama inggil* references are used in both the *ngoko* and the *krama* styles. Thus, in speaking to a second person who is of lower status about a third person who is higher, one speaks *ngoko* but uses *krama inggil* references with respect to the third person. In speaking to a higher person about a third higher person, one employs *krama* with *krama inggil* references. In speaking to a higher person about a third person who is higher than oneself but lower than the addressee, however, one employs the *krama* style with ordinary *krama* references.

The system of social styles in language usage requires that the Javenese have *krama inggil* equivalents for a number of their kinship terms of reference. A Javanese speaker must use these equivalents in three cases, namely:

1) in speaking to a higher or older person about a relative of the addressee;
2) in speaking to a distant acquaintance about a relative of the addressee;
3) in speaking to anyone about a higher or older third person's relative.

Although terms of address, according to Murdock (1949, p. 98), have less significance than terms of reference in kinship analysis, it is our opinion that they are equally important. Though they may not reflect the kinship system as fully, they often express patterns of kinship behavior more exactly. As compared with the reference terminology, the terms of address in the Javanese kinship system show a strong tendency toward classification by generation levels. Nevertheless, for the sake of brevity and simplicity, we list below only the Javanese terms of reference, and these only in their *ngoko* forms. An asterisk (*) after a term indicates that it has a *krama inggil* equivalent.

1 *bapaq**: father.
2 *ibu*: mother; mother's sister; father's sister; mother's brother's wife; father's brother's wife.
3 *uwa*: mother's elder brother or sister; father's elder brother or sister; mother's or father's elder brother's wife; mother's or father's elder sister's husband.
4 *bibiq*: mother's or father's younger sister; mother's or father's younger brother's wife.
5 *paman*: mother's or father's younger brother; mother's or father's younger sister's husband.
6 *kakang**: elder brother.
7 *mbaqju**: elder sister.
8 *adi**: younger brother or sister.
9 *anaq**: child, either son or daughter.
10 *naqsanaq*: first cousin of either sex, i.e., a parent's sibling's child.
11 *misanan*: second cousin of either sex, i.e., a grandparent's sibling's grandchild.
12 *mindoan*: third cousin of either sex, i.e., a great-grandparent's sibling's great-grandchild.
13 *keponaqan**: elder sibling's child.
14 *pelunan*: younger sibling's child.
15 *mbah, éjang**: grandparent, either maternal or paternal and of either sex.
16 *putu**: grandchild of either sex.
17 *bujut*: any relative of the third ascending or descending generations, including great-grandparents and great-grandchildren.

18 *tjanggah:* any relative of the fourth ascending or descending generations.
19 *warèng:* any relative of the fifth ascending or descending generations.
20 *udeq-udeq:* any relative of the sixth ascending or descending generations.
21 *gantung siwur:* any relative of the seventh ascending or descending generations.
22 *gropak-sénté:* any relative of the eighth ascending or descending generations.
23 *debok-bosoq:* any relative of the ninth ascending or descending generations.
24 *galih-asem:* any relative of the tenth ascending or descending generations.
25 *bodjo*:* spouse, either husband or wife. For variant designations see below.
26 *maratuwa (mertuwa)*:* spouse's parent of either sex.
27 *ipé:* spouse's sibling of either sex; sibling's spouse.
28 *pripé:* spouse's sibling's spouse.
29 *mantu:* child's spouse, either son-in-law or daughter-in-law.
30 *bésan:* child's spouse's parent.

The kinship terminology reflects the social importance of the nuclear family. Within the family, the criterion of sex differentiates the parents but is ignored in the case of children, although the latter can be distinguished by sex, if necessary, by employing the attributes *lanang* (male) and *wedoq* (female). Sibling terminology always reflects relative age, which is an important factor in the reciprocal behavior of siblings, but only elder siblings are differentiated terminologically by sex. The term *kakang* for elder brother, however, can also be applied to females, as when two girls are called *kakang-adi* to indicate that they are elder and younger siblings of each other. A special term, *sedulur* (or *sanaq*), is used to designate collectively all kinsmen outside the nuclear family, but it also embraces siblings. With this sole exception, the kinship terminology beyond the nuclear family is both completely distinctive and strongly classificatory on the basis of the principle of generation.

Cousin terminology conforms to the Eskimo pattern. Parallel and cross-cousins are referred to alike as *naqsanaq*, a compound (cf. Frake, 1955, p. 124), of *naq* (child) and *sanaq* (sibling). Second cousins are called *misanan*, a derivative term which, stripped of its morphemic elements, is the word *pisan*, meaning "once" or "first." The term therefore connotes a "first-degree" relative. Similarly *mindoan*, denoting a third cousin, is derived from *pindo*, "twice" or "second," implying a "second-degree" relative.

The terms for both avuncular and nepotic relatives are lineal in type and are extended collaterally to remoter relatives of the same generation. They also reflect strikingly the criterion of relative age. The *prijaji*, however, do not use the term *pelunan* (younger sibling's child); they call all nephews and nieces *keponaqan* regardless of the relative age of their parents.

Grandparental terms are also extended collaterally within the second ascending generation. Sex can be indicated, if necessary, by the attributes *kakung* (male) and *putri* (female). These are *krama inggil* references, since applied to older relatives, and thus contrast with the *ngoko* words *lanang* and *wedoq* that are used to differentiate the sex of children. Many families use the alternative grandparental terms *èjang* and *mbah* to make a distinction between paternal and maternal grandparents, but some use them one way and some the other. Sometimes, too, one of these terms is reserved for one pair of grandparents and the other is called *paqdé* and *budé*. Since *paq* is an abbreviation of *bapaq* (father), *bu* of *ibu* (mother), and *dé* of *gede*, these terms mean literally "grand father" and "grand mother." Hildreth Geertz (1955, p. 123) found these same two terms applied to parents' elder siblings in an East Javanese town. The term for grandchild, *putu*, is likewise classificatory in character, but collateral relatives of the second descending generation can be distinguished as *putu keponoqan*.

The terms for relatives of the third to the tenth ascending and descending generations are similarly classificatory within the generation. A distinctive feature emerges here, however, since all of them are used reciprocally, i.e., ignoring the criterion of polarity (see Murdock, 1949, p. 104). These terms are, of course, very seldom used. They formerly had a certain significance among the nobility and in other upper-class families who were interested in tracing their genealogies to prove relationship with one of the princely families. Few peasant families, even those of village headmen, remember even their great-grandparents.

The *ngoko* term for spouse, *bodjo*, has a *krama* equivalent, *simah*, and also a corresponding *krama inggil* term, *garwa*. All three refer to husband as well as wife without regard to sex. In addition, a native speaker must employ different designations in different status contexts. In talking about his wife to a younger person, for example, he refers to her as "your elder sister" or, if the addressee is much younger, as "your mother," the implication being that the speaker's wife, being older (or much older) than the addressee, might be the latter's elder sister or mother. A native speaker[18] of Javanese must alter the designation for spouse according to sixteen distinctly conceptualized situations. These are defined, on the one hand, by whether (1) the addressee is older or higher in status than himself, (2) younger or lower in status, (3) a distant acquaintance, or (4) an intimate friend and, on the other hand, by whether he is speaking about (1) his own spouse, (2) the addressee's spouse, (3) the spouse of a third person who is older or of higher status, and (4) the spouse of a third person who is younger or lower in status. The sixteen permutations are shown in the table on the opposite page.

KINSHIP BEHAVIOR

Underlying the patterns of behavior toward all kinsmen, affinal as well as consanguineal, is a general feeling of good will. Toward relatives who are older, higher in generation, or superior in rank there is, in addition, an ideal attitude of respect. This is manifested, in *prijaji* families and among the nobility, in the following ways: by adopting the proper style of speech, by employing the correct terms of address, by using gestures of respect, by sitting in a respectful attitude,[19] by avoiding starting a conversation, and by refraining from initiating an exchange of jokes. The reciprocal obligations and specific patterns of behavior prevailing

Ego speaks	about Ego's spouse	about addressee's spouse	about spouse of a lower third person	about spouse of a higher third person
to a higher or older person	teknonymy*	elder sister elder brother mother father	*krama* term	*krama inggil* term
to a lower or younger person	your elder sister your elder brother your mother your father	*ngoko* term	*ngoko* term	*krama inggil* term
to an intimate friend	personal name	personal name	*ngoko* term	*krama inggil* term
to a distant acquaintance	teknonymy	your younger sister your elder brother	*krama* term	*krama inggil* term

* Teknonymy is used, of course, only if the couple have children. Otherwise some such designation as "my female (male) friend" or "my friend from back home" is employed.

between relatives of particular categories are summarized in the following paragraphs.

Parents are expected to care for and rear their children with unconditional love, and in their old age reciprocal care is obligatory. Children must show respect to their parents, acknowledge their authority, and obey them. It is improper to contradict a parent, especially one's father. If a child disagrees with a parent's opinion, the matter should be discussed at another time and in an indirect and informal manner. Children resort to their mother for the satisfaction of most of their daily needs, but the father has the final decision in important matters, such as choosing a mate or a profession. Children very seldom discuss matters of sex with their parents or go to their mothers with intimate problems. In speaking to parents, especially to the father, the formal style of speech, *krama*, is theoretically obligatory, although there are numerous exceptions today. Children may not address their parents by name but must always use the kinship terms *bu* (or *ibu*) and *paq* (or *bapaq*). Parents, however, normally call their children by their nicknames.

Relationships between siblings reflect sex differences to only a very limited extent, but they are strongly channelized by relative age. A younger sibling is supposed to follow the advice of his older brothers and sisters, and to some extent to obey them. An elder sibling is expected to take good care of his younger brothers and sisters and to look after their welfare. If younger siblings become orphaned before adulthood it is obligatory for the older siblings to provide for them, and siblings must always help one another when financial problems arise. The use of *krama* in speaking to elder siblings is optional; though still customary in many noble families, it is little practiced among the *prijaji*. An elder brother is addressed by the term *mas*, an elder sister as *mbaq* (a contraction of *mbaqju*). Younger siblings are called by their names (*ndjangkar*).

In interacting with their uncles and aunts, children behave in a more formal manner than toward their parents, observing most of the aspects of respectful behavior enumerated above. The parents' siblings, however, have no authority over their nephews and nieces. Though formal and always marked by respect on the part of the siblings' children, the relationship can develop into one of friendship and intimacy. Nieces often form such warm attachments with an aunt that they discuss intimate problems with her. Nephews may also establish friendly, though less intimate, relationships with an uncle. The use of *krama* is obligatory in speaking to a parent's sibling, but it may change into *ngoko* if friendly relations develop. Such relations, however, tend to grow formal again as the sibling's children become adults. Aunts and uncles are addressed, like father and mother, as *bu* and *paq*. Nieces and nephews are called by their names, or by the term *naq* (a contraction of *anaq*), or by the terms of address for siblings, i.e., *mas*, *mbaq*, or *diq*.[20] The last custom, called *mbasaqaké anaqé* ("speaking the speech of one's children"), is practiced only by people who are themselves parents; in calling their nieces and nephews thus, they are adopting the position of their own children.

Though grandparents have no authority over their grandchildren, the latter must honor them throughout life and must exhibit toward them all the formal aspects of respectful behavior. Boys as well as girls often develop very friendly and intimate relations with one of their grandmothers to the extent that they come to her with their secret problems. The *krama* style of speech must always be used with a grandparent. The terms of address for grandparents are the same as the terms for reference, namely, *mbah* or *éjang*. A grandson is addressed as *lé* and a granddaughter as *nduk*, but names are often used instead.

Cousins are supposed to maintain mutually friendly relations without regard to their degree of collaterality. They are distinguished only by seniority, which is not identical with relative age. Senior cousins are the children of the parents' elder siblings; junior cousins, those of the parents' younger siblings. In address, sibling terms are extended to cousins—*mas* and *mbaq* for senior cousins, *diq* for junior cousins.

Husband and wife are supposed to show affection and love toward each other, though any open display of affection is disapproved in Javanese culture. Love and affection must, however, be consciously developed, especially in parentally arranged marriages where husband and wife meet for the first time at the wedding ceremony. A wife must always show respect toward her husband, since he is assumed to be the older of the two. The wife's sphere of interest centers mainly in the affairs of the household. The husband, to be sure, is the household head, but he is primarily concerned with matters on the outside. In urban *prijaji* families the wife commonly shares her husband's outside interests, but he seldom manifests an interest in the internal affairs of the household. Conflicts between husband and wife usually relate either to affairs outside the household or to matters concerning their children. The husband addresses his wife by name, but she addresses him as *mas* (elder sibling). More commonly, however, they use teknonymy; he calls her *bu*, and she calls him *paq*.

Conflict is unusual in the relations between parents-in-law and children-in-law. It occurs, as a rule, only when the husband brings his widowed mother to live in the household, as he is obligated to do if she has no income. Married people are expected to manifest formal respectful behavior, in all its aspects, toward their parents-in-law. The use of *krama* in speaking to them, for example, is obligatory, although they usually speak *ngoko* to their children-in-law. The spouse's parents are addressed by the terms for father and mother, and the child's spouse is reciprocally addressed as *naq* (child).

The relationship between siblings-in-law is not well defined, though it usually resembles that between own siblings. The spouse of an elder sibling must always be addressed, regardless of his age, by the terms for elder siblings, *mas* or *mbaq*. The spouse of a younger sibling, however, is not addressed by the terms for younger siblings, but is called *mas* if male or *djeng* if female.

The relationship between *bésan*, the two sets of parents of a married couple, though formal, is supposed to be characterized by mutual friendship and respect. The use of *krama* between them is obligatory unless they were already close friends when their children married. Males in this relationship are addressed as *mas* (elder sibling). The mother of the husband, however, is addressed as *mbaqju* (usually not *mbaq*), and the mother of the wife as *djeng*.

The relationship between neighbors deserves consideration in the context of kin relations. Though a person may not be particularly well acquainted with all the people who reside in his immediate neighborhood (*rukun tetangga*), he is obligated to render them assistance in case of sickness, accident, or death. Whenever a *slametan* is given the immediate neighbors are always invited, and at the annual Muslim holiday of *lebaran* it is obligatory to pay formal visits to the older members of the neighborhood. A neighbor is always addressed politely by kinship terms. This practice is rarely changed to the use of personal names even when a neighbor becomes a close friend.

Kinship, in its widest sense, can be conceived as extending to all the members of the same ethnolinguistic group. The Javanese divide people into four great ethnic categories: Javanese, i.e., members of their own group; Indonesians other than Javanese; Indonesian residents of non-Malayan race or language, e.g., Arabs and Chinese; and foreigners. Kinship terms are extended beyond the range of actual relatives to all Javanese and also, since the development of an Indonesian national awareness, increasingly to the members of other Indonesian ethno-linguistic groups, but not to non-Malayan peoples or to foreigners. Within this range of extension, everyone of the same generation as the speaker must be addressed by sibling terms, although schoolmates, colleagues, and other close acquaintances tend to substitute personal names. Those old enough to be placed in the generation of the speaker's parents are addressed by the parental terms *paq* and *bu*, and those of a younger generation are addressed as *naq* or, if small children, are called by name.

STRUCTURAL PRINCIPLES

From the foregoing account it is possible to identify the structural principles implicit in the Javanese kinship system. In general, the range of kinship affiliation is limited primarily by memory, acquaintance, and needs, rather than by structure, custom, or common residence, and therefore differs from individual to individual.

The nuclear family (*kulawarga*), both of orientation and of procreation, is the basic kin group in the life of every Javanese. Only toward members of this group does he have major obligations, and only from them can he expect maximal attention and care. Conflicts with his parents threaten to sever him from those who can most bless his life, and conflicts with his children imperil his security in old age. Neglect of obligations toward members of one's nuclear family, even though they are not specifically enforced by society, is always a serious matter.

Oustide the nuclear family, rights and duties toward kinsmen are less clearly defined and less strongly sanctioned. Patterns of kinship relations allow considerable latitude for individual variation. Nevertheless, the large number of strict and detailed rules for correct speech and behavior in formal kinship relations requires a keen awareness of differences in age, in seniority, in generation, and in rank, in order to conform to the demands of Javanese etiquette.

Despite the "loose structure"[21] of Javanese kinship relations outside of the nuclear family, there exists a definite conception of the importance of the kindred. This group consists of an individual's *sedulur* or relatives, consanguineal and often affinal as well, especially his lineal and closer collateral kinsmen of his own and the first ascending and descending generations. A person can rely on his *sedulur* for various kinds of support. In traveling, for example, he can drop in on a *sedulur* for overnight hospitality, and in giving a circumcision feast for his son he can expect assistance from his *sedulur*. Moreover, as noted earlier, the kindred plays some role in the determination of marriage choices.

Descent (*keturunan*) is likewise an important factor in the Javanese social system. It finds expression in the group of dispersed relatives called *alur waris*, who, in peasant communities, have the collective responsibility for tending and keeping in repair the graves of their common ancestors. Descent also played an important role in defining the social position of the individual among the *prijaji* of the pre-war period, when a bilateral kinship tie to a high-ranking official was a requisite for filling many posts in the colonial service. Descent is also involved in the rules of inheritance, especially in rural communities. Here, as we have seen, land is inherited according to the bilateral principle, albeit with some matrilineal bias; the status of *kuli* is inherited in the main according to the patrilineal principle; the house and garden matrilineally; and other property bilaterally.

The individual in Javanese society owes attention and assistance to, and receives them from, not only his nuclear family, his kindred, and his bilateral descent group (*alur waris*), but also his neighborhood (*rukun tetangga*). Etiquette requires that he treat the members of all these groups, and all other persons with whom he interacts, as kinsmen. The use of kinship terms, for example, extends far beyond the range of consanguineal and affinal relatives.

CHAPTER 7

THE SINHALESE OF THE DRY ZONE OF NORTHERN CEYLON

E. R. LEACH
Cambridge University

THE concept of social structure, as it is used by British social anthropologists, is closely linked with the notion of social continuity. It is an established convention among anthropologists that a "people" can survive the most startling changes of external circumstance. The Iroquois who build skyscrapers in New York are "the same" Iroquois that introduced Morgan to the mysteries of matrilineal kinship organization. Clearly, if we use such a terminology, the notion of sameness requires cautious analysis.

Over a period of time the actual composition of any "society" changes; the old die, children grow old, and new children are born. Customs change too, in primitive as well as in sophisticated cultures; in a single generation the headhunters of Sarawak have become prosperous rubber planters touring their rivers in outboard motorboats. In the face of such change, what is it that persists? The total situation is plainly very complex, for the perpetuation of language alone entails the maintenance of an elaborate mesh of "tradition" which is, to a high degree, impervious to immediate changes in the local situation. In developing their special theory of social structure the British social anthropologists have laid stress on only one particular aspect of this total problem.

If we consider a community of people at any given point in time, we can readily see that most interpersonal relations are governed by conventional rules which, in themselves, apply to statuses rather than to individuals. There are rules about how the young should respect the old, how men should treat women, how parents should deal with their children, and so on. Such rules, as a whole, can be said to form a "system." In principle, the system will not be altered by any mere progression of time, for at every point in time there will always be old and young, men and women, parents and children.

Going further, the British social anthropologists have claimed that, in societies where unilineal descent is given marked cultural emphasis, the continuing system of jural relationships to which I have referred turns out to be very largely a matter of kinship organization. The continuity of the society as a whole rests on the continuity of the system of lineages, each of which is a "corporation," the life span of which is independent of the individual lives of its individual members.

This mode of analysis has proved so fruitful, particularly with regard to African materials, that it has been easy to overlook its limitations. The argument is one which has developed specifically with regard to societies possessing clearcut unilineal descent groups (Fortes, 1953), and this poses two questions. First, what kind of ongoing corporation takes the place of the lineage in societies which lack unilineal descent groups? Second, if we are to distinguish societies with unilineal descent groups as a special type, where do we draw the line? For, considered as an organizing principle, unilineal descent is never simply present or absent; it can be present in varying degrees.

The justification for including a paper on Ceylon in a symposium on Southeast Asia is precisely that Sinhalese society may be considered a marginal case. Generally speaking, the tribal peoples of Borneo and the Philippines have kinship systems which are fully cognatic. Nothing could be more "bilateral" than the pattern described by Barton (1949) for the Kalinga or by Freeman (1958) for the Iban. Sinhalese society, however, though broadly speaking cognatic in type, also contains marked elements of unilinearity, and one authority (Ryan, 1953, p. 26) has even alleged that the Sinhalese have a lineage system. A discussion of the nature of structural continuity in the Sinhalese case may therefore serve to discriminate some of the critical issues.

The notion of a corporation, as derived from Maine, is that an estate comprises a "bundle of rights" over persons and things. At any one time the corporation embraces a number of individuals who share in the assets of the estate according to their particular relative status. Recruitment to such a property-owning corporation may be acquired in a variety of ways, e.g., by purchase, by initiation, or by inheritance. It is the general characteristic of unilineal descent groups that a child automatically inherits corporation membership from one or the other of its recognized parents, but not from both.

Clearly the principle of unilineal descent is a convenient one, but this should not blind us to the fact that several other kinds of "inheritance" are theoretically possible. A system in which all children inherited equal rights from both parents would plainly lead to total confusion, but a system in which children could choose to take particular rights from either the father or the mother (though not from both at once) would not, in principle, lead to a structure any more complex than one of straight unilineal descent. Alternatively, the status might depend not so much upon parentage as on place of residence. Ethnographic examples of both these alternatives have been recorded. The Sinhalese case contains something of both.

Sinhalese culture is by no means uniform. Common usage distinguishes the lowcountry Sinhalese of southwestern Ceylon from the Kandyans of the central and north central areas. Within the Kandyan category it is useful to distinguish further the population of the mountainous, and relatively densely populated, Central Province from that of the flat Dry Zone lying to the north and east.

The reasons for cultural differences here are partly historical, partly ecological. European colonialism made its impact upon the coastal regions and upon the southwest several centuries before the Kandyan kingdom was subjugated. Within the Kandyan area, on the other hand, the climatic contrast between the Dry Zone and the rest is very great, and in consequence quite different residential patterns have developed in different sections.

Formally considered, the whole Kandyan area possesses a unified system of customary law, much of which now has judicial sanction. The principles of this law, especially as regards matters of marriage and inheritance, have been described in a number of textbooks, notably that of Hayley (1923). Patterns of residence in relation to kinship have received less attention, but Tambiah (1958) has recently published an excellent account of the situation prevailing in hill villages close to Kandy itself. Still more recently Yalman (1960) has reported on other Kandyan hill communities.

Kandyan hill communities are mostly of substantial size, with populations exceeding 1,000 individuals. They usually include members of a number of different castes, and there is wide economic differentiation between rich and poor. The wealthier sections of the society set considerable value on the maintenance of the family estate as an intact entity. The *gedera,* i.e., the family house and its associated lands, is looked upon as a patrimony to be handed down mainly to the male heirs, who should ideally continue to reside in, or close to, the parental home. With this patrilineal ideology, however, is associated a bilateral principle of inheritance. Daughters as well as sons inherit from both parents, and in equal degree. The patrimonial landed estate can therefore be conserved on behalf of the sons only if the daughters can take their share of the inheritance in some other form, usually that of money or other movable assets given as a dowry at the time of the daughter's marriage.

Although the same ideology concerning property rights prevails throughout the community, it is in general only the wealthier families that are able to provide their daughters with cash dowries. Hence it is only among the wealthy that the *gedera* emerges as a named group with many of the attributes of a corporate patrilineage. Among poorer families, property in land, such as it is, is dispersed among both sons and daughters, and the appearance of unilinearity disappears.

The situation in the northern Dry Zone is rather different. The general region of Anuradhapura has a very long history of human occupation. It was the site of the classical kingdom of Ceylon, the virtues of which are extolled in the Mahavamsa. What is relevant in a highly complex history is only that a sophisticated civilization flourished there from the third century B.C. until the thirteenth century after Christ. It was a "hydraulic civilization" in the sense in which Wittfogel (1957) uses the term; the whole countryside was very intensively developed by a great variety of irrigation works of various types and sizes.

In later centuries the more elaborate of these works fell into decay, but village life continued to be possible on a limited scale. If we ignore the consequences of the intensive reconstruction work over the past thirty years, the general ecological pattern of the North Central Province today may be summarized as follows. Each village constitutes a separate economic entity. Its population subsists by the cultivation of irrigated rice in a small permanent field which is watered from a rain-fed reservoir (tank) which is particular to that village alone. The villagers are alone responsible for the maintenance of the tank and, subject to certain supervisory governmental controls, have sole rights in its water.

The village field necessarily lies below the level of the tank where it is easily irrigated with a controlled water supply. The houses of the village are clustered together immediately below the earthwork of the tank, where water seepage makes it possible to grow fruit trees and moisture-demanding vegetables. Although the total annual precipitation is considerable—50 to 75 inches—it is concentrated in brief periods, and the rate of evaporation in dry weather is very high. Some cultivation in unirrigated areas is possible, but only erratically so. Generally speaking, permanent human habitation is impossible without irrigation.

It follows that there is a peculiarly intimate relationship between any particular tank and the village and field that are associated with it. The size of any tank depends upon its position. Once the main earthwork has been constructed the capacity of the tank is fixed within quite narrow limits. This sets consequential limits on the size of the field which can be irrigated, and more indirectly on the size of the village population which can derive its subsistence from that field.

Since the field is fixed in size and position, it is not surprising to find that land is owned according to rules which we might describe as "freehold private tenure," i.e., which allow land to be bought and sold, leased, and mortgaged. Such a description, however, masks the really crucial element in the situation. The scarce valuable is not land but water. Although the villagers appear at first sight to be concerned with the ownership of land, closer investigation shows that land is measured in terms of the water to which it is entitled. This fact has considerable social implications.

While plots of land can be divided, the unity of the tank is permanent and inescapable. The villagers who derive their sustenance from a single tank may have their petty rivalries, but in larger matters, such as the maintenance of the tank earthwork and the proper operation of the tank sluices, they must cooperate closely lest disaster befall them all. We consequently find that, although the ownership of land (i.e., water) is meticulously fragmented into small individual parcels, the work of the agricultural cycle is closely coordinated and operated according to a strict collective timetable. We find too that the villagers who derive their sustenance from a single tank are almost invariably members of a single small sub-caste (*variga*), that they tend strongly to be endogamous, and that they are consequently all close kin.

Although both men and women own and inherit property, it is the husband who is normally its manager. Since it is humiliating for a man to be exclusively dependent upon his wife's property, every man endeavors to marry virilocally (*diga*). If he must marry uxorilocally (*binna*), he looks for a girl from his own village, where he is likely to have assets of his own. While the ideal preference for *diga* as opposed to *binna* marriage is quite explicit, the actual numerical proportion of *binna* marriages may be 40 per cent or more.

Binna marriages belong to several clearly defined types. There is the *binna* husband who is himself landless and makes himself the servile dependent of his father-in-law; there is the *binna* heiress who has no brothers and whose parents have insisted that she stay at home to maintain the family estate; and there is the *binna* marriage where the spouses are cross-cousins. In this last instance there is again an economic motive. Since a man normally inherits land both from his father and from his mother, he may be co-heir with his mother's brother's daughter of land located in his mother's village of birth, so that by marrying her he consolidates the estate. Sinhalese even say that a man has a "right" to marry his mother's brother's daughter for this purpose. In practice, although cross-cousin marriages occur quite frequently, they are in no special sense preferred or prescribed.

Properly speaking there is no dowry system. What is sometimes called a dowry (*dävädda*) is simply an advance of inheritance in the form of land. There is in this region no technique of preserving the patrimonial estate for males by giving movable assets to the daughters. Nevertheless, since it is the more prosperous families who marry *diga*, there is observable among them a statistical tendency in the direction of patrilineal rather than cognatic inheritance. What happens is roughly as follows. Both the male head of a household and his wife may separately own property in land. Both parcels will be separately inherited by the sons and daughters. Those who remain resident in the village will all receive equal shares, but those who marry far away will, in practice, get smaller shares or even nothing at all.

It is mainly a question of the practicability of fragmentation. A poor man with several children can not in practice divide his assets equally, and the family usually disperses, leaving a single son to inherit the patrimony and buy out his co-heirs as the occasion demands. A wealthy household with only one son and one daughter, on the other hand, is likely to arrange an exchange marriage with some equally wealthy household in a nearby village or even in the same village. The property may be fragmented for the time being, but the possibility, indeed the probability, exists that it will be brought together again by further marriages between the same two families at a later date. Such procedures do not have the effect of conserving property within a patrilineage, but they do tend, in the long run, to conserve property within particular co-resident compound groups. The heads of such groups are normally male and are usually descended from previous owners by male rather than female links.

If the total population of a cluster of closely adjacent villages is analyzed over a period of time, it will be found that, in each village, the occupants of a small number of particular compounds (*watte*) persistently retain most of the economic and political influence. None of the various positions of influence and title which villagers can hold, either by governmental appointment or in their own private affairs, are hereditary, but the constancy with which such positions remain within a narrow circle of kin plainly demonstrates that, among the wealthy, the strategy of marriage can be used to circumvent the apparently disruptive influence of bilateral inheritance.

In one village studied, for example, the leadership over a period of about half a century was transmitted successively (the dates are approximations) as follows:

In 1905 to A, a resident in Compound 1;
In 1925 to B, a resident in Compound 2, son-in-law to A;
In 1938 to C, a resident in Compound 1, son of a cross-cousin of A's wife;
In 1948 to D, a resident in Compound 2, sister's son to C and cross-cousin's son to B;
In 1952 to E, a resident in Compound 1, cross-cousin to D and son to C.

There were nine compounds in the village, but the other seven were entirely excluded from positions of influence during the period in question. This was not because Compounds 1 and 2 had any special hereditary right but was directly due to the fact the A and B arranged a series of highly astute marriages both for themselves and for their descendants. In 1886 the occupants of Compounds 1 and 2 had both been nearly bankrupt; by 1954 their successors owned all the best land in the village.

It is against this background of property maneuver that we can best understand the peculiar attitude of the Dry-Zone Sinhalese toward marriage. By European standards the villagers are scandalously promiscuous. A girl ordinarily starts having love affairs as soon as she reaches puberty, and most women have been pregnant at least once by the time they reach sixteen. According to customary law the resulting children are always legitimate, provided always that the girl is not foolish enough to have a liaison with a man of the wrong sub-caste.

This kind of "marriage" can be entered into in the most casual manner. Any woman who cooks for a man is considered to be his wife for the time being, and the relationship can be broken off as easily as it is started. When a child is born, the villagers go to great pains to see that the birth is registered and that the father's name appears on the birth certificate, for this may potentially affect the child's ultimate status as an heir. The ordinary obligations of parents toward children, however, are treated in a highly casual way. It is quite common to find that a man and woman who are living together and rearing a family have each had several other children by several different spouses. One consequence of this is that half-brother and step-brother relationships are extremely common.

In addition to these casual "common-law" marriages, we find that the villagers sometimes turn a wedding into a ceremony of the utmost elaboration. Ceremonial weddings are the occasion for expensive feasting and the demonstrative gathering of rival groups of kinsmen. From a legal point of view the formal wedding is no more binding than an informal liaison, though in practice the collapse of a formally established marriage is likely to lead to bitter recriminations. The formal marriages, as one might expect, are mainly those of influential people, or of those who are seeking to gain influence. In terms of village politics they represent treaties of alliance between potentially hostile groups of kinsmen. The two types of marriage are identical from the point of view of the children, who are legitimate in either case. They differ in the fact that, whereas informal marriage is a private affair between husband and wife, a formal marriage is arranged by the parents. Formal unions are part of the long-term strategy whereby property and influence are conserved within particular compound groups.

Since all the inhabitants of a Sinhalese Dry-Zone village are likely to be related to one another in several different ways, it would be misleading to suppose that kinship behaviors conform to rigid stereotypes. Nevertheless, some general tendencies deserve to be noted. Relations between a man and his children are never close. As soon as a young man marries he begins to be treated as a separate householder, and his relations with his parents become increasingly formal and remote. Separation of the sexes is extreme. Although men and women sometimes work together in the field, there are few other occasions when they can, with propriety, be seen close together.

Relations between co-resident siblings, who are likely to be heirs to the same property, are formal rather than friendly. In contrast, the relationship between brothers-in-law, which is assimilated to that of cross-cousins, is characteristically one of cooperative equality. Where brothers-in-law reside in the same compound their friendship often assumes the form of a joking relationship. This stereotyped pattern is, however, complicated by the high incidence of half-sibling and step-sibling relationships alluded to above. Since the total area of irrigated land available to the villagers is unalterable, the inheritance of land inevitably becomes a source of bitter jealousy. The restrained formality with which a younger brother is expected to treat an elder brother is in accord with this. Co-resident "brothers," however, may well be of partly or completely different parentage, so that their potential rights of inheritance are quite different. In such cases much of the potential strain inherent in the sibling relationship disappears, and half-brothers who are not co-heirs to the same property are often close allies.

Neat summary of these facts is difficult, but underlying the whole complex one can discern two contradictory, yet complementary, structural principles. On the one hand there is the principle of bilateral inheritance by all sons and all daughters in roughly equal proportions. While property can be transmitted in other ways, e.g., by will or by sale, inheritance remains the main process by which rights in land are transferred from one generation to another. Considered simply in kinship terms, bilateral inheritance must lead to the fragmentation of holdings and to rivalry between co-heirs. It thus stands in contradiction to the ideology which requires the co-heirs of an estate to remain co-resident in the same ancestral compound, and which presupposes that a band of brothers will always act together as a united family.

On the other hand, the principle that women, despite their inferior political status, have rights to land means that the transmission of property to children serves to unite disparate holdings as well as to fragment them, for the separate properties of a man and his wife are unified in their children. Heirship separates property; marriage brings it together. It is a reflection of this that full brothers, though formally united, seldom cooperate, whereas brothers-in-law, though formally opposed, are characteristically close allies.

Space is lacking for more than the barest outline of the system of land tenure which provides the economic basis for Sinhalese Dry-Zone society, but its essence can be briefly summarized. The village field is not only fixed in size; it is also fixed in layout. It consists of a set number of permanent shares (*pangu*), which are so laid out on the ground that each share receives a precisely equal proportion of the total available tank water. One share may be divided among several owners, or one owner may possess several shares, but the layout of the field, which is plain for all to see, remains the same from generation to generation.

Let me sum up. The study of social structure in societies organized according to unilineal descent has not only thrown the emphasis on kinship but has given the impression that kinship structures can be considered in isolation, without reference to the economic background. It has also suggested that social structure is a matter of clearly defined rules, e.g., of descent, of inheritance, and of preferential marriage. In the society considered in this essay social structure is likewise a matter of kinship, but kinship arrangements are not clearly constrained by rules. In all issues of inheritance, succession, marriage, and residence the individual is faced with choice. It is not implied that choice is random, but by and large choices are governed by economic ends.

In such a society the continuing entity is the pattern of the man-made economic context—the village tank, the compounds, the layout of the village field. Within narrow limits these are unalterable facts to which each generation of inhabitants must adjust their domestic lives. Although, as in other primitive and peasant societies, the language of kinship plays a dominating role in the expression of social relationships, social behavior is not constrained by the prior existence of kinship corporations. It is not so much that the Sinhalese order their economic lives in accord with kinship relations as that their kinship relations are an expression of the way in which they order their economic lives.

The relevance of this analysis in the present context of a survey of Southeast Asian societies is that it should make us cautious of embarking upon typological generalizations. Freeman's analysis of Iban society might, on first inspection, suggest a polarization of types—the social structure of bilateral societies in contrast to the social structure of societies with unilineal descent groups. But we need to be careful. My analysis of Sinhalese social structure has followed lines closely analogous to those of Freeman for the Iban, even though less quantitative evidence has been provided. But Sinhalese society, though lacking a fully developed lineage system, is by no means fully cognatic in a sense applicable to the Iban and the Kalinga. More important than typology is the implication, in both

Freeman's work and my own, that social structures are sometimes best regarded as the statistical outcome of multiple individual choices rather than a direct reflection of jural rules. For this approach both of us are indebted to a highly germinal essay by Fortes (1949).

KINSHIP TERMINOLOGY

It will be apparent from the foregoing analysis that in my personal view the kinship terminology is not of any great significance for the understanding of Sinhalese social structure. By request, however, and for comparison with the data in other papers, I append a list of the kinship terms used colloquially by the Sinhalese of the northern Dry Zone, followed by a summary of the facts. Unless otherwise noted, all terms are subject to rather wide collateral extension as discussed hereinafter.

1 *kiriāttā:* grandfather, either paternal or maternal.
2 *kiriamma:* grandmother, either paternal or maternal.
3 *appa:* father.
4 *loku appa:* father's elder brother; mother's elder sister's husband.
5 *bāppa:* father's younger brother; mother's younger sister's husband.
6 *amma:* mother.
7 *loku amma:* mother's elder sister; father's elder brother's wife.
8 *kudamma:* mother's younger sister; father's younger brother's wife.
9 *māmā:* mother's brother; father's sister's husband; spouse's father. Not subject to collateral extension.
10 *nāndā:* father's sister; mother's brother's wife; spouse's mother. Not subject to collateral extension.
11 *ayiyā:* elder brother; elder male parallel cousin; elder female cross-cousin's husband.
12 *malli:* younger brother; younger male parallel cousin; younger female cross-cousin's husband.
13 *akkā:* elder sister; elder female parallel cousin; elder male cross-cousin's wife.
14 *namgi:* younger sister; younger female parallel cousin; younger male cross-cousin's wife.
15 *massinā:* male cross-cousin; brother-in-law. Not subject to collateral extension.
16 *nānā:* female cross-cousin; sister-in-law. Not subject to collateral extension.
17 *putā:* son; sister's son (w.s.); brother's son (m.s.).
18 *duvā:* daughter; sister's daughter (w.s.); brother's daughter (m.s.).
19 *bānā:* sister's son (m.s.); brother's son (w.s.); daughter's husband. Not subject to collateral extension.
20 *leli:* sister's daughter (m.s.); brother's daughter (w.s.); son's wife. Not subject to collateral extension.
21 *munuburā:* grandson. Not subject to collateral extension.
22 *minibiri:* granddaughter. Not subject to collateral extension.

An accurate and adequate brief summary of Sinhalese kinship terminology is given by Tambiah (1958). The other principal accounts are those of Ariyapala (1956), Hocart (1928), and Pieris (1956). Superficial differences between the various descriptions are due to several factors. First, certain literary terms (e.g., *piyā*, father) are seldom used in colloquial speech. Second, some terms which occur in Low-Country Sinhalese are not used by the Kandyans, and *vice versa*. Third, the language is particularly prolific in terms of endearment. Thus where colloquial English has such terms as "dad," "daddy," "pa," "papa," and "pop" as alternatives for the formal "father," Sinhalese has *appa, appocci,* and *tatta* as alternatives for *piyā*. Analogous alternatives exist for most other terms, e.g., *bālappa, bāpocci,* and *kudāppa* for *bāppa* (father's younger brother). Such variations differ somewhat by caste as well as by region, but usage is not necessarily standardized even among households of the same caste group within the same village.

When complications of this sort are ignored, the structural pattern of Sinhalese kinship terminology is identical to that of the Tamil, which was first fully analyzed by Morgan (1870) and classed by him as Turanian. This circumstance may be partly responsible for the widespread belief that the Sinhalese have or have had a patrilineal descent system (cf. Pieris, 1956, p. 219). At the present time Sinhalese society is "patrilineal" only to about the same extent as is English society, i.e., with surnames normally derived from the father rather than from the mother, and there is no evidence that patrilinearity was any more emphatic in the past.

It must be remembered that Sinhalese kinship terminology is associated with a system of sub-caste endogamy; all recognized kinsmen are members of the same sub-caste. The functional purpose of the terminological categories is not to divide up the total society into discrete unilineal descent groups but rather to distinguish, among the general body of kinsmen, those who are classed as affines from the rest. Marriage establishes an affinal (*massinā*) relationship between a man and his brother-in-law, and this relationship is perpetuated in the next generation so that the sons of brothers-in-law are likewise *massinā* to one another. The structural facts have been correctly analyzed by Dumont (1957), who points out that in societies of this type the sociological facts are better expressed by saying that "my cross-cousin is the child of my father's brother-in-law" than by the more conventional statement that "my cross-cousin is the child of my mother's brother or of my father's sister."

Tambiah (1958, p. 22) has summarized the Sinhalese terminological system so succinctly that it seems advisable to quote him directly:

"All kin within Ego's own and adjacent generations fall into one or other of two major categories. On the one hand own patrilineal kin constitute a theoretically exogamous grouping consisting of fathers (*appa*) and father's sisters (*nāndā*); elder brothers (*ayiyā*) and elder sisters (*akkā*); younger brothers (*malli*) and younger sisters (*namgi*); sons (*putā*) and daughters (*duva*). Ranged against these are the categories of affinal relatives: mothers (*amma*) and mother's brothers (*māmā*); male cross cousins (*massinā*) and female cross cousins (*nānā*); sons of siblings of opposite sex (*bānā*) and daughters of siblings of opposite sex (*leli*). The terminology is used as if the entire society consisted only of two intermarrying exogamous patrilineal groups. Thus the wives of all *appa* are *amma*; the husbands of all *nāndā* are *māmā;* and so on. One consequence of this is that Ego's mother's sister's child is classed as a sibling even if there is no real patrilineal link at all. It will be observed that any term category is specific as to the sex and the generation of the individual referred to. Within each sex-generation category individuals are further distinguished by various prefixes, e.g., father's elder brother, *loku appa* (big father); father's younger brother, *kudā appā* (little father)."

Practical usage does not correspond strictly to this formal design. For example, I found that *bāppa* (a variant form of *kudā appā*) was often given a very wide extension, being applied to any male of Ego's sub-caste of the senior generation whose precise kinship status was unknown. Similarly the terms *ayiyā* (elder brother) and *malli* (younger brother) may be used indiscriminately, even of individuals who should, according to formal principles, be classed as *massinā* (cross-cousin). The term *hūrā* is often used in addressing a cross-cousin who is considerably older than Ego. It is, I think, less formal and respectful than *ayiyā*. Its reciprocal is to address the younger *massinā* by his personal name.

In general the "matrilateral" or "affinal" terms (*māmā, nāndā, massinā, nānā, bānā*, and *leli*) have a much more restricted usage than their "patrilateral" counterparts (*appa, amma, ayiyā, malli, akkā, namgi, putā* and *duva*). The former group of terms are applied only to relatives who are effectively in an affinal relationship with Ego. Since affinal relationship entails various kinds of obligation, the use of affinal kinship terminology implies an assertion of kinship rights. In certain kinds of polite society, indeed, the use of the terms *massinā, nānā*, and *leli* seems to be altogether taboo except in reference to third parties. In this connection it should be remembered that, although marriage with a true cross-cousin is not particularly common, all of a man's legitimate mates are his *nānā*, so that the use of this term has definite sexual connotations. The distinction between "patrilineal" kinsmen and "affines" disappears in the second ascending and descending generations.

Rights of domicile in the Dry Zone are a jealously guarded privilege which, in theory, can only be derived by inheritance from an ancestor. There is thus a set of terms denoting ancestors of different generations without regard to sex. My informants professed to distinguish seven such terms for as many degrees of ancestry: *āttā*, grandparent; *nāttā*, great grand-parent; *panāttā*, ancestor of the fourth ascending generation; *kittā*, ancestor of the fifth ascending generation; *kirikittā*, ancestor of the sixth ascending generation; *kirikimuttā*, ancestor of the seventh ascending generation; and *dōvikittā*, ancestor of the eighth ascending generation. While I do not think these terms were invented simply to amuse the anthropologist, I got no evidence that they are ever actually used.

CHAPTER 8

THE ABORIGINAL PEOPLES OF FORMOSA

TOICHI MABUCHI
Tokyo Metropolitan University

ALL the aboriginal inhabitants of Formosa belong linguistically to the Austronesian or Malayo-Polynesian family. Their languages appear to form a distinct sub-grouping within this family, with the exception of Yami, spoken on the off-lying island of Botel Tobago, which affiliates more closely with the languages of the northern Philippines. The original population of the western and northern lowlands of Formosa has long since been overrun by South Chinese immigrants and is completely Sinicized in language and culture. The indigenous ethnic groups of this region, whose former distributions are shown in lower-case letters on Map 3, are the following, arranged in north-to-south order: (a) Luilang, (b1) Ketangalan or Basai, (b2) Turubiawan, (b3) Qauqaut and Linau, (c) Kavalan, (d) Taokas, (e) Pazeh, (f) Papora, (g) Babuza, (h1) Arikun, (h2) Hoanya and Lloa, (i) Sau or Thau, (j1) Siraya or Sideia, (j2) Taivoan, and (j3) Makatau.

The ethnic groups which are still extant, and which still retain substantial elements of their aboriginal culture, are shown in capital letters on Map 3. According to the Japanese census report for 1931, they had a total population of nearly 143,000 at that time. The officially recognized groups, with the population recorded for each in the same census, are listed below.

Ethnic groups	*1931 population*
Atayal (A1) and Sedeq (A2)	33,302
Saisiyat (B)	1,340
Bunun (C)	18,179
Tsou (D1)	1,718
Kanakanabu (D2) and La'arua (D3)	479
Rukai (E) and Paiwan (F and G2)	36,457
Puyuma (G1)	5,289
Ami (H)	44,187
Yami (I)	1,673

The Ami and Puyuma of the coastal plains in eastern Formosa subsist primarily by the cultivation of irrigated rice, which they adopted from the Chinese in the late nineteenth century. Other groups, however, still preserve in large measure their aboriginal economy based on slash-and-burn agriculture, depending mainly on cereals (especially millet but also some dry rice) and root crops (especially

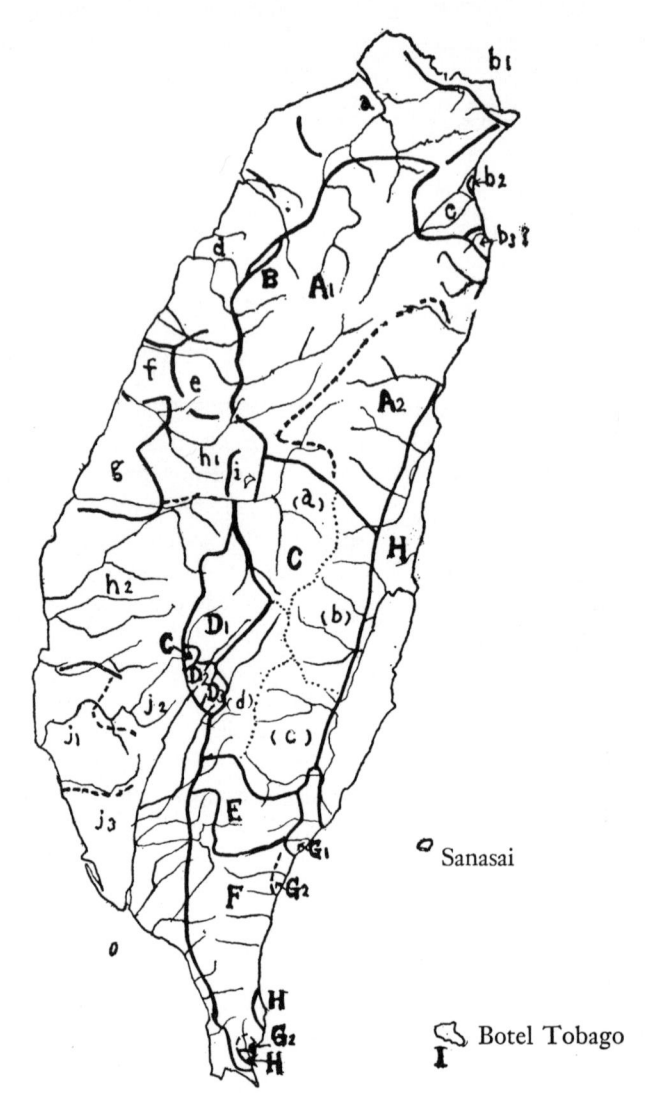

MAP 3
DISTRIBUTION OF ETHNIC GROUPS IN FORMOSA
(see text for explanation of symbols)

sweet potatoes but also considerable taro). In their social organization the Formosan indigenous peoples, like those of Sumatra, run the full gamut from fully patrilocal and patrilineal systems to strictly matrilocal and matrilineal ones, and exhibit a diversity of nonunilineal or bilateral structures. These can be comprehended most easily if the twelve ethnic groups are combined into six clusters for separate presentation.[1] The Saisiyat and Sedeq have therefore been grouped with Atayal; the Kanakanabu, La'arua, and Tsou with the Bunun; and the Rukai and Paiwanized Puyuma (G2) with the Paiwan. The Ami, Puyuma, and Yami will receive individualized attention.

THE ATAYAL AND THEIR NEIGHBORS

The Atayal and Sedeq live in settlements with an average population of about 165 persons. The component households are sometimes dispersed but more often clustered in relatively compact villages or hamlets. The average household, according to one survey, has 4.8 members. In general, each married couple has a dwelling of its own, but one adult child, usually a son, normally continues to reside with or near his parents after his marriage. Settlements show no marked tendency toward either exogamy or endogamy. Incest taboos are extended bilaterally to all second cousins, but third cousins are marriageable. Residence reveals a definite trend toward patrilocality, but matrilocal residence prevails in nearly 10 per cent of all marriages, notably where the bride's family has a larger amount of land. Private property in cultivated and fallow land, including the power of sale, is recognized in at least the more densely settled regions. The inheritance of land rights tends to be patrilineal, but it shows some variation depending upon the choice of residence.

The Saisiyat in the west have exogamous patrilineal clans like the Bunun farther south, and, like the Tsou and Kanakanabu, they extend marriage prohibitions to all members of the mother's clan and to children of the mother's own sisters. Among the eastern Sedeq each hamlet often consists of a localized patrilineage five or six generations in depth descended from a founding ancestor. Most of the Atayal and Sedeq, however, completely lack clans and unilineal exogamy, though they exhibit some tendency toward a patrilineal form of organization. Among the northern Atayal each settlement has several ritual groups, numbering about ten households on the average, which center around an influential man and typically bear his name. Such a group usually has as its core a patrilineage several generations in depth, comprised of patrilineal kinsmen of its leader, but it normally also includes affinal kinsmen and even attached non-relatives. It is united less by unilineal kinship than by common residence, shared rituals, and the fame and influence of its leader. Although such ritual groups may occasionally be in fact exogamous, owing to the bilateral extension of incest taboos, informants differ as to whether or not they are characterized by the ideal of exogamy.

In the original homeland of the Atayal, the southwestern part of their present habitat, such ritual groups, often called "feast groups," are linked into larger ritual groups, which may extend throughout the area of a subtribe. The feast groups assemble for marriage festivities and for ceremonial pig sacrifices, as well as more informally to distribute the meat of wild game and to drink millet beer and feast on pork in slack periods of the agricultural cycle.

Political authority within the settlement is exercised chiefly by "men of influence," especially the leaders of the local ritual groups. They select one of their number as headman of the village, but he is merely *primus inter pares*. In the areas of more recent settlement each village tends to be politically autonomous, but in the southwest the villages of a drainage basin or along a river are loosely organized in "subtribes" or districts, based mainly on military considerations. The headman of one of the villages may be recognized as chief of the larger unit, but the component settlements are not integrated by a network of affinal ties, as among the Bunun. Two of the three independent subtribes of the Saisiyat are, however, bound into a tribal unit by bonds of ritual solidarity, expressed in a common exorcistic ceremony performed by a hereditary priest who belongs to a particular lineage in one of the subtribes.

The kinship terminology of the Atayal, Sedeq, and Saisiyat reflects the generation principle in both Ego's and the first descending generations; terms for siblings are extended to all first and second cousins, and those for children are applied to nephews and nieces as well. In the first ascending generation, however, the Atayal and Sedeq employ terms of the lineal type for uncles and aunts. The Saisiyat refer to these relatives by derivative parental terms, and some Sedeq similarly use *lêleh-tama* and *lêleh-bubu* instead of lineal terms. All three groups distinguish grandparents by sex but call grandchildren by the term for child. The relevant terms are tabulated below.

	Atayal	*Sedeq*	*Saisiyat*
Grandfather	yutas	vake	bake
Grandmother	yake	pai	kuku
Father	yaba	tama	yama
Mother	yaya	bubu	ina
Uncle	mama	mama	pina-yama
Aunt	yata	ata	pina-ina
Elder sibling of same sex	qĕbusuyan	qĕbusuran	mina-tini
Younger sibling of same sex	sĕsuwai	suwaye	mina-ite
Sibling of either sex	mĕtsĕ-sĕsuwai	mĕn-suwaye	ahal
Sibling of opposite sex	nĕqun	halmadan	—
Child of either sex	laqe	laqe	kurkuring

In regard to affinal relatives, the Formosan peoples in general tend to extend the kinship terms for consanguineal relatives, e.g., uncles and aunts, to the spouses of the latter, and in the case of relatives of the spouse to employ the consanguineal terms which the spouse himself (or herself) uses for them. The Atayal and to a lesser extent the Sedeq, however, are characterized by an exceptional proliferation of special affinal terms. Those current among the Atayal, all of which have a classificatory extension, are listed below.

1 *yanai:* brother-in-law (m.s.).
2 *nana:* elder sister's husband (w.s.); husband's elder brother; husband's elder sister's husband.
3 *suwage:* younger brother's wife (m.s.); younger sister's husband (w.s.); wife's younger sister; husband's younger brother; wife's younger brother's wife; husband's younger sister's husband.
4 *irah:* elder brother's wife; spouse's elder sister; spouse's elder brother's wife.
5 *yango:* younger brother's wife (w.s.); husband's younger sister; husband's younger brother's wife.
6 *mawan:* wife's sister's husband.
7 *yama:* son-in-law; son's wife's brother; daughter's husband's brother.
8 *yina:* daughter-in-law; son's wife's sister; daughter's husband's sister.

The relationship between siblings and cousins of opposite sex among the Atayal and Sedeq is characterized by a rigid avoidance of obscenity and any reference to sexual matters. They may not even discuss together a proposal of marriage made by a third person. Any violation of this taboo is believed to anger the ancestral spirits and to pollute and endanger the community. A person guilty of such a violation must sacrifice a pig in a purificatory "communion ceremony" for the entire ritual group. Similar rites expiate the breach of various other taboos and are also held whenever a new member joins, or an old member severs his ties with, the ritual group. The relationship between brothers-in-law, who are called *yanai* by the Atayal, is affected by brother-sister avoidance. When a woman marries or gives birth to a child, this is believed to pollute her brothers and male cousins, and her husband must pay them a small "purification price" in millet beer, cloth, or shell beads.[2]

THE BUNUN AND THEIR NEIGHBORS

The peoples of the central highlands of Formosa—particularly the Bunun, Kanakanabu, and Tsou—are characterized by strict rather than incipient patrilineal descent. They reveal a segmentary organization into patrilineal lineages, subclans, clans, and usually also phratries, with exogamy prevailing at every level from the minimal lineage to the clan and among the Bunun to the phratry. Only the small La'arua tribe deviates substantially from this pattern; exogamy has largely broken down and extends today only to second cousins within the lineage and to first cousins outside. The other three groups, however, extend their exogamous prohibitions to all members of the mother's clan as well as to those of the father's clan or phratry. The Bunun even forbid marriage between two individuals whose mothers belong to the same clan, but the Tsou apply this prohibition only to persons whose mothers are actually sisters.

In contrast to the compact villages of the Atayal, the Bunun reside in neighborhoods of dispersed homesteads or, especially in the north, of isolated small hamlets. Clans and phratries are not localized. Their members are widely scattered, and several such groups are normally represented in a community, which is thus usually an agamous rather than an exogamous unit. The settlement as such lacks any formal political organization. Even local headmen are absent except where they have been appointed by the administration. Nevertheless, groups of settlements are aggregated into "subtribes" through magico-spiritual ties and a complex network of affinal relationships, which find expression in ceremonial exchanges and which operate effectively to maintain law and order over areas of substantial size. Bunun subtribes number, on the average, about 3,600 people—a population more than three times that of their average counterparts among the Atayal.

Among the Tsou the settlement pattern takes the form of a capital village and ceremonial center with a number of outlying satellite villages and hamlets. Each village has a men's house, where its "men of influence" meet. The men's house of the core village is the meeting place for the council of the entire complex or subtribe, and serves as a center for ritual activities concerned with warfare and headhunting. Within each village the households of the same patrilineage constitute a distinct ritual, economic, and landholding unit.

Marriage is exclusively monogamous and normally involves the payment of a modest bride-price. Among both the Bunun and the Tsou, however, sister-exchange marriages are by no means infrequent. Incest taboos prevent union between first cousins of any kind, but second cousins are marriageable unless their fathers or mothers belong to the same patrilineal clan. Residence is strictly patrilocal; no exception was noted in 313 cases among the Bunun (1935). Small patrilocal extended families are characteristic of the Bunun and Tsou but not of the Kanakanabu or La'arua. The average size of the household among the Bunun—9.4 persons—exceeds that of any other Formosan people. The rule of inheritance, like that of descent, is patrilineal.

The Bunun rarely extend the use of kinship terms beyond the subclans of both parents, but the Tsou apply them throughout the clan. Terms of reference reflect a modified generation pattern in Ego's and in the first ascending and descending generations. In address, however, the Bunun apply the honorific vocatives for father and mother to all adult members of the mother's patriclan, regardless of generation, and they may refer to the same relatives as uncle or aunt. This overriding of the generation principle results in an approximation to the Omaha pattern in the terms of address for cross-cousins, presumably an incipient reflection of the lineage principle (Mabuchi, 1953). Some of the terms of reference of the three principal ethnic groups are tabulated below.

	Bunun	*Kanakanabu*	*Tsou*
Grandfather	tama-qo'daš	tamu	ake'i
Grandmother	tina-qo'daš	tamu	ba'i
Father	tama	tsuma	amo
Mother	tina	tsina	ino

Uncle	man-tama	tsuma-vuravurau	amo-tsoni
Aunt	man-tina	tsina-vuravurau	ino-tsoni
Sibling	taš'an	kinturanga	ohaesa
Cousin	man-taš'an	kinturanga-varavurau	popu'e-nanato'to'-ohaesa
Child of either sex	uvath	manu	oko
Nephew, niece	man-uvath	manu	popu'e-o-oko-a
Grandchild	uvath, man-uvath	namu	popu'e-o-oko-a

THE AMI

The Ami of the coastal plains of eastern Formosa reside in compact permanent villages with an average of 600 to 700 inhabitants. Each village is politically autonomous under an elective headman, and the relations between local groups were formerly characterized by perpetual conflict and sometimes by reciprocal headhunting. Local endogamy, moreover, is nearly universal. Marriage is monogamous and does not require the payment of a bride-price. Inheritance is matrilineal, and residence is regularly matrilocal except in strongly acculturated sections. Matrilocal extended families occur among the central and southern Ami but are rare in the north. The size of the average household reflects this difference; the statistical average is 7.8 persons, but this falls to 5.2 among the northern Ami and rises to 9.5 in the center and south.

The bilateral extension of incest taboos characterizes all branches of the Ami, but its range varies; marriage is forbidden with any fourth or closer cousin among the central Ami but only with first and second cousins in the north and south. In some northern Ami villages the relatives of certain priests, distinguished by the observation of particular rituals, form matrilineages of three or four families each, but with this exception the northern Ami reveal no evidences of matrilineal organization.

The central and southern Ami, on the other hand, are organized into about fifty matrilineal clans, subdivided into more or less local lineages. Each clan bears a distinctive name, often that of the village where it traditionally originated, and is commonly, though by no means universally, distinguished from others by special food taboos, characteristic rituals, and distinctive funerary practices. Though their membership is ordinarily dispersed, clans do not exert an integrating influence beyond the local community. Nor are they strongly functional even within the community, where their solidarity, to the extent that it exists, is greatly overshadowed by that of the village.

Matrilineal exogamy, extending not only to the local matrilineage but also to the clan, is definitely reported for a number of scattered villages among the southern Ami and also, as late as the beginning of the present century, among some of the central Ami. Even today in certain parts of the central Ami country marriage is strongly disapproved with any known matrilineal kinsman, including those more remote than fourth cousins, who would be excluded by the bilateral extension of incest taboos. Nevertheless, clan exogamy is not generally characteristic of either the central or the southern Ami.

There are reasons for believing that matrilineal exogamy, where it exists among the Ami, is incipient rather than residual. Since the middle of the eighteenth century the Ami have been subjected to severe headhunting raids from the Sedeq in the north and the Bunun in the west, and to strong military pressure from the Puyuma in the south. This has precipitated considerable internal migration, with the result that many villages tend to be composed of matrilineages of heterogeneous origin. Under these circumstances a small immigrant lineage in a particular village might often remain exogamous for several generations by virtue of the bilateral extension of incest taboos alone, and a tradition of lineage exogamy might thus become established and perpetuated for a period. Eventually, however, such an incipient rule of matrilineal exogamy would tend to disappear as contacts and reciprocal borrowing gradually obliterated the original differences in customs and ritual observances among the lineages of the community. We conclude, therefore, that the sporadic appearance of lineage and clan exogamy among the southern and central Ami is more reasonably to be regarded as a local development under a special set of circumstances than as a vestige of a formerly general rule of matrilineal exogamy.

Kinship terminology among the Ami conforms in the main to the generation principle. Some of the more important terms, with regional variations, are listed below.

1 *vake:* grandfather; grandson (in the north only); maternal or paternal uncle (mainly in the north).
2 *vai:* grandmother; granddaughter (in the north); maternal or paternal aunt (mainly in the north).
3 *ama:* father; maternal or paternal uncle (mainly in the center and south).
4 *ina:* mother; maternal or paternal aunt (mainly in the center and south).
5 *kaka:* elder sibling of either sex.
6 *sava:* younger sibling of either sex.
7 *malĕ-kaka-ai:* cousin.
8 *wawa:* child of either sex; nephew or niece; grandchild (in the center and south).
9 *sina-wawa* (as an alternative to *wawa*): nephew or niece; grandchild (in the center and south).
10 *are:* spouse's sibling; sibling's spouse.
11 *aput:* wife's sister's husband.

THE PUYUMA

The Puyuma, southern neighbors of the Ami, live in permanent villages with an average population of about 600. Villages tend strongly toward local endogamy and political autonomy, although some villages have vassal hamlets. The inhabitants fall into two social classes, nobles and commoners, but intermarriage between them is not interdicted. The noble class comprises the members of certain chiefly families, of whom there are several in each village, each with its own men's house. The heads of these families exercise political control. One of them fills the office of local headman, to which, however, succession is not automatic. When a headman dies, the noble elders and other influential men informally choose his successor from among his sons or other close bilateral relatives.

Marriage is monogamous and involves no significant bride-price. Extended incest taboos prevent unions with any first or second cousin. Residence is predominantly matrilocal, but patrilocality occurs with moderate frequency both today and in the past. The small size of the average household—4.8 persons—reflects the prevalence of independent nuclear families and the absence of any form of extended family organization.

The social unit of outstanding importance is the ritual group, which revolves around common participation in agrarian, hunting, headhunting, and curing rituals. Each village comprises several such groups of varying size. Each has a ritual house (*ka-lumah-an*) and its own priest, priestess, or both. The larger ritual groups of a village are associated with the several chiefly families. The smaller ones are usually subordinate to one or another of the larger groups, with whom they join for major rituals though they perform minor rites independently. Some of the lesser ritual groups have originated by fission from larger ones, usually on the advise of a divinatory priestess following some disaster. Instances are also known where two previously independent groups have fused into one.

Though ritual groups are not exogamous, the Puyuma consider them to be composed of actual or presumptive kinsmen. Descent, however, is irregular and even capricious. When the parents belong to different ritual groups, the children may be affiliated with either group, or with both at the same time, or sons may join the father's group for participation in the hunting and headhunting rituals performed by males while daughters join the mother's group for the agrarian rituals in which females play an important role. Of these alternatives, the third is exceptional and is rarely followed in two successive generations. The second alternative, that of dual affiliation, though somewhat more common, is likewise seldom perpetuated in the next generation. The alternative most frequently chosen is the first, and here the decision as to whether the child will adhere to the father's or the mother's group is normally determined by the parents' place of marital residence. Since residence is much more often matrilocal than patrilocal, matrilineal descent preponderates numerically in ritual group affiliation.

Membership in a ritual group is not only subject to choice; it can also be changed. If a person falls ill and consults a *ka-lumah-an* priestess or a shamaness, she may, in the role of an oracle speaking for the ancestral spirits or deities of some other ritual group, tell him that his sickness has resulted from negligence in participating in the rites of that group. The ritual group in question may be one with which the individual might have chosen to affiliate on the basis of known bilateral or "multilineal" genealogical connections, or it may be one whose membership has declined and whose ancestral spirits allegedly wish to recruit new members by invoking a genealogical tie forgotten by the living.

The victim has the choice either of accepting an additional membership, at least temporarily, or of renouncing his previous membership and affiliating exclusively with the ritual group indicated by the oracle. Some individuals change memberships in this way several times during their lifetime. In certain northern Puyuma villages an adult does not affiliate with any ritual group until he receives such a supernatural warning. In general, however, parents persuade their children to join tentatively one of the groups to which they themselves belong, and if nothing untoward happens such membership may endure for life.

In the conception of the people themselves a ritual group is always a kin group with membership dependent upon some genealogical connection, known or hypothetical. The rule of descent or mode of affiliation, however, deviates notably from those characteristic of unilineal kin groups. Matrilineal affiliation, to be sure, is the norm, but optional deviations occur too frequently to be regarded as genuine aberrations. The term "optional," as here used, connotes the choice either of the individual himself or of the ancestral spirits as revealed through oracles. Optional descent among the Puyuma is strongly reminiscent of the "ambilateral" rule described by Firth (1929, p. 8) for the Maori *hapu* and of other cases, fairly widespread in Oceania, to which Goodenough (1955) has called attention.

Kinship terminology conforms in general to the generational pattern. Thus the term for father (*ama*) is extended to both maternal and paternal uncles, that for mother (*ina*) to both maternal and paternal aunts, and that for child (*alak*) to sororal as well as fraternal nephews and nieces. In addition to use of a sibling term for cousin (*wa-wadi-an*), the Puyuma, like many Philippine peoples, distinguish cousins by their collateral distance as *kinar-asa* (first cousin), *kinar-papuan* (second cousin), *kinar-taluluan* (third cousin), and *kinar-papatun* (fourth cousin). Grandparents of either sex are called *imo,* and an alternative term (*těmoan*) is employed reciprocally between grandparents and grandchildren. Other Puyuma kinship terms include *iva* (elder sibling, elder sibling's spouse, spouse's elder sibling), *wadi* (younger sibling), *omos* (younger sibling's spouse, spouse's younger sibling), *yanai* (wife's brother, sister's husband), *aput* (wife's sister's husband), and *musavak* (son-in-law, daughter-in-law).

THE PAIWAN AND THEIR NEIGHBORS

The Paiwan and Rukai of southeastern Formosa live in concentrated villages with an average of 300 inhabitants each. This settlement pattern, as contrasted with the dispersion of households among the Bunun and some of the more northern tribes who practice a similar primitive agriculture, presents disadvantages because it increases the distance between dwellings and fields, especially since good arable land is irregularly distributed on account of the mountainous terrain. Private holding in arable land seems to be more fully and widely recognized than among other Formosan slash-and-burn tillers, including even the Atayal.

Village endogamy prevails among both the Paiwan and the Rukai, and incest taboos are extended bilaterally to include all second cousins. Nobles are distinguished from commoners, as among the Puyuma, but intermarriage somewhat blurs the distinction between them. A bride-price is required, but marriage is monogamous and normally involves the establishment of an independent household. The average number of individuals per household is 4.9. Residence is ambilocal—about 70 per cent patrilocal and 30 per cent matrilocal in a 1935 survey of 370 marriages. The parental dwelling is inherited by the eldest child, regardless of sex, among the Paiwan, but usually by the eldest son among the Rukai.

Political authority is vested in chiefs. A village may have a single chief or several independent ones, or, as occasionally happens among the Paiwan, one chief may exercise hegemony over several villages, either directly or through vassal subchiefs. A chief is regarded as having eminent domain over all the land in his jurisdiction, and this gives him the privilege of levying tribute from his subjects in the products of hunting, agriculture, and animal husbandry. In theory, the chief is the individual of the highest genealogical seniority among the nobles in his territory. Succession, consequently, follows the principle of primogeniture and parallels exactly the rule governing the inheritance of dwellings; the successor is the eldest son among the Rukai, the eldest child regardless of sex among the Paiwan. Chiefly families strive to maintain and enhance their seniority by intermarrying with families of high rank, oftentimes in other villages. While this tends to improve intergroup relations, the effect is usually transitory and can be nullified by jealousies and by, for example, inveterate enmity between two villages with which the chief of a third establishes affinal ties.

The literature yields no intimation of unilineal kin groups. Each Paiwan and Rukai family has its own "house name," which is transmitted by primogeniture in accordance with the prevailing rule of inheritance. The younger siblings of the heir either marry into other families or establish branch families which ultimately acquire their own "house names." A child's acceptability as family heir depends heavily upon his previous choice of marital residence, with the result that transmission often deviates from the patrilineal principle, especially among the Paiwan.

The sources also suggest that the Paiwan and Rukai recognize more or less definite "spheres of relatives" which are aggregated on the basis of bilateral or "multilineal" ties around an individual and his siblings as a core. In some west central Paiwan villages, on the other hand, the inhabitants are reported to be divided into two moiety-like divisions, which are neither endogamous nor exogamous. When the parents belong to opposite divisions, their choice of residence apparently determines the affiliation of their children. The latter may never affiliate with the groups of both parents at the same time, so that the situation resembles that which Freeman (1958) has called "utrolateral" in the case of the Iban of Borneo.

The kinship terminology, as tabulated below, strongly reflects the generation principle. The Torulukane are one of three northwestern Rukai villages which diverge rather sharply in language from the rest of the Rukai.

	Paiwan	Rukai	Torulukane
Grandfather	vuvu	tomo	momo
Grandmother	vuvu	kaingo	kakurongo
Father	kama	tama	mama
Mother	kina	tina	nina
Uncle	kama-lavavau	tama	mati-amama
Aunt	kina-lavavau	tina	mati-nina
Elder sibling	kaka-a-cavulung	taka-taka	kaka
Younger sibling	kaka	agi-agi	agi-agi
Sibling	kaka	lama-taka-taka	malamunganĕ
Cousin	malĕ-kaka	lama-taka-taka	malamunganĕ
Child of either sex	alak	lalakĕ	velakĕ
Nephew or niece	alak	lalakĕ	velakĕ
Grandchild	vuvu	aganĕ	aganĕ

THE YAMI

The Yami of the isolated island of Botel Tobago subsist by irrigated and brand-tillage agriculture, supplemented by fishing and shellfishing. The staple crop is wet taro, but sweet potatoes, millet, yams, and bananas are also grown. The indigenous domestic animals include pigs, goats, and chickens. Men clear the land and grow yams and millet, whereas women cultivate taro and sweet potatoes. Men do the offshore fishing, but women tend pigs and do most of the shellfishing.[3]

The prevailing settlement pattern is one of compact villages, which are agamous and politically autonomous. In size, villages average about 240 inhabitants. Authority resides in an informal council; there were no local headmen under aboriginal conditions. Private property in land exists mainly with respect to taro plots. Other land belongs collectively to the village, with individuals holding only usufruct rights to fields under cultivation. Inheritance is mainly patrilineal, sons sharing equally in the paternal estate. Intergroup relations are characterized by the absence of headhunting, in which respect the Yami differ from all other indigenous Formosan peoples.

Marriage involves no bride-price or other material consideration. Exclusive monogamy prevails, and each household comprises a single nuclear family with an average membership of 4.7 persons. Residence is patrilocal; matrilocality is rare and occurs only when the bride has no brothers.

The Yami divide kinsmen into two categories: (1) "true relatives" and (2) "those a bit related." The former, who include first cousins (*kateisa*), form an exogamous sphere and constitute a kindred whose solidarity is emphasized in various ways in both secular and ritual life. Second cousins (*kapuisin*), who are considered only "a bit related," are permitted to marry. Third cousins (*kapologan*) are regarded as non-relatives. The social system reveals no trace of unilineal organization.

Kinship terminology conforms to the lineal pattern in the first ascending generation. Paternal and maternal uncles are called by the same term (*malan*) and distinguished from father (*ama'*), and aunts (*kaminan*) are similarly differentiated from mother (*ina'*). On Ego's generation the terms for elder sibling (*tsi-kaka'*) and younger sibling (*tsi-wali'*) are not extended to cousins; the terms for the latter, cited above, are of the so-called Eskimo type. On the first descending generation, however, terminology accords with the generation pattern; the terms for son (*atsita'*) and daughter (*bita'*) are extended respectively to nephews and nieces. Other Yami kinship terms include *akai'* (grandfather), *akĕs* (grandmother), *anak* (child), and *apu'* (grandchild).

SUMMARY AND CONCLUSIONS

The aboriginal peoples of Formosa have, on the whole, achieved only a minimal level of political integration. The eastern groups (the Ami and Yami) reveal no socio-political units which transcend the level of the local community. The northern peoples (the Atayal and their neighbors) exhibit little more complexity, although the political unit sometimes embraces a small cluster of adjacent villages. An institutionalized chiefship with hereditary succession has developed only in the south (among the Paiwan, Puyuma, and Rukai), and even here its evolution, with occasional exceptions, has fallen short of achieving the integration of a number of villages. Only in the center (among the Bunun and their neighbors) are communities effectively organized into subtribes. The cohesion of the latter, however, is juridical rather than strictly political, being based, not on chiefship, but on a ramifying network of affinal kin relationships through which it has been found possible to maintain a measure of law and order over areas comprising a considerable number of settlements.

Unilineal kin groups have evolved in only two of the six clusters into which we have classed the Formosan peoples—the matrilineal Ami and the patrilineal Bunun cluster. Elsewhere kinship is bilateral, and kinsmen form either personal kindreds, as among the Yami, or some kind of unit characterized by an ambilateral or multilineal mode of affiliation, exemplified most clearly in the ritual groups of the Puyuma. Inheritance assumes a unilineal form mainly among the matrilineal Ami and the patrilineal Bunun cluster. In the bilateral societies it is variable and tends strongly to depend upon the choice of marital residence, which is always to some extent optional and which commonly reflects the relative amounts of arable land available to the bride's and the groom's families. Primogeniture is confined exclusively to the Paiwan cluster. Extended forms of family organization are likewise confined to the unilineal peoples, as is apparent from the statistics on average household size. Elsewhere the residential unit normally assumes the form of an independent nuclear family. Incest taboos and exogamous rules conform closely to the pattern of descent. Marriage prohibitions are extended unilaterally in the patrilineal Bunun cluster and to a limited extent among the matrilineal Ami but only bilaterally in all other Formosan groups.

The kinship terminology of the Formosan peoples reveals an overwhelming predominance of the generational principle of classification, which on Ego's generation results in cousin terminology of the Hawaiian type. The evidence supports the conclusion of Murdock (1949, p. 350) "that the original Malayo-Polynesian speech community had a social organization of Hawaiian type." Bifurcation, whether in the form of bifurcate merging or of bifurcate collateral terminology (Lowie, 1928), occurs only rarely among the Malayo-Polynesian peoples in general, even in unilineal societies, and does not appear at all in Formosa. Deviation from the generation pattern, where it occurs, is invariably in the direction of the lineal pattern of classification. In such a shift, "modified generation terminology"—i.e., avuncular, nepotic, and cousin terms which are morphological variants or derivatives of the terms for parents, children, and siblings respectively —presumably represents an intermediate step. Full-fledged lineal terminology in Formosa is largely confined to the Atayal, who have lineal terms for uncles and aunts, and to the Yami, who, in addition, use "Eskimo" terminology for cousins. Modified generation terminology is somewhat more common, especially in the Bunun cluster, where it prevails alike in Ego's and in the first ascending and descending generations.

The reasons for this distribution may well reside in the well-known paucity of independent elementary kinship terms in the Malayo-Polynesian languages as a whole. When a particular people of this stock is faced with a social structural change which makes it advantageous to distinguish collateral from lineal kinsmen, the paucity of nomenclature compels them to make shift with some combination or modification of the terms for primary relatives. The resulting modified generation terminology may then ultimately evolve into full-fledged lineal terminology. In so far as any developmental trend is observable in Formosan kinship terminology, it would appear to be this.

CHAPTER 9

SUPPLEMENTARY NOTES ON THE FORMOSAN ABORIGINES

WEI HWEI-LIN
National Taiwan University

[Professor Wei's paper at the Bangkok symposium covered essentially the same subject matter as that prepared by Professor Mabuchi. The latter, being considerably longer and more detailed, has been given precedence, and only such portions of Professor Wei's contribution as do not overlap Professor Mabuchi's are reproduced herewith. On topics covered by both, the two accounts reveal a most encouraging measure of agreement. The only serious discrepancy concerns the Puyuma tribe, which Professor Wei classifies as matrilineal. (Ed.)]

In the segmentary organization of the Bunun and Tsou each phratry has one leading clan, each clan has a senior subclan, and each subclan has a ranking household. The head of the ranking household of the senior subclan is the priest of the clan and the guardian of the power of its ancestral spirits. This power is symbolized by sacred millet seeds and by the preserved mandibles of slain game animals. Among the matrilineal Ami, though the mother is always the head of the family, the maternal uncle holds the position of priest and chief of the clan. Chiefly and priestly office among the Paiwan and Rukai is transmitted by primogeniture within the senior noble household.

Each unit in the segmentary patrilineal structure of the Bunun acts as a group in social functions. The phratry (*kaviath*), for example, is the unit in the communion feast of sacred millet. The clan, which has collective rights in particular hunting grounds, is the unit for the distribution of game. The subclan holds collective rights in fallow arable land, acts as a unit in blood vengeance, has collective responsibility for the payment of penalties, and conducts rituals with captured heads after a headhunting expedition.

The Arisan branch of the Tsou perform all ceremonies in the capital village (*hosa*) of the subtribe, where the members of all clans assemble, afterwards dispersing for separate rituals in their individual meeting houses. In the matrilineal societies ceremonial functions are conducted in part by the leading household of the clan in its spirit house, in part by age-sets in the men's houses.

Private ceremonials connected with the life cycle, e.g., at childbirth, weddings, and funerals, are performed collectively by the near relatives, or kindred, of the individuals concerned. Among the Yami, in addition to the kindred (*lipus*), there are patrilineages (*asa itatoaŋ*) which have communal rights in land and cooperate in agricultural labor; there are also special bilateral groups, called *asasoinawaŋ*, which act as units in intra-village and intervillage warfare.

CHAPTER 10

THE MAGPIE MIAO OF SOUTHERN SZECHUAN

RUEY YIH-FU
National Taiwan University

THE people now generally known as the Miao (literally "rice shoot") are frequently referred to in the Chinese classics under the names Miao-Min, Yu-Miao, or San-Miao. When first mentioned, they occupied the country south of the territory of the legendary Emperor Shun (2255–2206 B.C) in the central Yangtze plain, in the region now embraced by the provinces of Hupeh, Hunan, and Kiangsi. According to the *Shu Ching* or *Classic of History*, they were banished by Yü the Great (2205–2198) to San-Wei, which subsequent commentators have identified with San-wei-san, a locality in the vicinity of Tun-huang-hsien in northwestern Kansu.

Later records commonly failed to distinguish the Miao from other indigenous peoples, employing the name Man ("barbarians") or Nan-Man ("southern barbarians") collectively for all tribal groups of the general area. Some of these were incorporated by Emperor Ch'en (1115–1078 B.C.) of the Chou dynasty in the feudal state of Ch'u, and all of them were brought under administrative control soon after 221 B.C., when the Ch'in dynasty succeeded for the first time in unifying all of China.

The name Miao does not reappear until the Sung dynasty (960–1279 A.D.), when Yeh Ch'ien, a scholar of the twelfth century, clearly distinguished five ethnic groups among the Wu-Chi-Man or "barbarians of the five streams" on the upper Yuan River in western Hunan: the Miao, the Yao, the Lao, the Chuang or Tai, and the Keh-Lao. Subsequent writers, nevertheless, often employed Miao or Miao-Man as a loose general term for the tribes of this region. From the Ming dynasty (1368–1643) to the present, however, many works have restricted the name to the people who now call themselves Hmo, Hmu, Hmong, or Hmung.

The Miao-Tze or (more politely) Miao-Chia, as these people are designated by the Han Chinese, are concentrated in Kweichow, their heartland, but are also found in the provinces of Yunnan, Szechuan, Hunan, and Kwangsi and on the island of Hainan. Some groups have migrated southward into the mountainous northern parts of Burma, Thailand, Laos, and Vietnam, where they are usually called Meo. They commonly live at altitudes of several thousand feet above sea level. The Statistical Bureau of Peking reports their population in China in 1954 as 2,511,389. Since the late nineteenth century they have been visited by a number of western missionaries, travelers, and scientists, as well as by Chinese and Japanese scholars. The bibliography by Embree and Dotson (1950) lists 79 titles on their ethnology and 15 on their linguistics in European languages alone.

Repeatedly defeated in uprisings against the Han Chinese during the Yuan, Ming, and Ch'ing dynasties, and oppressed by the Chinese bureaucracy (see Wiens, 1954, pp. 87-88), the Miao today lack any sense of political unity. What they share is an essentially common culture, although wide dispersion in different environments has inevitably produced appreciable regional differentiation in institutions, beliefs, and arts. A number of subgroups are readily distinguished, e.g., the Red Miao, Black Miao, Blue Miao, White Miao, Flowery Miao, Magpie Miao, and Cowrie-shell Miao.

The particular group described herewith was visited by the writer in 1943 on an ethnographic survey of southern Szechuan. It is one of those designated collectively but inaccurately by Graham (1937) as the Ch'uan Miao. They call themselves Hmong Ntsu and are known to the Chinese as the Yachio Miao or "Magpie Miao," or alternatively as the Han Miao or "Sinicized Miao." They number about 10,000 and live interspersed among the Han Chinese in the mountainous region around the headwaters of the Yungning River in southern Szechuan on the borders of Kweichow and Yunnan provinces (28° to 29° N and 105° to 106° E). The writer has previously published two papers (Ruey, 1949 and 1954) on the kinship system of this group.

The Magpie Miao subsist primarily by agriculture, with techniques and tools influenced by centuries of contact with the Han Chinese. Arable land being scarce, all that is available is intensively used, with two crops a year. Millet, barley, buckwheat, maize, kaoliang, cabbage, turnips, and tea are grown by slash-and-burn techniques on the higher mountain slopes, depending for moisture exclusively on rainfall and subsoil seepage. Rice, together with smaller quantities of beans, hemp, indigo, and tobacco, is raised in paddy fields on the rare stretches of level ground, along the river banks, and behind terraces laboriously constructed on the lower slopes of the mountains. Water for irrigation is supplied by an elaborate system of bamboo pipes and water-powered mills. Cattle, pigs, and chickens are raised, and sometimes sheep, ducks, and bees as well. Hunting, conducted during the winter, and fishing provide a by no means negligible supplement to the subsistence economy.

Handicraft manufactures include a variety of bamboo objects, such as baskets, boxes, mats, hats, and fish traps. Cloth is woven from hemp, is dyed dark blue or patterned by batik, and is sometimes elaborately embroidered. A few men have specialized as silversmiths, blacksmiths, and carpenters, but only very rarely as shopkeepers. Surplus produce, handicrafts, and game obtained by hunting are sold at Han Chinese markets in exchange for such necessaries as salt, sugar, and cloth. Men do the hunting and fishing, as well as all basketry, metalwork, and carpentry. They also plow, but both sexes participate in other agricultural operaations. Women tend the domestic animals and do the weaving, sewing, dyeing, and embroidery.

The Magpie Miao live in villages, occasionally compact but normally consisting of a cluster of separate hamlets. These are located on mountain slopes, usually far enough away from main transportation routes to be inaccessible and readily defensible. The Miao lack any political organization of their own, and are thoroughly integrated into the Chinese administrative system. The basic political, as well as economic and social unit, is the village. Villages are grouped into townships and divided into hamlets of about ten to twenty households each. The headmen of both the village and the hamlet are appointed by the chief of the township. The members of different villages or hamlets are bound principally by affinal ties. They may cooperate for the common good, but they lack any formal organization of an indigenous character. Disputes between members of the same hamlet are settled, if possible, within the hamlet. Those between members of different hamlets of the same village are adjudicated by a council composed of the village headman and the heads of the hamlets involved. If this council cannot effect a settlement, the litigants have a right to carry their dispute to the chief of the township or even to the Chinese court of the county.

The core of the Miao hamlet, or occasionally of an entire village, is a localized patrilineal kin group, consisting mainly of the families of men who bear the same surname, commonly augmented by persons of other surnames who have voluntarily come to reside with them more or less permanently. The surnames have been borrowed from the Han Chinese, and, as will be indicated below, the rule of descent may once have been bilateral rather than patrilineal.

Although there are instances of independent nuclear families, consisting of a married couple with their own or adopted children, the normal residential unit is a patrilocal extended family of the small or lineal type. So long as the parents are alive, their unmarried children and their married sons with their families live with them in the same house. When the parents die, the married sons usually establish independent households, and unmarried children reside with their older brothers. Not infrequently, however, brothers continue to live together after the death of their parents, or a young married couple may go to live with an older brother of the husband, so that extended families of considerable size do occur. These seem, however, to reflect the influence of the Han Chinese family organization.

Marriage is normally monogamous, but non-sororal polgyny is permitted and exists to a limited extent. Co-wives usually live together in the same house. A substantial bride-price is required, and is paid in money, cattle, or pigs. The levirate is practiced in an attenuated form; it is optional rather than compulsory. Secondary unions with a father's widow, however, are forbidden. Marriage is also prohibited between members of families bearing the same surname, but it is not clear whether patrilineal exogamy is an old Miao custom.

Incest taboos prevent marriage with any primary or secondary consanguineal kinsman and with any parallel cousin. Cross-cousin marriage, however, is favored today, though by no means obligatory, and sex relations between unmarried cross-cousins are freely permitted and taken as a matter of course. According to the *Kweichow Tungchih* or *Historical Geography of Kweichow* (1742, vol. 7), a man formerly had the privilege of marrying his father's sister's daughter, and if a man had no son to exercise this right his sister's husband was required to make him a money payment to extinguish the right before marrying his daughter to another man. Asymmetrical patrilateral cross-cousin marriage must thus once have been the rule. The shift to symmetrical cross-cousin marriage doubtless reflects the influence of the Han Chinese, who have long practiced it.

Though residence is normally patrilocal, and descent patrilineal, when a man has daughters but no sons, one daughter remains at home and her husband comes to live with her in matrilocal residence, thus continuing the paternal line for one generation through a female. Graham (1937, p. 37) reports that matrilocal residence formerly prevailed among the Ch'uan Miao of Kunghsien in a neighboring county. Possibly this refers only to the initial period of marriage, or to what Murdock (1949, p. 17) calls "matri-patrilocal residence," since Mickey (1947, p. 51) specifically reports this rule among the Cowrie-shell Miao of Kweichow: "After a girl was married she returned at once to her parents' home, where she stayed, except for short periods in her husband's home, during the busy season and at feasts, until she was pregnant. Before the child was born she went to live in his home permanently."

The core of the patrilocal extended family, plus its outmarrying female members, approaches the usual conception of a patrilineage. The patronymic surname group, with its associated exogamy and the obligation of its members to participate in certain memorial ceremonies for its traditional ancestors, similarly approximates the typical characteristics of a patrilineal sib. The local group, moreover, meets essentially the criteria advanced by Murdock (1949, pp. 66–68) to define a compromise kin group and may thus be designated, in his terminology, as a patriclan. Despite these patrilineal features, however, the Miao social system reveals unmistakable bilateral elements. An individual maintains close associations with a group of his nearest kinsmen, regardless of their genealogical connection to him, and expects from them certain kinds of services which he cannot demand of non-relatives or of remoter kinsmen. This group, which includes maternal as well as paternal uncles and aunts, approximates the definition of a bilateral kindred (Murdock, 1949, pp. 46, 60–62). Moreover, the Miao of western Hunan, when they were visited by the writer in 1933, still maintained to a large extent what was purportedly their old tradition of neolocal residence and independent nuclear families (Ling and Ruey, 1947, p. 93). Finally, as has been pointed out elsewhere (Ruey, 1954), the kinship terminology gives internal evidence of ultimate derivation from a system of the generation or Hawaiian type, which is widely associated with bilateral descent. From these facts the writer tentatively concludes that the Miao may once have been characterized by bilateral descent and perhaps also by neolocal residence, and that their present patrilineal and patrilocal social structure has developed under influence from the Han Chinese.

In transcribing the kinship terminology we shall employ the orthography of the International Phonetic Association to represent the phonemes of Miao, with the following modifications:

à   for a low back unrounded vowel somewhat like that in English "art"
c   for a fronto-palatal sibilant like the sh sound in English
gn   for a fronto-palatal nasal like the ny in English "canyon"
ll   for a voiceless lateral spirant like the ll in Welsh
ng   for a dorso-velar nasal like the ng sound in English

Superscript numerals will be employed to represent the nine tonemes of Miao, as follows:

1 high level, as in mi^1, "small"
2 high-middle level, as in $nts'ai^2$, "daughter"
3 high to middle falling, as in to^3, "son"
4 high to low falling, as in tsi^4, "father"
5 middle to high-middle rising, as in $llà^5$, "wife's younger sister"
6 middle level, as in jeu^6, "husband"
7 middle to low falling, as in $gnang^7$, "father's sister"
8 low to middle rising, as in na^8, "mother"
9 low level, as in $làu^9$, "husband's elder brother"

The terms of reference used by the Magpie Miao are compounded from 27 elementary terms, of which 23 have primary reference to a particular kinsman, while the remaining four are employed solely as modifiers in the formation of derivative terms. The terms and their compounds are presented below.

1 tsi^4: father. Compounded with term 22, it yields tsi^4 je^9: FaYoBr. In combination with terms 21 and 22, it is employed, as an expression of respect, by female speakers (and their husbands) for certain own and classificatory brothers-in-law.

2 na^8: mother. Compounded with term 23, it yields na^8 $llà^5$: MoYoSi, FaYoBrWi, WiMoYoSi, HuMoYoSi. In combination with term 23, it is employed by male speakers (and their wives) for certain own and classificatory sisters-in-law. For WiMo, na^8 tai^2 is an alternative to term 15.

3 to^3: son. Compounded with term 26, it yields to^3 ntu^6: BrSo (m.s.), FaBrSoSo (m.s.), SiSo (w.s.), FaBrDaSo (w.s.), HuBrSo, and WiSiSo. Further suffixing term 27 yields to^0 ntu^9 $mpeu^9$: FaSiSoSo (m.s.), MoBrSoSo (m.s.), MoSiSoSo (m.s.), FaSiDaSo (w.s.), MoBrDaSo (w.s.), MoSiDaSo (w.s.), and the same relatives of Ego's spouse. For SoWi, to^3 $gnang^3$ is an alternative to term 19, with which to^3 also enters into other compounds.

4 $nts'ai^2$: daughter. In compounds it commonly has the meaning of "female," as in $nts'ai^2$ ntu^9: BrDa (m.s.), FaBrSoDa (m.s.), SiDa (w.s.), FaBrDaDa (w.s.), and the same relatives of Ego's spouse; $nts'ai^2$ ntu^9 $mpeu^9$: daughter of any first cousin of Ego's sex other than FaBrCh; $nts'ai^2$ ku^4: SiDa (m.s.), FaBrDaDa (m.s.), BrDa (w.s.), FaBrSoDa (w.s.), and the same relatives of Ego's spouse;

*nts'ai*² *ku*⁴ *mpeu*⁹: daugter of any first cousin of opposite sex other than FaBrCh. It also enters into other compounds to which term 20 is suffixed.

5 *ti*⁷: elder brother (m.s.), and by extension FaBrSo older than Ego. Compounded with term 27, it yields *ti*⁷ *mpeu*⁶: FaSiSo (m.s.), MoBrSo (m.s.), MoSiSo (m.s.), in each case if older than Ego. The tone changes from *ti*⁷ to *ti*⁶ following a term which has tone 3 or 7, e.g., *gnang*³ *ti*⁶: ElBrWi (m.s.).

6 *ku*⁴: younger brother (m.s.), and by extension FaBrSo (m.s.) older than Ego. Compounded with term 27, it yields *ku*⁴ *mpeu*⁹: FaSiSo (m.s.), MoBrSo (m.s.), MoSiSo (m.s.), in each case if older than Ego. The tone changes from *ku*⁴ to *ku*¹ when the term immediately follows another which has tone 3 or 7, e.g., *gnang*³ *ku*¹: YoBrWi (m.s.). When suffixed to terms 7 or 4, *ku*⁴ denotes a cross, as opposed to a parallel, collateral relative of the first descending generation, e.g., *no*⁹ *ku*⁴: SiSo (m.s.), FaBrDaSo (m.s.), BrSo (w.s.), FaBrSoSo (w.s.), and the same relatives of Ego's spouse; *no*⁹ *ku*⁴ *mpeu*⁹: son of a cross-cousin (or MoSiCh) of opposite sex, and the same relatives of Ego's spouse; *nts'ai*² *ku*⁴: SiDa (m.s.), BrDa (w.s.), etc.

7 *no*⁹: brother (w.s.), and by extension FaBrSo (w.s.), WiBr, and WiFaBrSo. Compounded with *mpeu*⁹, it yields *no*⁹ *mpeu*⁹: FaSiSo (w.s.), MoBrSo (w.s.), MoSiSo (w.s.), and the same relatives of Ego's wife. Its compounds with term 6 have already been noted. The tone changes from *no*⁹ to *no*⁶ when the term immediately follows another which has tone 3 or 7, e.g., *gnang*³ *no*⁶: BrWi (w.s.).

8 *mà*⁶: sister (m.s.), and by extension FaBrDa (m.s.), HuSi, and HuFaBrDa. Compounded with term 27, it yields *mà*⁶ *mpeu*⁹: FaSiDa (m.s.), MoBrDa (m.s.), MoSiDa (m.s.), and the same relatives of Ego's husband. It also enters into various compounds with term 20.

9 *ve*⁴: elder sister (w.s.), and by extension FaBrDa (w.s.) older than Ego. Compounded with term 27, it yields *ve*⁴ *mpeu*⁹: FaSiDa (w.s.), MoBrDa (w.s.), and MoSiDa (w.s.), in each case if older than Ego.

10 *ntcàu*⁹: younger sister (w.s.), and by extension FaBrDa (w.s.) younger than Ego. Compounded with term 27, it yields *ntcàu*⁹ *mpeu*⁹: FaSiDa (w.s.), MoBrDa (w.s.), and MoSiDa (w.s.), in each case if younger than Ego.

11 *jeu*⁶: husband, and by extension through ellipsis WiFa [alternatively *tai*² *jeu*⁶]. This term, meaning "man," by change in tone becomes *jeu*⁸, a more respectful term meaning "old man." Either tonal form may be used in certain compounds applying to wife's older male relatives, namely, *jeu*⁶ *làu*⁹: WiFaElBr, WiMoElSiHu; *jeu*⁶ *je*⁹: WiFaYoBr; *jeu*⁶ *klang*³: WiMoBr; *jeu*⁶ *vàu*⁴: WiFaSiHu; *jeu*⁶ *llà*⁵: WiMoYoSiHu.

12 *jeu*⁸: father's father, and by extension HuFa. This term appears in such compounds as *jeu*⁸ *tai*²: MoFa, WiFaFa; *jeu*⁸ *làu*⁹: FaElBr, MoElSiHu, WiFaElBr, WiMoElSiHu, HuMoElSiHu; *jeu*⁸ *klang*³: MoBr [alternatively simply *klang*³], WiMoBr, HuMoBr; *jeu*⁸ *vàu*⁴: FaSiHu, WiFaSiHu, HuFaSiHu; *jeu*⁸ *llà*⁵: MoYoSiHu, WiMoYoSiHu, HuMoYoSiHu; *jeu*⁸ *je*⁹: HuFaYoBr, WiFaYoBr.

13 *po*⁷: wife. In compounds this yields *po*⁷ *klang*³: MoBrWi, HuMoBrWi; *po*⁷ *làu*⁶: MoElSi, FaElBrWi, HuMoElSi, HuFaElBrWi; *po*⁷ *je*⁶: HuFaYoBrWi.

14 *po*⁶: father's mother, and by extension HuMo and HuFaMo. Compounded with term 15, it yields *po*⁶ *tai*²: MoMo [alternatively simply *tai*²], WiMoMo, HuMoMo.

15 *tai*²: mother's mother [alternatively *po*⁶ *tai*²], and by extension WiMoMo [alternatively *po*⁶ *tai*²], HuMoMo [alternatively *po*⁶ *tai*²], WiFaMo, and WiMo [alternatively *na*⁸ *tai*²]. The compounds with terms 12 and 14 have been pre-

viously noted. Other compounds are tai^2 $làu^9$: WiMoElSi, WiFaElBrWi; tai^2 $llà^5$: WiMoYoSi [alternatively na^8 $llà^9$]; tai^2 je^9: WiFaYoBrWi; tai^2 $gnang^7$: WiFaSi; tai^2 $klang^3$: WiMoBr; tai^2 jeu^6 [or simply jeu^6]: WiFa.

16 ki^4: grandson. Compounded with term 4, it yields $nts'ai^2$ ki^4: SoDa, DaDa. Suffixing term 20 to this yields $nts'ai^2$ ki^4 $vàu^4$: SoDaHu, DaDaHu. The tone changes from ki^4 to ki^1 following a term which has tone 3 or 7, e.g., $gnang^3$ ki^1: SoSoWi, DaSoWi.

17 $klang^3$: mother's brother [alternatively jeu^8 $klang^3$], and by extension WiBr [alternatively no^9]. Its compounds with terms 11, 12, 13, and 15 have already been noted.

18 $gnang^7$: father's sister [alternatively me^2 $gnang^7$], and by extension HuFaSi and occasionally HuSi. WiFaSi is tai^2 $gnang^7$.

19 $gnang^3$: son's wife, who may alternatively be called to^3 $gnang^3$. Prefixed to another term, it connotes "wife of" the relative denoted by that term. Its principal compounds are $gnang^3$ ti^6: ElBrWi (m.s.), FaBrSoWi older than Ego (m.s.); $gnang^3$ ti^5 $mpeu^9$: wife of a FaSiSo, MoBrSo, or MoSiSo who is older than Ego; $gnang^3$ ku^1: YoBrWi (m.s.), FaBrSoWi younger than Ego (m.s.); $gnang^3$ ku^1 $mpeu^9$: wife of a FaSiSo, MoBrSo, or MoSiSo who is younger than Ego; $gnang^3$ no^6: BrWi (w.s.), FaBrSoWi (w.s.), WiBrWi, WiFaBrSoWi; $gnang^3$ no^6 $mpeu^9$: FaSiSoWi (w.s.), MoBrSoWi (w.s.), MoSiSoWi (w.s.); $gnang^3$ no^9 ku^4: SiSoWi (m.s.), FaBrDaSoWi (m.s.), BrSoWi (w.s.), FaBrSoSoWi (w.s.), and the same relatives of Ego's spouse; $gnang^3$ to^3 ntu^9: BrSoWi (m.s.), FaBrSoSoWi (m.s.), SiSoWi (w.s.), FaBrDaSoWi (w.s.), and the same relatives of Ego's spouse; $gnang^3$ ki^1: SoSoWi, DaSoWi.

20 $vàu^4$: daughter's husband, who may alternatively be called $nts'ai^2$ $vàu^4$. Suffixed to another term, it connotes "husband of" the relative denoted by that term, e.g., jeu^8 $vàu^4$: FaSiHu, WiFaSiHu, HuFaSiHu; ma^6 $vàu^4$: SiHu (m.s.), FaBrDaHu (m.s.), HuSiHu, HuFaBrDaHu; $nts'ai^2$ ntu^9 $vàu^4$: BrDaHu (m.s.), SiDaHu (w.s.), and the same relatives of Ego's spouse; $nts'ai^2$ ku^4 $vàu^4$: SiDaHu (m.s.), BrDaHu (w.s.), and the same relatives of Ego's spouse; $nts'ai^2$ ki^4 $vàu^4$: SoDaHu, DaDaHu.

21 $làu^9$: husband's elder brother, and by extension HuFaBrSo older than Ego. Compounded with term 27, it yields $làu^9$ $mpeu^9$: husband of a FaSiSo, MoBrSo, or MoSiSo who is older than Ego. Its principal compounds are jeu^8 $làu^9$: FaElBr, MoElSiHu, WiFaElBr, WiMoElSiHu, HuMoElSiHu; jeu^6 $làu^9$: WiFaElBr, WiMoElSiHu; tai^2 $làu^9$: WiMoElSi, WiFaElBrWi; na^8 $làu^9$: WiElSi, HuElBrWi, WiFaBrDa older than wife; tsi^4 $làu^9$: ElSiHu (w.s.), WiElSiHu, husband of a FaBrDa older than Ego (w.s.); tsi^4 $làu^9$ $mpeu^9$: husband of a FaSiDa, MoBrDa, or MoSiDa who is older than Ego (a woman or her husband speaking). The tone changes from $làu^9$ to $làu^6$ following a term which has tone 3 or 7.

22 je^9: husband's younger brother, and by extension HuFaBrSo younger than Ego. Compounded with term 27, it yields je^9 $mpeu^9$: husband of a FaSiSo, MoBrSo, or MoSiSo younger than Ego. Its principal compounds are tsi^4 je^9: FaYoBr; jeu^8 je^9: WiFaYoBr, HuFaYoBr; po^7 je^6: HuFaYoBrWi; tai^2 je^9: WiFaYoBrWi. The tone changes from je^9 to je^6 following a term which has tone 3 or 7, as in po^7 je^6 above.

23 $llà^5$: wife's younger sister, and by extension HuYoBrWi. Compounded with term 27, it yields $llà^5$ $mpeu^9$: spouse's younger FaSiDa, MoBrDa, or MoSiDa. Term 25 is often prefixed to any of the above. Important compounds are jeu^8 $llà^5$: MoYoSiHu, WiMoYoSiHu, HuMoYoSiHu; tai^2 $llà^5$: WiMoYoSi [alterna-

tively na^8 $ll\grave{\partial}^5$]; na^8 $ll\grave{\partial}^5$: MoYoSi, FaYoBrWi, WiMoYoSi, HuMoYoSi; tsi^4 $ll\grave{\partial}^5$: YoSiHu (w.s.), etc.

24. me^2: "beautiful." This term, the first of four which have no primary kinship meanings, is commonly prefixed as a compliment to term 18: me^2 $gnang^7$: FaSi.
25. mi^1: "small." This term is commonly prefixed to term 23 and some of its compounds, e.g., mi^1 $ll\grave{\partial}^5$: WiYoSi.
26. ntu^9: "parallel." The tone changes from ntu^9 to ntu^6 following a term which has tone 3 or 7. When suffixed to terms 3 or 4, this term contrasts with term 6 in denoting a parallel, as opposed to a cross, collateral relative of the first descending generation, e.g., to^3 ntu^6: BrSo (m.s.), SiSo (w.s.), etc.; $nts'ai^2$ ntu^9: BrDa (m.s.), SiDa (w.s.), etc.; $nts'ai^2$ ntu^9 $v\grave{a}u^4$: SiDaHu (w.s.), etc.; $gnang^3$ to^3 ntu^6: BrSoWi (m.s.), SiSoWi (w.s.), etc.
27. $mpeu^9$: "outside." The tone changes from $mpeu^9$ to $mpeu^6$ following a term which has tone 3 or 7. When suffixed to another term, this term denotes a remote or classificatory relative of the same generation and type of connection, especially one involving the distinction between cousins and siblings [the Miao, however, consistently classify ortho-cousins, i.e., the children of a FaBr, with siblings rather than with cousins]. Numerous examples have already been cited, e.g., ti^7 $mpeu^6$: FaSiSo (m.s.), MoBrSo (m.s.), and MoSiSo (m.s.) if older than Ego; $m\grave{a}^6$ $mpeu^9$: FaSiDa (m.s.), MoBrDa (m.s.), MoSiDa (m.s.); no^9 $mpeu^9$: FaSiSo (w.s.), MoBrSo (w.s.), MoSiSo (w.s.).

Since the mode of classifying relatives and the principles governing it do not readily emerge from a mere listing of kinship terms it will be advantageous to group the terms into a few major categories for purposes of analysis.

Grandparents and grandchildren. The Magpie Miao have one elementary term (12) for paternal grandfather and a second (14) for paternal grandmother. A third term (15) is suffixed to the one or the other to designate maternal grandparents or may stand alone for MoMo. A single elementary term (16) denotes grandson; when prefixed by the term for daughter (4) it denotes a granddaughter.

Parents, uncles, and aunts. On the first ascending generation there are separate elementary terms for father (1), mother (2), maternal uncle (17), and paternal aunt (18). Paternal uncles and maternal aunts are called by descriptive terms and are further differentiated according to relative age. A father's elder brother is called by the term for "paternal grandfather" (12) followed by term 21 as a modifier; his younger brother is "father" (1) modified by term 22. A mother's younger sister is called by the term for "mother" (2) modified by term 23. Her elder sister is called po^7 $l\grave{a}u^6$ (terms 13 and 21), of which the first element, curiously enough, carries the tone for "wife" rather than that for "grandmother" (term 14). The terminology in this generation thus conforms to the bifurcate collateral pattern of Lowie (1928) and to the A type of Kirchhoff (1932, pp. 46–49).

Siblings and cousins. There are six elementary terms for siblings: term 5 for elder brother (m.s.), 6 for younger brother (m.s.), 7 for brother (w.s.), 8 for sister (m.s.), 9 for elder sister (w.s.), and 10 for younger sister (w.s.). All six are extended to ortho-cousins, i.e., children of a FaBr. They are also applied to other first cousins, the children of a FaSi, MoBr, and MoSi, but only as derivative terms with term 27, meaning "outside," as the modifying element. The terminology for consanguineal kinsmen on Ego's generation thus conforms essentially to the generation type of Lowie (1928), the C type of Kirchhoff (1932), and the Hawaiian type of Murdock (1949, p. 223).

Children, nephews, and nieces. On the first descending generation there are elementary terms only for son (3) and daughter (4). Nephews and nieces are called by derivative terms, and these are distinguished from one another both by sex and by the sex of the connecting relative. Suffixed elements, terms 26 and 6, denoting "parallel" and "cross" relatives respectively, are normally added to the terms for son (3) and daughter (4) to indicate a nephew or niece, but term 7, for brother (w.s.), is used instead of that for son in forming the terms for SiSo (m.s.) and BrSo (w.s.). On the first descending generation the terms for consanguineal relatives thus reveal characteristics of both the bifurcate merging and the bifurcate collateral types of Lowie (1928).

Affines. There are separate terms for husband (11) and wife (13). A spouse's parent is usually called by a grandparental term, e.g., term 12 for HuFa, 14 for HuMo, and 15 for WiMo. For wife's father, however, the term *jeu*[6] carries the tone for husband (term 11) rather than that for paternal grandfather (term 12). There are distinct elementary terms for son's wife (19) and daughter's husband (20), and on Ego's generation for HuElBr (21), HuYoBr (22), and WiYoSi (23). The term for WiElSi, however, is derived from that for mother (term 2 plus term 21). A wife's brother is called by the term for brother (w.s.) or alternatively by that for MoBr, terms 7 and 17 respectively, and a husband's sister by that for sister (m.s.), term 8. We here encounter a feature widely applied in the terminology for remoter affines, namely the adoption for a spouse's relatives of the terms used for them by the spouse himself.

The Magpie Miao never equate terms for the affines of a consanguineal kinsman with those for kinsmen of Ego's own spouse. Thus a man's SiHu (terms 8 plus 20) is distinguished from the other brother-in-law, his WiBr; a woman's BrWi (terms 19 plus 7) from her other sister-in-law, her HuSi. The remaining terms for siblings-in-law are compounds: terms 19 plus 5 for ElBrWi (m.s.), 19 plus 6 for YoBrWi (m.s.), 1 plus 21 for ElSiHu (w.s.), and 1 plus 23 for YoSiHu (w.s.). The spouses of consanguineal kinsmen may be equated with consanguineal kinsmen, e.g., FaBiWi with MoSi and MoElSiHu with FaElBr, but such is not the case with MoYoSiHu (terms 12 plus 23), MoBrWi (13 plus 17), or FaSiHu (12 plus 20). Nephew and niece terms are regularly extended to the spouse's nephews and nieces.

Various factors other than strictly historical and sociological ones have clearly exerted a significant influence on the kinship terminology of the Magpie Miao. Several of these merit brief discussion.

1. *Teknonymy.* The widespread practice of teknonymy rests basically upon

the identification of parents with their children, resulting in a tendency for the former to adopt for certain relatives the terms which their children use for them. Among the Miao this tendency is reflected in the extension of the term for MoBr (17) to WiBr, and of that for FaSi (18) to HuSi, which would result from the adoption, by fathers and mothers respectively, of the same terms as are used by their children for the relatives who are siblings-in-law to the former but uncles and aunts to the latter.

2. *Tekeisonymy.* This term, derived from Greek *tekeis*, parent, and *onoma*, name, has been proposed by the writer (Ruey, 1955, pp. 51–57, 61–62), in connection with observations among both the Han Chinese and the Miao, for practices opposite to teknonymous ones, namely those reflecting the identification of children with their parents. Examples among the Magpie Miao include the use of the term for HuElBr (21) in the compound for FaElBr (12 plus 21), of the term for HuYoBr (22) in that for FaYoBr (1 plus 22), and of the term for WiYoSi (23) in that for MoYoSi (2 plus 23).

3. *Spousal identification.* Identification with a spouse, rather than with a parent or child, can result in the adoption by one spouse of the terms used by the other for the latter's kinsmen. Chen and Shryock (1932, p. 649), for example, note that among the Chinese "the wife generally uses the same terms as her husband in referring to members of his own clan," and Kroeber (1933, p. 157) compares this to the habit among some Americans of referring to a mother-in-law as "mother," a brother-in-law as "brother," etc. This type of extension, as previously noted, is very prevalent in Magpie Miao kinship usage.

4. *Ellipsis.* Han Chinese who have visited the Miao have commonly been perplexed by certain elliptical usages of the latter in regard to descriptive terms. Thus a spouse's grandfather, $jeu^8\ tai^2$, is frequently called simply jeu^8, "paternal grandfather," and a wife's father, $tai^2\ jeu^6$, simply jeu^6, "husband."

5. *Respect.* Tax (1955, pp. 21–22) propounds the general principle that "persons of one generation tend to respect those of the generation above." Among the Magpie Miao, as among the Han Chinese, the higher in generation a relative stands the more respect his juniors are expected to accord him in their behavior. This is frequently reflected in kinship terminology. Thus the term for FaFa (12), implying great respect, is frequently prefixed to that for MoBr (17) in referring to a maternal uncle, and the term for paternal aunt (18) is commonly preceded by the complimentary me^2 (term 24). The term for paternal grandfather (12) is also prefixed in honorific fashion to term 21 in designating the elder brother of one's father, and the term for father (1) is similarly prefixed to terms 21 and 23 to denote respectively a woman's elder and younger sister's husband.

Of the various criteria recognized by Kroeber (1909) and Murdock (1949, pp. 101–106) for the differentiation of kin types, the Magpie Miao utilize in varying degrees those of generation, sex, affinity, collaterality, bifurcation, polarity, relative age, and speaker's sex. Despite many evidences that the kinship system is basically of generation type, the criterion of generation is rather frequently overridden. Significantly, however, this never results from the intrusion of the lineage principle, as happens in so many unilineal societies. In some instances it reflects teknonymy, tekeisonymy, or ellipsis, as illustrated above, but the principal factor overriding the criterion of generation is that of respect. The preceding paragraph cites only a few of the many instances.

The criterion of sex is rigorously observed throughout the system. That of affinity finds numerous exceptions, mainly resulting from spousal identification but also including such instances as the equating of FaBrWi with MoSi and of MoElSiHu with FaElBr. The criterion of collaterality is widely observed, especially through the use of the suffixed term $mpeu^9$ (27), meaning "outside." The most noteworthy exception is the extension of sibling terms to ortho-cousins. The criterion of bifurcation prevails except in the second descending generation, and is emphatically expressed in the two terms which mean essentially "cross" (6) and "parallel" (26). The criterion of polarity is strictly adhered to; in no instance, even in Ego's generation, do a pair of relatives employ the same reciprocal term for one another. Relative age is differentiated only for siblings of the same sex, siblings-in-law of opposite sex, and parallel aunts and uncles (affinal as well as consanguineal). The criterion of speaker's sex exerts a differentiating influence only in the terms for siblings, for siblings-in-law, and for nephews and nieces, both affinal and consanguineal.

A kinship system, like any other aspect of social structure or culture, is always the product of a historical process. Boas (1920, p. 137) has stated that "each cultural group has its own unique history, dependent partly on the peculiar inner development of the social group, and partly upon the foreign influence to which it has been subjected." In any historical process, however, the forms of social organization exert a steady pressure upon the structure of a kinship system, producing what Sumner (1906, pp. 5–6) has called a "strain toward consistency" which tends ultimately to bring the terminological classification of kinsmen into harmony with their alignment in social groups. The lack of striking internal consistency in this respect among the Magpie Miao leads us to seek a historical explanation.

We have already suggested, on the basis of both internal and distributional evidence, that the Miao may once have had a social system characterized by bilateral descent, either an independent nuclear or a stem type of family organization, a kinship system of generation type, and possibly a neolocal rule of residence. Overwhelmingly the most important factor in bringing about modifications in such a system must have been the long contact with and penetration by the Han Chinese. From the earliest historical period to the present culture of the peasants with whom the Miao have been in close contact for centuries, the Han Chinese have had a social system characterized by patrilocal residence, exogamous patrilineal sibs, patrilocal extended families, and localized patriclans.

As we have already seen, the Magpie Miao today share all these traits, at least incipiently if not always completely. And these have unquestionably exerted an influence on the Miao kinship system. This is reflected, for example, in the widespread recognition of the principle of bifurcation and in the differentiation of sib members from other kinsmen, e.g., by classifying ortho-cousins with siblings and by using the suffixed term *mpeu*[9] (27) to distinguish non-unilineal kinsmen much as the term *piao* is used in Chinese (Feng, 1948, p. 10). That these changes have occurred, at least in part, through independent adaptation rather than through direct borrowing is suggested by the development of special terms for "cross" (6) and "parallel" (26), which are alien to the kinship system of the Han Chinese.

Other influential factors, including teknonymy, tekeisonymy, spousal identification, and respect, seem also to have been borrowed from the Han Chinese. The effects of these various influences have often been contradictory, thus presumably accounting for the lack of any thoroughgoing consistency between the kinship system and the sociological organization of the Magpie Miao. We can thus agree with Murdock (1949, p. 126) in his conclusion that "the casual factors actually operating in any particular situation are always multiple. No single factor or simple hypothesis can account for all observable effects. From this it follows that different determinants must often exert their pressure in opposite directions. What operates is therefore a sort of parallelogram of forces, and the phenomena which ensue represent, not the effects of particular forces but the resultant of them all."

In conclusion, it will be relevant to record certain observations on patterned kinship behavior among the Magpie Miao. Although both parents are concerned with the welfare of their children, a father is primarily responsible for the training of his son, and hence usually exacts a higher degree of obedience from him than from a daughter. The converse is true of the relationship between a mother and her children. If the parents die, the responsibility for the care and socialization of the children devolves upon a paternal uncle; in default of such, upon a maternal uncle or occasionally upon an adult older brother or sister. In general, the parent-child relationship or its surrogate involves authority on the part of the senior relative and respect on the part of the junior.

In the relationship between spouses a higher degree of respect is expected from the wife. The division of labor by sex in economic matters has already been described. Beyond this, the husband is more concerned with social and ceremonial activities, the wife with household affairs.

The interaction between grandparents and grandchildren is characterized by helpfulness and affection on the part of the former and by deference on the part of the latter. A grandfather often instructs his grandson in ritual observances, and a grandmother assists in the domestic training of her granddaughter. Both manifest a warm interest in their grandchildren and take pleasure in playing with them in their leisure time.

The relationships between affines are more complex. A son-in-law defers to the opinions of his wife's parents, and his respect for them approaches avoidance in the case of his mother-in-law. Avoidance also prevails between a daughter-in-law and her husband's father, and the former is expected to be obedient toward her mother-in-law. A woman displays reserve in her relationship with her husband's elder brother. She avoids familiar conversation with him and refrains from walking beside him in public.

The interaction of cousins, both cross and parallel and regardless of sex, is characterized by privileged familiarity, which permits teasing and mild joking. This takes a much more extreme form between cross-cousins, where such behavior becomes obligatory and finds expression in singing and dancing, in practical jokes, and in sexual play.

A man is more restrained in his behavior toward his maternal parallel cousins than with his cross-cousins, though he calls them by identical kinship terms, and he can neither marry nor have sex relations with his mother's sister's daughter. Moreover, in cases where a term for a relative of an older generation is extended out of respect to a relative of a younger generation, the actual behavior exhibited toward the two may often differ appreciably. There is, consequently, no perfect correlation between the categories of kinship terminology and the patterns of behavior prevailing between kinsmen.

NOTES

Chapter 1

1. The writer has previously used "bilocal," but "ambilocal" is clearly preferable for a rule of residence which permits a choice between two unilocal alternatives, the one uxorilocal (matrilocal), the other virilocal (patrilocal or avunculocal).
2. Defined in Murdock, 1957, p. 669. The term "lineal," as here used, should now be recognized as inappropriate. A new term is clearly needed.
3. The so-called "stem kindreds" described by Davenport (1959, p. 565) may possibly constitute an exception. See Murdock, 1958, for a description of the kindred among the Tenino Indians of Oregon.

Chapter 2

1. Cf. Condominas, 1953, où nous avons essayé de donner un schéma des différentes cultures de l'Indochine orientale.
2. Pour une description détaillée de la vie mnong gar, cf. Condominas, 1957, dont le titre est la traduction de l'expression mnong désignant l'année 1949 à Sar Luk. Le but de cet ouvrage est de fournir des documents purement ethnographiques, reproduisant, par des exemples précis, le jeu des institutions dans leur contexte épisodique; bref, de les restituer pour ainsi dire *in vivo*. Le lecteur qui voudrait approfondir la question traitée dans la présente étude aurait intérêt à se reporter à cet ouvrage en s'aidant de l'*Index analytique*. On trouvera un essai d'analyse structurale du système de parenté de cette tribu un ouvrage en preparation sur la société mnong gar. Rappelons que les matériaux utilisés au cours de la présent étude (comme dans ceux élaborés dans mes précédents écrits) ont été recueillis au cours d'une mission au Viêt-Nam effectuée de novembre 1947 à février 1950 sous l'égide de l'Office de la Recherche Scientifique et Technique Outre-Mer et de l'École Française d'Extrême-Orient.
3. Le mode de transcription adopté ici est celui que nous avons suivi dans nos précédents écrits. C'est celui qui a été recommandé pour l'ensemble des langues proto-indochinoises par la Commission de Dalat réunie le 1ᵉʳ Août 1949 sous la direction du professor F. Martini. Pour son étude détaillée cf. Condominas, 1954. En voici les caractéristiques essentielles:

Consonnes
k, g, t, d, n, p, b, m, l, s, se prononcent sensiblement comme en française.
h, marque une aspiration.
jj, dd, bb, nn, sont les équivalents préglottalisés de j, d, b, n.
ng gutturale nasalisée équivalent à l'anglais *ng* dans *sing*.
ny, palatale nasalisée équivalent à *gn* de *oignon*.
c, palatale sourde mouillée, ressemble au *ti* de *tiare*.
j, palatale sonore, rappelle le *j* anglais de *John*.
r, se prononce toujours du bout de la langue.
', occlusion glottale.

Voyelles
  e, ouvert comme dans *cher*.
  ê, fermé comme dans *été*.
  o, ouvert comme dans *robe*.
  ô, fermé comme dans *rose*.
  u, semblable au français *ou* de *chou*.
  ö, la longue öö rappelle le français *eu* (ou *oeu*) dans *noeud;* la brève o rappelle plutôt la voyelle de l'anglais *but*.
  ü, voyelle médiane correspond au "u dit barbu" du viêtnamien.
  Une voyelle redoublée signifie qu'on a affaire à une longe, par opposition à une brève: ansi *maang* (corbeille à riz), *mang* (nuit).
  4. Cf. Condominas, 1957, pp. 427, 473-474.
  5. Cf. Condominas, 1957, chapitre II.
  6. Ce mot lorsqu'il est appliqué aux animaux veut dire "troupeau" ou "variété, sorte."
  7. Lévi-Strauss, 1949, p. 270.
  8. Cf. Condominas, 1957, chapitre III.
  9. Tel qu'il a été dégagé par Lévi-Strauss, 1949, pp. 13-31.
  10. Comparable à celle des Katchins de Birmanie: dix-huit termes élémentaires, d'après les tableaux fournis par Leach, 1945. L'un et l'autre recommandent le mariage avec la cousine croisée matrilatérale et l'interdisent avec la cousine croisée patrilatérale. Ils sont, d'autre part, harmoniques l'un et l'autre. Mais alors que Katchins sont patrilinéaires, les Mnong Gar sont matrilinéaires. Sur le lien entre ces deux caractères, communs aux deux systèmes, cf. Lévi-Strauss, 1949, chapitre XV.
  11. "FaSiDa and MoBrDa called by different terms and terminologically differentiated from sisters and parallel cousins, but FaSiDa is terminologically classed with FaSi and/or MoBrDa with BrDa" (Murdock, 1949, p. 224). Dans le système mnong gar, du fait de la dichotomie entre aînés et cadets, on obtient des analogies plus précises: la fille de la soeur aînée du père est appelée *mei* (mère) et la fille du frère cadet de la mère *koon* (enfant), alors que les soeurs et cousines parallèles d'un home sont ses *rôh*. La fille de la soeur aînée du père est classée avec la soeur cadette du père (*mei*) et la fille du frère cadet de la mère avec la fille du frère (*koon*).
  12. Les mots mnong sont invariables; il n'existe aucune forme permettant de distinguer le masculin du féminin, ni le pluriel du singulier. Certains mots contiennent en eux-mêmes l'idée d'appartenance à un sexe déterminé (exemple: *mei*) ce qui permet, en les accolant à un nom d'animal, par exemple, de spécifier le sexe de celui-ci. Mais en dehors des chiffres, il n'y a guère que les pronoms personnels, ou des mots comme *mpôol* ("clan, troupeau") qui possèdent en eux l'idée de nombre.
  13. Cf. Condominas, 1957, pp. 77, 356-357.
  14. Condominas, 1953, p. 556, note 2; Sabatier et Antomarchi, 1940, p. 130.

Chapter 3

  1. Kroeber, 1928, p. 146.
  2. Kroeber, 1919, p. 82.
  3. These field studies are by Dr. Robert B. Fox, Dr. Charles Kaut, and Alfredo Evangelista in the Tagalog region; by Rev. Frank Lynch, S. J., in the Bicol area; by George Smith, Jr., in the Central Bisayan region; and by Mr. and Mrs. Melvin Mednick in the Moro communities near Lake Lanao and in Cotabato, Mindanao.
  4. The author is indebted to a Fulbright Research Fellowship in 1949-1950 for field work in the Mountain Province and to a Guggenheim Award and a Ford Faculty Grant for assistance in preparing these and other materials for publication. Felix Keesing, Alfredo Pacyaya, William H. Scott, and Leonard Aclop have provided useful data, and profitable comments were received from Fellows at the Center for Advanced Study in the Behavioral Sciences at Stanford, California, during 1958-1959. The paper represents part of a projected

study of Philippine social structure under the auspices of the Philippine Studies Program of the University of Chicago, the Newberry Library, and the Chicago Natural History Museum, which is supported by the Carnegie Corporation of New York and the Rockefeller Foundation.

5. Based on the researches of the late R. F. Barton in 1940; of Fred Eggan and Alfredo Pacyaya in 1950 and, briefly, in 1958; and of William H. Scott in 1954-1957 and continuing.

6. From a census of wards made in 1952 by Alfredo Pacyaya.

7. Goodenough (1955), in surveying the various types of bilateral kin groups found in Oceania, has found it useful to distinguish the group of bilateral relatives surrounding any particular individual or sibling group (the "kindred" of Rivers and Murdock) from the group of relatives descended from a common ancestor (the "kindred" of *Notes and Queries*, 5th edition, 1929). The latter, which Goodenough calls "non-unilinear descent groups," can take several forms, as he notes. In our studies of the Igorots of the Mountain Province I have found it convenient to refer to the first type as the "personal kindred," following Leach, or the "kinship circle," and to the local variant of the second type as the "bilateral descent group." The term "conical clan," proposed by Kirchhoff (1955) and used by him in a discussion of Igorot society, is also apt, but he gives it a wider meaning and a broader significance than we believe is warranted at present.

8. Beyer and Barton, 1911, pp. 228-229.

9. Beyer and Barton, 1911, p. 228.

10. The materials on kinship were gathered through the use of genealogical methods and by observation of village life, supplemented by independent accounts from Alfredo Pacyaya, a native of Sagada who was the late R. F. Barton's assistant in 1940 and mine in 1950, and from Leonard Aclop, a native of Tetepan, a neighboring village. Our orthography for kinship terms follows that in Scott, 1957, except that accents are omitted. For convenience, we frequently employ English equivalents in our analysis, since the Sagada system exhibits certain parallels with our own, but these terms need to be understood with reference to their Sagada applications and meanings.

11. The following data are summarized from a chapter on the life cycle prepared for a general study of the social and ceremonial system of the Sagada Igorots on the basis of the researches of the late R. F. Barton, Fred Eggan, W. H. Scott, and Alfredo Pacyaya.

12. For a preliminary account of growing up in Sagada see Scott, 1958.

Chapter 4

1. As a geographical designation, Zamboanga refers to the area included in the political units of Misamis Occidental Province, Zamboanga del Norte Province, Zamboanga del Sur Province, and Zamboanga City.

2. This term is now established in the literature (see Conklin, 1957, p. 1). In most areas, Subanun agriculture is of the type which Conklin calls "integral swidden farming" (Frake, 1955).

3. See Christie, 1909, pp. 17-32; Combés, 1667; Finley and Churchill, 1913, pp. 8-15; Forrest, 1779, p. 325.

4. Based on field work among the Subanun in 1953-54 and 1957-58 financed by grants from the United States Government (under the Fulbright Act) and the Yale University Southeast Asia Studies Program. The data, especially all linguistic forms cited, pertain specifically to a group of about 500 Eastern Subanun inhabiting the area drained by the upper Diaakan, Muyu, and Duhinob (*duinid*) Rivers in north-central Zamboanga del Norte, but surveys made in other areas indicate that the analysis presented herewith is generally applicable to the Eastern Subanun as a whole.

5. Discrete social groups are those that divide a population in such a way that if individual A belongs to the same group as B, and B belongs to the same group as C, then A and C belong to the same group. Discrete groups are mutually exclusive; every individual belongs to one and only one group of the same kind. Lineages, army platoons, and Hindu castes

are examples of discrete groups. Non-discrete groups, in contrast, divide a population in such a way that one can not predict common membership of A and C in a group from the fact that A and B belong to one group and that B and C belong to one group. Friendship groups are usually non-discrete; that Joe and Bill are friends, and that Bill and Tom are friends, does not imply that Joe and Tom are friends. Other examples of non-discrete groups include bilateral kindreds and suburban neighborhoods.

6. Conklin, 1951; Schneider and Homans, 1955; Naroll, 1958; Koentjaraningrat, 1957.

7. It should be noted that the family exhibits independence in many spheres not discussed here, e.g., in trade with lowlanders (Frake, 1957b) and in attending to life-crisis events (Frake and Frake, 1957).

Chapter 5

1. The Iban are also known as Sea Dayaks. In Sarawak it so happened that the first Iban with whom the British came into contact, in the early 1940's, were inhabitants of the Lupar and Saribas Rivers who, in league with Malays, had taken to coastal piracy. The British called them Sea Dayaks. From an ecological point of view, however, the term Sea Dayak is misleading; the vast majority of the Iban have always been a hill people living many miles from the coast with an economy based on the cultivation of dry rice. Today, among the tribes of the interior, the name Iban (a borrowing from the Kayan) is in general use; it was first introduced into ethnographic literature by Haddon (1901, p. 325).

2. My first period of field work among the Iban was carried out under the auspices of the Colonial Social Science Research Council of Great Britain, and the second from the Australian National University. I wish to express my thanks to both these institutions.

3. Freeman, 1958. This published paper, prepared before my second period of field research among the Iban, incorporates much of the material which I presented at the symposium in Bangkok.

4. *Bilek* is a term used by the Iban to refer to the living room of a long-house apartment; the same term is also used to refer to the family which owns and occupies the whole of such an apartment. The other main sections of an apartment are the *ruai* or gallery and the *tanju* or open platform. When a series of family apartments are joined together they form what is, in effect, a terrace of attached houses. The *ruai* and *tanju* have no side walls and so run the full length of the long-house.

5. In the event of a marriage not producing a child, the usual course is for the child of a close cognate to be adopted. Many families follow this course to ensure their survival. Such adopted members acquire full parcenary rights in the *bilek* estate, and in the account which follows adoption should be regarded as jurally equivalent to descent based on consanguinity.

6. This statement is based on the assumption that the marriage of the affine concerned is a stable and enduring one. An out-marrying member does retain the contingent residual right to return to his (or her) natal *bilek* should a marriage end in divorce.

7. From the Latin, *uter*, either of two, one or the other, one of two. I prefer "utrolocal" to "bilocal" on the ground that for Iban society it is more precise etymologically. Similarly, the Iban system of filiation is best described by the term *utrolateral;* to call the Iban system "bilateral" is to invite misunderstanding, for filiation is always to one side or the other, never to both.

8. See Freeman, 1958, and note 7 above.

9. Goodenough, in a recent discussion of Malayo-Polynesian social organization, points with perspicacity to the feasibility of a solution to the problem of forming corporations in cognatic societies which is, in essence, the same as that reached by the Iban. "Kindreds," he writes (Goodenough, 1955, p. 71), cannot . . . function as land-owning bodies. Bilocal extended families could so function, but this would require that all out-marrying members of a family lose membership in the land-owning group while all in-marrying spouses acquire such membership."

10. I.e., the long-houses of the districts of Pengulu Jenggut and Pengulu Grinang, during the year 1948.

11. For a fuller account of Iban land tenure and usage see Freeman, 1955.

12. According to Radcliffe-Brown, "Kith were one's friends by vicinage, one's neighbors; kin were persons descended from a common ancestor" (Radcliffe-Brown and Forde, 1950, p. 15).

13. E.g., Nadel, 1947, p. 17.

14. Cf. *Oxford English Dictionary;* Pollock and Maitland, 1952, Vol. 2, p. 241; Phillpotts, 1913, p. 2; Rivers, 1924, p. 16; Evans-Pritchard, 1940, p. 193; Murdock, 1949, p. 46.

15. According to Pollock and Maitland (1952, Vol. 2, p. 242), "there were as many blood-feud groups as there were living persons; at all events each set of brothers and sisters was the centre of a different group." The term "personal kindred" was introduced to the literature by Leach (1950, p. 62).

16. In Iban society, in which the marriage of cognates is preferred, it frequently happens that a married pair are close collateral kin, i.e., first, second, or third cousins. In many cases, however, the cognatic relationship of spouses is either more remote than this or is nonexistent.

17. I have not the space in an outline paper of this kind to discuss the changes in kinship terminology and relationship which are adopted when cognates of different generations do marry. Because of the marked generational emphasis of the Iban kinship system these changes always result in incongruities which cause resentment and irritation among many of the other cognates involved. Indeed, I would hypothesize that Iban marital prohibitions beyond the *bilek* family are chiefly concerned with the avoidance of this sort of dysnomia.

18. In 1936, when a section of the *adat* of the Third Division Iban was codified under the authority of the Third Rajah, this fine was set at $15. In 1952 it was increased to $30. A Malay dollar is valued at 2s. 4d. sterling. See *Sea Dayak Fines,* 1940; *Tusun Tunggu Iban,* 1955.

19. If first cousins marry there is an overlap of 50 per cent, but this will be increased if they are related on more than one side, as sometimes happens. Theoretically, universal first cousin marriage (i.e., in all generations) would result in the complete coincidence of the two categories *kaban mandal* and *kaban tampil.*

20. At Rumah Nyala, for example, the linkage of *bilek* families to the rest of the long-house community was traced either exclusively or predominantly from a natal *bilek* member in 62 per cent of instances, and from an in-married *bilek* member in 38 per cent.

21. This statement applies only to pioneer areas, like the Baleh, where land is not in short supply. In some parts of Sarawak, such as the Second Division, the adverse population-land balance prevents or severely inhibits the movement of *bilek* families from one long-house to another. In the Baleh region rubber is now becoming widely established as a cash crop, and already the population has become more sedentary than under the traditional subsistence economy based on shifting cultivation.

22. As early as 1889, for example, Starcke (1889, p. 207) wrote: "A consideration of the whole series of our researches ... will show that ... the nomenclature was in every respect the faithful reflection of the juridical relations which arose between the nearest kinsfolk of each tribe. Individuals who were, according to the legal point of view, on the same level with the speaker, received the same designation. The other categories of kinship were formally developed out of this standpoint."

23. Hence Ego, in Figures 6–8, may be either male or female. This has been indicated by superimposing a circle (the symbol for a female) on a triangle (the symbol for a male).

24. *Petunggal* is the classificatory term applied to all cousins of whatever degree. It is applied, however, only to collateral cognates on the same generation level as Ego; the Iban have no concept comparable to "cousin once removed" in the English kinship system. First cousins are more exactly described as *petunggal diri menyadi* ("cousins sprung from siblings") or *petunggal se kali* ("cousins for the first time"). More remote degrees of cousin-ship are indicated by numerical phrases, e.g., *petunggal dua kali,* second cousins; *petunggal tiga kali,* third cousins.

25. It often happens that differential ease of communication results in an individual be-

coming more closely associated with one side of his (or her) kindred than the other. This, however, does not alter the fact that, beyond the *bilek,* both sides are *de jure* equally available for all the purposes of kinship.

26. As a term of address *menyadi* is commonly extended to include all cousins. Alternative terms of address for cousins are *petunggal* and *unggal.* Again, both siblings and cousins (male and female) may be addressed by the terms *aka and adi,* the former for siblings and cousins older than oneself and the latter for those younger. These terms of address have about them a tone of affection associated with the sentiments that arise from the interdependence of siblings and cousins who grow up together. The vocatives *aka* and *adi* are in no way related to jural rights; during disputes between siblings, for example, they are dropped in favor of the more formal term *menyadi.*

27. In its terms of address, however, the Iban system conforms to Murdock's Hawaiian type, for as a vocative the term *menyadi* may be used in a classificatory way to address any cousin on either side of the personal kindred.

28. This term may be used in addressing cognates of Ego's own generation and, in joking, those of the second ascending or second descending generations, but it is not permissible between cognates of adjacent generations. Personal names are interdicted only for cognates of the first ascending generation, but they are not commonly used for those of the second ascending generation.

29. The term of reference for a great-grandchild is *ichit.* This term, however, is never used as a vocative; instead, great-grandchildren are always addressed as *ucho.*

30. *Ipar* is also used as a term of address. Alternatively, an *ipar* may be addressed as *ika* if older than Ego's spouse, or as *adi* if younger. *Duai* refers to the relationship between the spouses of a pair of siblings, i.e., a double affinal relationship.

31. In many respects the kinship system of the Iban resembles that of the contemporary United States. Cf. Parsons, 1943.

32. Of the world ethnographic sample of 565 societies compiled by Murdock (1957), 247 have patrilineal descent, 85 have matrilineal descent, 29 have double descent, and 204 have bilateral descent.

33. Radcliffe-Brown and Forde, 1950; Fortes, 1953.

Chapter 6

1. Tjelapar, a mountain village of 1,880 inhabitants about 15 kilometers north of Kebumen (a regency town in south central Java), and Madjasari, a lowland village of 1,200 inhabitants about 15 kilometers southwest of the same town.

2. Widjojo Nitisastro (1956, p. 21), on the basis of recent field research in the lowland village of Djabres in south central Java, estimates population density in that region at 1,022 per square kilometer. Of the 181 households living in Djabres, he reports (p. 20) that only 125 possess plots of irrigated rice land and that the holdings of 110 of these amount to less than half a hectare each.

3. On agriculture in overcrowded Java see Pelzer, 1945, pp. 160–176.

4. See Heyning, 1954, pp. 130-134, for recent census material, which for the most part is spotty. The last complete census was that of 1930.

5. See Rouffaer, 1921, for historical details concerning the four principalities.

6. The families of many Central Javanese village headmen consider themselves descended from, or related to, members of the nobility who participated in the revolts against the Dutch in Central Java in the eighteenth and nineteenth centuries and who, after their defeat, took refuge as outlaws or fugitives in the mountainous sections of that region.

7. Geertz is wrong, however, in asserting (1956, p. 152) that "religiously the prijaji have been particularly interested in neither the stlametans nor the Qur'an." The author knows from his own experience that many *prijaji* families still practice the *slametan* periodically.

8. The Javanese child is already a center of social attention while still in its mother's womb (see Djojodigoeno and Tirtawinata, 1940, pp. 1–2).

9. This period is called *ngedah*, from Arabic *'iddah*, the taboo period for a woman during menstruation, after childbirth, and following divorce. For details concerning the Javanese taboos, see Juynboll, 1903, p. 175.

10. See Koperberg, 1934, for details of an elaborate example of this ceremony.

11. The *wajang* is a Javanese folk puppet play. Of its several types, the two-dimensional leather puppet play is the most popular today. The central actor not only recites the story and sings the song but also manipulates the puppets and directs the *gamelan* orchestra which provides the sound effects which accompany the movements of the puppets. A good story-teller must have a variety of artistic talents. In addition to knowing the story, the songs, and their sequence by heart, he must be able to improvise personal remarks, jokes, and satirical comments on current events in harmony with the characters of the puppets and in time with the music. Many anthropological theories have been advanced to account for the integration of the *wajang* into the social life of the people. To the Javanese these puppet plays have both an artistic and a ritual value, which helps to explain their popularity. In addition to a wide repertory of stories, there are several kinds of *wajang*. Plays with three-dimensional wooden puppets are popular among the Sundanese of western Java. South Sumatra, Bali, and Lombok have plays with two-dimensional leather puppets resembling those of the Javanese. A huge literature exists on the subject. See, in particular, Hazeu, 1897.

12. Cf., for example, the highly inadequate paper on childbearing in Indonesia by Fischer (1950, pp. 39–64).

13. During his fieldwork in the Kebumen area the author noticed girls engaged in herding, but in relatively much smaller numbers than boys.

14. Muslim law books of the Sjafiitic school regard circumcision as *wadjib* (obligatory) despite the fact that nothing is said about it in the Qur'ân. Muslim theologians cite the Qur'ân, IV, 124, where Allah ordered the people to "follow the religion of Abraham," which means, they assert, that the people must follow the Jewish custom of circumcision.

15. The native explanation of this disapproval seems very logical. The bride's guardian (*wali*), an important figure in the Javanese wedding ceremony, must be a close relative of the bride (e.g., her father, brother, or father's brother). He represents the bride's party in the ceremonial interaction with the groom's party. If a girl marries her father's brother's son, her guardian and the groom's father might well be the same person.

16. As is correctly reported by Djojodigoeno and Tirtawinata (1939, pp. 175-177).

17. According to Djojodigoeno and Tirtawinata (1939, pp. 257-260), however, there may be exceptions to this principle.

18. It is necessary to specify a "native speaker" since a foreign speaker of Javanese does not need to consider age or status distinctions and has to differentiate only whether the addressee is a good friend or a distant acquaintance.

19. In the presence of a relative of very advanced age who is two generations or more older than Ego, and formerly also in the presence of a person of higher rank, one is expected to sit on a lower level, namely, on the floor.

20. The term *diq* is an abbreviation of *adi*, the term of reference for a younger sibling, with the addition of a glottal stop at the end.

21. This term, used by Embree (1950) in characterizing the social organization of the Thai, is applicable to the Javanese only in respect to the absence of clearly defined rights and duties alluded to above. The other features of Thai culture cited by Embree as evidence of a loosely structured social system are absent in Javanese culture.

Chapter 8

1. Since the paper submitted by Professor Mabuchi exceeded in length the space that could be alloted to it in this publication, the editor has taken the liberty of eliminating portions concerned with historical and distributional problems, retaining the material pertaining directly to the social organization of the Formosan aborigines. The author had arranged his ethnographic data according to a topical organization, but the editor has taken the further

liberty of recording them according to ethnic groups. This, he feels, will considerably facilitate comparison with the information presented in the other contributions to this volume. Professor Mabuchi draws primarily upon his own extensive first-hand knowledge of the cultures he deals with, and upon his own previous publications, which are cited in the Bibliography. He also utilizes the publications of the former Japanese Government-General of Formosa and the works of other Japanese anthropologists, notably, Furuno, 1950; Kano, 1944; Kano and Segawa, 1956; Koizumi, 1932 and 1933; Miyauchi, 1938; Okada, 1942 and 1949; and Utsurikawa et al., 1935. The author points out, in correspondence, that the Saisiyat, though placed in the Atayal cluster on geographical grounds, belong more properly in the Bunun cluster in terms of social structural classification. (Ed.)

2. According to sources in the Human Relations Area Files, the Atayal are further characterized by strict monogamy; by the requirement of a substantial bride-price, or sometimes, in lieu thereof, two or three years of bride-service; by the former prevalence of head-hunting; and by a sexual division of labor in accordance with which the men do the hunting, fishing, and land clearance whereas the women perform the rest of the agricultural work. (Ed.)

3. The above information and occasional items mentioned below are drawn from Professor Mabuchi's introduction to Kano and Segawa (1956) to supplement the less complete summary contained in his manuscript. (Ed.)

BIBLIOGRAPHY

ARENSBERG, C. M., and S. T. KIMBALL
1940. *Family and Community in Ireland*. Cambridge.

ARIYAPALA, M. B.
1956. *Society in Mediaeval Ceylon*. Colombo.

BARNES, J. A.
1951. The Fort Jameson Ngoni. *Seven Tribes of British Central Africa*, ed. E. Colson and M. Gluckman, pp. 194–252. London.

BARTON, R. F.
1919. Ifugao Law. *University of California Publications in American Archaeology and Ethnology*, XV, 1–186.

1930. *The Half-Way Sun*. New York.

1940. The Igorots of Sagada. Unpublished Ms.

1946. The Religion of the Ifugaos. *Memoirs of the American Anthropological Association*, LXV, 1–219.

1949. *The Kalingas*. Chicago.

1955. The Mythology of the Ifugaos. *Memoirs of the American Folklore Society*, XLVI, 1–244.

BERG, C. C.
1938. Javaansche geschiedschrijving. *Geschiedenis van Nederlandsch-Indië*, ed. F. W. Stapel, II, 5–148. Amsterdam.

BERTLING, C. T.
1936. Huwverbod op grond van verwantschaps posities in Middel-Java. *Indisch Tijdschrift van het Recht*, CXLIII, 119–134.

BEYER, H. O., and R. F. BARTON
1911. An Ifugao Burial Ceremony. *Philippine Journal of Science*, VI, 227–249.

BOAS, F.
1897. The Social Organization and the Secret Societies of the Kwakiutl Indians. *Report of the U. S. National Museum for 1895*, pp. 311–738.

1920. The Method of Ethnology. *American Anthropologist*, XXII, 311–321.

BOGORAS, W.
1907. The Chukchee, Pt. 2. *Memoirs of the American Museum of Natural History*, XI, 277–733.

BUCK, P. H.
1934. Mangaian Society. *Bulletins of the Bernice P. Bishop Museum*, CXXII, 1–207.

1938. Ethnology of Mangareva. *Bulletins of the Bernice P. Bishop Museum*, CLVII, 1–519.

BURROWS, E. G.
1936. Ethnology of Futuna. *Bulletins of the Bernice P. Bishop Museum*, CXXXVIII, 1–239.

CHEN, T. S., and J. K. SHRYOCK.
1932. Chinese Kinship Terms. *American Anthropologist*, XXXIV, 623–669.

CHRISTIE, E. B.
1909. The Subanuns of Sindangan Bay. *Philippine Bureau of Science Division of Ethnology Publications*, VI, 1–121.

COMBÉS, F.
1667. Historia de las islas de Mindanao, Iolo. y sus adyacentes. Madrid.
[New edition, Madrid, 1897].

CONDOMINAS, G.
1953. L'Indochine. *L'ethnologie de l'Union Française, Territoires extérieurs*, ed. A. Leroi-Gourhan, II. Paris.

1954. Enquête linguistique parmi les populations montagnardes du Sud-Indochinois. *Bulletin de l'École Française d'Extrême-Orient*, XLVI, 573–597.

1955. Introduction au *Klei Khan Kdam Yi*: Observations sociologiques sur deux chantes épiques rhadés. *Bulletin de l'École Française d'Extrême-Orient*, XLVII, 555–568.

1957. *Nous avons mangé la forêt de la pierre-génie Gôo*. Paris.

CONKLIN, H. C.
1951. Co-existing Sets of Relationship Terms among the Tanay Tagalog. Unpublished Ms.

1957. Hanunóo Agriculture. *Food and Agricultural Organization of the United Nations, Forestry Development Papers*, XII, 1–209. Rome.

DAVENPORT, W.
1959. Nonunilinear Descent and Descent Groups. *American Anthropologist*, LXI, 557–572.

DEMPWOLFF, O.
1938. *Vergleichende Lautlehre*, Band III: *Austronesisches Wörterverzeichnis*. Berlin.

DJOJODIGOENO, M. M. M., and R. TIRTAWINATA
1940. *Het adatprivaatrecht van Middel-Java*. Soekamiskin.

DUMONT, L.
1957. Hierarchy and Marriage Alliance in South Indian Kinship. *Occasional Papers of the Royal Anthropological Institute*, XII, 1–45.

EGGAN, F.
1941. Some Aspects of Culture Change in the Northern Philippines. *American Anthropologist*, XLIII, 11–18.

1954. Some Social Institutions in the Mountain Province and Their Significance for Historical and Comparative Studies. *Journal of East Asiatic Studies*, III, 329–335. Manila.

1956. Ritual Myths among the Tinguian. *Journal of American Folklore*, LXIX, 331–339.

EMBER, M.
1959. The Nonunilinear Descent Groups of Samoa. *American Anthropologist*, LXI, 573–577.

EMBREE, J. F.
1950. Thailand—A Loosely Structured Social System. *American Anthropologist*, LII, 181–193.

EMBREE, J. F., and L. O. DOTSON
1950. *Bibliography of the Peoples and Cultures of Mainland Southeast Asia.* New Haven.

EVANS-PRITCHARD, E. E.
1940. *The Nuer.* Oxford.

FENG HAN-YI
1948. *The Chinese Kinship System.* Cambridge.

FINLEY, J. P., and W. CHURCHILL
1913. The Subanu. *Carnegie Institution of Washington Publications,* CLXXXIV, 1–236.

FIRTH, R.
1929. *Primitive Economics of the New Zealand Maori.* London.

1957. A Note on Descent Groups in Polynesia. *Man,* LVII, 4–8.

1959. "Bilateral" Descent Groups: An Analytical View. Unpublished Ms.

FISCHER, H. T.
1950. *Kinderaantal en kinderleven in Indonesië.* Den Haag.

FORCE, R. W.
1960. Leadership and Cultural Change in Palau. *Fieldiana: Anthropology,* L, 1–211.

FORREST. T.
1779. *A Voyage to New Guinea.* London.

FORTES, M.
1949. Time and Social Structure: An Ashanti Case Study. *Social Structure,* ed. M. Fortes, pp. 54–84. Oxford.

1953. The Structure of Unilineal Descent Groups. *American Anthropologist,* LV, 17–41.

1959. Descent, Filiation and Affinity. *Man,* LIX, 193–197, 206–212.

FRAKE, C. O.
1955. Social Organization and Shifting Cultivation among the Sindangan Subanun. Unpublished Ms.

1956. Malayo-Polynesian Land Tenure. *American Anthropologist,* LVIII, 170–173.

1957a. Litigation in Lipay. *Proceedings of the Ninth Pacific Science Congress* (in press). Bangkok.

1957b. Sindangan Social Groups. *Philippine Sociological Review,* V, ii, 2–11.

1957c. The Subanun of Zamboanga: A Linguistic Survey. *Proceedings of the Ninth Pacific Science Congress* (in press). Bangkok.

FRAKE, C. O., and C. M. FRAKE
1957. *Post-Natal Care among the Eastern Subanun.* Silliman Journal, IV, 207–215. Dumaguete City.

FREEMAN, J. D.
1955. Iban Agriculture. *Colonial Research Studies,* XVIII, 1–148. London.

1958. The Family System of the Iban of Borneo. *Cambridge Papers in Social Anthropology,* I, 15–52.

FURUNO, K.
1940. *Takasago-zoku no Saigi Seikatsu* [Ritual Life of Formosan Native Peoples]. Tokyo.

GEDDES, W. R.
1954. The Land Dayaks of Sarawak. *Colonial Research Studies*, XIV, 1–113. London.

GEERTZ, C.
1956. Religious Beliefs and Economic Behavior in a Central Javanese Town. *Economic Development and Culture Change*, IV, 134–158. Chicago.

GEERTZ, H.
1955. Family and Life-Cycle in Modjokuto. Unpublished Ms.

GLUCKMAN, M.
1950. Kinship and Marriage among the Lozi of Northern Rhodesia and the Zulu of Natal. *African Systems of Kinship and Marriage*, ed. A. R. Radcliffe-Brown and D. Forde, pp. 166–206. London.

1951. The Lozi of Barotseland in North-Western Rhodesia. *Seven Tribes of British Central Africa*, ed. E. Colson and M. Gluckman, pp. 1–93. London.

GOLDMAN, I.
1940. The Alkatcho Carrier of British Columbia. *Acculturation in Seven American Indian Tribes*, ed. R. Linton, pp. 333–389. New York.

GOODENOUGH, W. H.
1951. Property, Kin, and Community on Truk. *Yale University Publications in Anthropology*, XLVI, 1–192.

1955. A Problem in Malayo-Polynesian Social Organization. *American Anthropologist*, LVII, 71–83.

1957. Notes on the Bwaidoga People of Goodenough Island. Unpublished Ms.

GRAHAM, D. C.
1937. The Customs of the Ch'uan Miao. *Journal of the West China Border Research Society*, IX, 13–70.

HADDON, A. C.
1901. *Head-Hunters: Black, White and Brown.* London.

HAYLEY, F. A.
1923. *A Treatise on the Laws and Customs of the Sinhalese.* Colombo.

HAZEU, G. J. A.
1897. *Bijdrage tot de kennis van het Javaansche tooneel.* Leiden.

HENRY, T.
1928. Ancient Tahiti. *Bulletins of the Bernice P. Bishop Museum*, XLVIII, 1–651.

HEYNING, N.
1954. Recente bevolkingscijfers van Java en Madoera. *Geographisch Tijdschrift*, VII, 130–134.

HOCART, A. M.
1928. The Indo-European Kinship System. *Ceylon Journal of Science*, Section G, I, 179–186.

HOGBIN, H. I.
1934. *Law and Order in Polynesia.* New York.

HULSTAERT, G.
1938. Le mariage des Nkundó. *Mémoires de l'Institut Royal Colonial Belge, Section des Sciences Morales et Politiques*, VIII, 1–519.

INGGERIS
1921. Volksgewoonten in Bagelen. *Djawa*, I, 89–91. Djokjakarta.

IVENS, W. G.
1927. *Melanesians of the South-east Solomon Islands.* London.
JAPANESE GOVERNMENT-GENERAL OF FORMOSA
1913–21. *Banzoku Chôsa Hôkokusho* [Survey Reports of Formosan Aborigines]. 8 vols. Taipei.
1915–22. *Banzoku Kanshû Chôsa Hôkokusho* [Survey Reports on the Customs of the Formosan Aborigines]. 8 vols. Taipei.
1936–39. *Takasago-zoku Chôsa-sho* [Survey Reports on Formosan Native Peoples]. 6 vols. Taipei.
JENKS, E. A.
1905. The Bontoc Igorot. *Philippine Islands Ethnological Survey Publications,* I, 1–266.
JOCHELSON, W.
1905-08. The Koryak. *Memoirs of the American Museum of Natural History,* X, 1–842.
JUYNBOLL, T. W.
1903. *Handleiding tot de kennis van de Moehammedaansche wet.* Leiden.
KANO, T.
1944. Kôtôsho Yami-zoku to Tobi-uo [The Yami of Botel Tobago and Flying-Fish]. *Taiheiyô-ken* [Pacific Circle], Vol. I: *Minzoku to Bunka* [Peoples and Cultures], pp. 503–573. Tokyo.
KANO, T., and K. SEGAWA
1956. *An Illustrated Ethnography of Formosan Aborigines,* Vol. I: *The Yami.* Tokyo.
KEESING, F. M.
1949. Some Notes on Bontok Social Organization. *American Anthropologist,* LI, 578–601.
1950. A Brief Characterization of Lepanto Society. Unpublished Ms.
KEESING, F. M., and M. KEESING
1934. *Taming Philippine Headhunters.* London.
KENNEDY, D. G.
1931. Field Notes on the Culture of Vaitupu. *Memoirs of the Polynesian Society,* IX, 1–326.
KEUR, J. Y., and D. L. KEUR
1955. The Deeply Rooted. *Monographs of the American Ethnological Society,* XXV, 1–208.
KIRCHHOFF, P.
1932. Verwandtschaftsbezeichnungen und Verwandtenheirat. *Zeitschrift für Ethnologie,* LXIV, 41–71.
1955. The Principles of Clanship in Human Society. *Davidson Journal of Anthropology,* I, 1–10. Seattle.
KOENTJARANINGRAT, R. M.
1957. *A Preliminary Description of the Javanese Kinship System.* New Haven.
KOIZUMI, M.
1932. *Bankyô Fûbutsu-shi* [Descriptive Notes on Aboriginal Formosa]. Tokyo.
1933. *Taiwan Dozoku-shi* [Ethnographic Notes on Formosa]. Tokyo.

KOPERBERG, S.
1934. Het betreden der aarde (*tedaq sitèn*). *Djawa*. XIV, 213-214. Djokjakarta.

KROEBER, A. L.
1909. Classificatory Systems of Relationship. *Journal of the Royal Anthropological Institute*, XXXIX, 77-84.
1919. Kinship in the Philippines. *Anthropological Papers of the American Museum of Natural History*, XIX, 69-84.
1928. *Peoples of the Philippines*. 2nd edit. New York.
1933. Process in the Chinese Kinship System. *American Anthropologist*, XXXV, 151-157.

LAMBRECHT, F.
1953. Genealogical Trees of Mayawyaw. *Journal of East Asiatic Studies*, II, 21-27. Manila.
1954. Genealogical Tree of Kiangan. *Journal of East Asiatic Studies*, III, 366-369.

LANTIS, M.
1946. The Social Culture of the Nunivak Eskimo. *Transactions of the American Philosophical Society*, XXXV, 153-323.

LEACH, E. R.
1945. Jinghpaw Kinship Terminology. *Journal of the Royal Anthropological Institute*, LXXV, 59-72.
1950. Social Science Research in Sarawak. *Colonial Research Studies*, I, 1-93. London.

LÉVI-STRAUSS, C.
1949. *Les structures élémentaires de la parenté*. Paris.

LING SHUN-SHENG and RUEY YIH-FU
1947. *The Miao Tribe of Western Hunan* [In Chinese]. Shanghai.

LOEB, E. M.
1926. History and Traditions of Niue. *Bulletins of the Bernice P. Bishop Museum*, XXXII. 1-226.

LOUNSBURY, F. G.
1956. A Semantic Analysis of the Pawnee Kinship Usage. *Language*, XXXII, 158-194.

LOWIE, R. H.
1928. A Note on Relationship Terminologies. *American Anthropologist*, XXX, 263-267.

MABUCHI, T.
1934. *Bunun-Tsou-ryozoku no Shinzoku-meisho* [Kinship Terms of the Bunun and Tsou]. *Nampo Dozoku* [Ethnography of the Southern Countries], III, 1-35. Taipei.
1935. Chûbu Takasago-zoku no Saidan [Ritual Groups among the Native Peoples of Central Formosa]. *Monzokugaku Kenkyû* [Japanese Journal of Ethnology], III, 1-29. Tokyo.
1938. Chûbu Takasago-zoku no Fukei-sei ni okeru Bozoku no Chii [The Place of Maternal Relatives under the Patrilineal System among the Native Peoples of Formosa]. *Minzokugaku Nempô* [Annual Report of Ethnology], I, 1-68. Tokyo.
1940. Bunun-zoku ni okeru Jûniku no Bumpai to Zôyo [Distribution and Presentation of Meat among the Bunun]. *Minzokugaku Nempô*, II, 368-452.
1941. Sanchi Takasago-zoku no Chiri-teki Chishiki to Shakai-Seiji Soshiki [Geographical Knowledge and Socio-Political Organization of the Mountain Peoples of Formosa]. *Minzokugaku Nempô*, III, 267-311.

1951. Social Organization of the Central Tribes of Formosa. *Journal of East Asiatic Studies*, I, 43-69. Manila.

1952. Social Organization of the Central Tribes of Formosa. *Internationales Archiv für Ethnographie*, XLVI, 182–211. 1952. [A republication].

1953. The Omaha Type of Kinship Terminology among the Bunun. *Proceedings of the Eighth Pacific Science Congress* (in press). Manila.

1954a. Takasago-zoku no Bunrui: Gakushi-teki Kaiko [Retrospect on the Classification of Formosan Native Peoples]. *Minzokugaku Kenkyû*, XVIII, 1–11.

1954b. Takasago-zoku ni kansuru Shakai-minzoku-gaku [Social Anthropology of Formosan Native Peoples]. *Minzokugaku Kenkyû*, XVIII, 86–104.

1954c. Takasago-zoku no Idô to Bumpu [Migration and Distribution of Formosan Native Peoples]. *Minzokugaku Kenkyû*, 123–154, 319–368.

1957. Land Tenure among the Central Tribes of Formosa. *Proceedings of the Ninth Pacific Science Congress* (in press). Bangkok.

1958. Two Types of Kinship Rituals among Malayo-Polynesian Peoples. *Proceedings of the Ninth International Congress for the History of Religions* (in press). Tokyo.

Marshall, L.
1957. The Kinship Terminology System of the !Kung Bushmen. *Africa*, XXVII, 1–25.
1959. Marriage among the !Kung Bushmen. *Africa*, XXIX, 335–365.

Mayer, L. H.
1897. *Een blik in het Javaansche volksleven*. 2 vols. Leiden.

McCulloch, M.
1950. *Peoples of Sierra Leone Protectorate*. London.

McIlwraith, T. F.
1948. *The Bella Coola Indians*. 2 vols. Toronto.

Meek, C. K.
1931. *A Sudanese Kingdom*. London.

Métraux, A.
1940. Ethnology of Easter Island. *Bulletins of the Bernice P. Bishop Museum*, CLX, 1–432.

Mickey, P. M.
1947. The Cowrie Shell Miao of Kweichow. *Papers of the Peabody Museum of American Archaeology and Ethnology, Harvard University*, XXXII, 1–83.

Miyauchi, E.
1938. Iwayuru Paiwan-zoku no Tsûkon-ken ni tsuite [On the Marriage Circle among the so-called Paiwan]. *Minzokugaku Kenkyû* [Japanese Journal of Ethnology], Vol. III.

Monzon, A.
1949. *El calpulli en la organización de los Tenochca*. Mexico.

Morgan, L. H.
1870. Systems of Consanguinity and Affinity of the Human Family. *Smithsonian Contributions to Knowledge*, XVII, 1–590.

Murdock, G. P.
1949. *Social Structure*. New York.
1957. World Ethnographic Sample. *American Anthropologist*, LIX, 664–687.

1958. Social Organization of the Tenino. *Miscellanea Paul Rivet*, pp. 299–315. Mexico.

NADEL, S. F.
1947. *The Nuba*. Oxford.

NAROLL, R.
1958. German Kinship Terms. *American Anthropologist*, LX, 750–755.

OKADA, Y.
1942. *Mikai Shakai ni okeru Kazoku* [The Family in Primitive Society]. Tokyo.
1949. Atayaru-zoku no Shakai Kôsei [Social Structure of the Atayal]. *Essays presented to Professor Teizo Toda*, pp. 393–433. Tokyo.

PACYAYA, A.
1953. A Sagada Dirge. *Journal of East Asiatic Studies*, II, 49–53. Manila.

PACYAYA, A., and F. EGGAN
1953. A Sagada Igorot Ballad. *Journal of American Folklore*, LXVI, 239–246.

PARSONS, T.
1943. The Kinship System of the Contemporary United States. *American Anthropologist*, XLV, 22–38.

PEHRSON, R. N.
1954. Bilateral Kin Groupings as a Structural Type. *Journal of East Asiatic Studies*. III, 199–202. Manila.

PELZER, K. J.
1945. *Pioneer Settlement in the Asiatic Tropics*. New York.

PHILLPOTTS, B. S.
1913. *Kindred and Clan*. Cambridge.

PIERIS, R.
1956. *Sinhalese Social Organisation: The Kandyan Period*. Colombo.

POLLOCK, F., and F. W. MAITLAND
1952. *The History of English Law*. 2nd edit. Cambridge. [1st edit., 1895].

RADCLIFFE-BROWN, A. R.
1935. Matrilineal and Patrilineal Succession. *Iowa Law Review*, XX, 286–303.
1952. *Structure and Function in Primitive Society*. London.

RADCLIFFE-BROWN, A. R., and D. FORDE (eds.)
1950. *African Systems of Kinship and Marriage*. London.

REED, S. W. (ed.)
1956. *Indonesia*. 3 vols. New Haven.

RIVERS, W. H. R.
1924. *Social Organization*. New York.
1926. *Psychology and Ethnology*. London.

ROUFFAER, G. P.
1921. Vorstenlanden. *Encyclopaedie van Nederlandsch-Indië*, 2nd edit., IV, 626–636. 'sGravenhage and Leiden.

RUEY YIH-FU
1949. Miao Kinship Terms [in Chinese]. *Bulletin of the Institute of History and Philology, Academia Sinica*, XIV, 307–340.
1954. On the Original Type of Kinship Terminology among the Miao Tribe in the Region on the Sources of the Yungning River [in Chinese with English summary]. *Bulletin of the Department of Archaeology and Anthropology, National Taiwan University*, III, 1–13.

1955. Parent-Child Identity Kinship Terminology [in Chinese with English summary]. *Bulletin of the Ethnological Society of China*, I, 45–62.

Ruopp, P.
1953. *Approaches to Community Development*. The Hague and Bandung.

Ryan, B.
1953. *Caste in Modern Ceylon*. New Brunswick.

Sabatier, L., and D. Antomarchi
1940. *Recueil des coutumes rhadées du Darlac*. Hanoi.

Schneider, D. M., and G. C. Homans
1955. Kinship Terminology and the American Kinship System. *American Anthropologist*, LVII, 1194–1208.

Schrieke, B.
1921. Allerlei over de besnijdenis in de Indische Archipel, Deel 1. *Tijdschrift voor Indische Taal-, Land- en Volkenkunde*, CX, 423–507.

Scott, W. H.
1957. A Vocabulary of the Sagada Igorot Dialect. *Transcripts of the Philippine Studies Program, University of Chicago*, No. 6.

1958. Boyhood in Sagada. *Anthropological Quarterly*, XXXI, 61–72.

Spencer, R. F.
1959. The North Alaskan Eskimo. *Bulletins of the Bureau of American Ethnology, Smithsonian Institution*, CLXXI, 1–490.

Spier, L.
1922. A Suggested Origin for Gentile Organization. *American Anthropologist*, XXIV, 487–489.

1925. Distribution of Kinship Systems in North America. *University of Washington Publications in Anthropology*, I, 69–88.

1928. Havasupai Ethnography. *Anthropological Papers of the American Museum of Natural History*, XXIX, 81–392.

Spoehr, A.
1954. Saipan. *Fieldiana: Anthropology*, XLI, 1–383.

Starcke, C. N.
1889. *The Primitive Family in Its Origin and Development*. New York.

Subandrio, H.
1951. Javanese Peasant Life. Unpublished Ms.

Sumner, W. G.
1906. *Folkways*. Boston.

Tambiah, S. J.
1958. The Structure of Kinship and Its Relationship to Land Possession and Residence in Pata Dumbara, Central Ceylon. *Journal of the Royal Anthropological Institute*, LXXXVIII, 21–44.

Tax, S.
1955. Some Problems of Social Organization. *Social Anthropology of North American Tribes*, ed. F. Eggan, 2nd edit., pp. 1–32. Chicago.

Teit, J. A.
1906. The Lillooet Indians. *Memoirs of the American Museum of Natural History*, IV, 193–300.

UKUN SURJAMAN
1956. Tempat pemakaian istilah klasifikasi kekerabatan pada orang Djawa dalam susunan masjarakat. *Bahasa dan Budaja*, V, ii, 7–29. Djakarta.

UTSURIKAWA, N., N. MIYAMOTO, and T. MABUCHI
1935. *Takasago-zoku Keitô Shozuku no Kenkyû* [The Formosan Native Tribes: A Genealogical and Classificatory Study]. 2 vols. Tokyo.

WHITAKER, I.
1955. Social Relations in a Nomadic Lappish Community. *Norsk Folkemuseum Samiske Samlinger*, II, 1–178. Oslo.

WIDJOJO NITISASTRO
1956. *Some Data on the Population of Djabres, a Village in Central Java*. Djakarta.

WIENS, H. J.
1954. *China's March toward the Tropics*. Washington.

WITTFOGEL, K. A.
1957. *Oriental Despotism*. New Haven.

YALMAN, N.
1960. The Flexibility of Caste Principles in a Kandyan Community. *Cambridge Papers in Social Anthropology*, II, 78–112.

Index

INDEX

Abipon, 6, 7
Abortion, 99
Acculturation, 27, 144–47, 153–54
Adolescence, 42, 98–99
Adoption, 84, 103
Adultery, 41
Affinal kin, 20–21, 35–36, 40–41, 45, 60–62, 73–76, 81–85, 130–31, 151, 154–55
Age-sets, 141
Aged, status of, 37–38, 45, 105
Agriculture, 15, 17, 25, 46–47, 51, 65, 88, 118–19, 127–29, 138, 144
Ainu, 6
Albanians, 6
Aleut, 8
Alkatcho Carrier, 12–13
Alsea, 13
Ambil-anak, 12, 146
Ambilineal descent, 2, 9–14, 29–30, 135–36, 139
Ambilocal residence, 2, 6, 10, 12, 13, 14, 28, 66–68, 75, 102, 109, 129, 135, 157
Americans, 6
Ami, 127, 133–34, 139, 140, 141
Ancestor cult, 38, 44–45, 105
Andamanese, 6
Animal husbandry, 25, 138, 144
Apayao, 25, 47, 50
Arapaho, 13
Arensberg, C. M., 6, 165
Argentinians, 6
Ariyapala, M. B., 124, 165
Atayal, 9, 10, 127, 129–32, 139, 140, 164
Avoidance relationships, 81–83, 131, 155
Avunculocal, 1–2
Aztec, 13

Bacairi, 7
Bahnar, 17
Barnes, J. A., 8, 165
Barrios, 13
Barton, R. F., 6, 13, 29, 31, 37, 41, 46, 50, 117, 159, 165
Basic kinship terms, 60–62
Bellacoola, 10, 11
Bertling, C. T., 100, 165
Betrothal, 55, 100
Beyer, H. O., 29, 30, 159, 165

Bifurcate collateral terminology, 6, 8, 20, 124–26, 140, 150
Bifurcate merging terminology, 3, 7, 8, 14, 140
Bilateral descent, 2–7, 24, 29–31, 49, 67–68, 85, 139, 141, 146–47, 159
Boas, F., 10, 11, 153, 165
Bogoras, W., 6, 165
Bontok, 6, 24, 25, 27, 28, 31, 40, 45, 47, 50
Bride-price, 7, 55–56, 132, 137, 145, 164
Bride-service, 56, 164
Buck, P. H., 10, 12, 165
Bunun, 127, 131–34, 139, 140, 141
Bureaucracy, 89–92
Burial. See Mortuary rites
Burrows, E. G., 12, 165
Bwaidoga, 12

Caddo, 13
Camayura, 7
Camba, 6
Cambodians, 6, 7
Carib structural type, 8
Caribou Eskimo, 7
Carinya, 6
Caroline Islands, 5
Catawba, 6
Cayapa, 6
Ceremonial. See Life cycle ceremonies
Chamorro, 6
Chen, T. S., 152, 166
Cheyenne, 13
Child care, 96–97
Childbirth, 95–96
Childhood, 97–98
Chinese, 143–47, 152–54
Chorti, 13
Christie, E. B., 63, 159, 166
Chukchee, 6
Circumcision, 98
Circumscriptive groups, 5
Clans, 1–2, 4, 5, 11, 29, 145, 153–54, 159. See also Sibs
Class stratification, 31, 89–93, 118, 134–35, 137
Cognatic descent, 1–14, 24, 70–73, 85, 117, 123
Comanche, 13
Combés, F., 51, 159, 166

177

Community, 69–70, 76–77, 93–94, 118–19. See also Political organization
Complementary filiation, 12
Componential analysis, 60–62
Condominas, G., 15–23, 157, 158, 166
Conjugal tie, 84–85
Conklin, H. C., 159, 160, 166
Contraception, 103
Coos, 8
Corporate groups, 2, 4–5, 29–30, 54–58, 63, 66–69, 93, 116–17, 141
Courtship, 40, 42, 99
Cousin marriage, 3, 6, 7, 8, 10, 13, 14, 15, 18–19, 30, 40, 55, 75–76, 79, 100, 120, 126, 129, 131, 132, 133, 135, 137, 139, 145–46, 155, 158
Crow cousin terminology, 15, 20, 158
Cultural drift, 50
Culture change, 116
Czechs, 6

Dakota structural type, 7
Davenport, W., 2, 5, 9, 10, 11, 12, 13, 157, 166
Death, causes of, 37, 57. See also Mortuary rites
Definitive affiliation, 11
Dempwolff, O., 48, 166
Descent, 3, 9, 114–15, 123, 135. See also Ambilineal, Bilateral, Cognatic, Double, Matrilineal, Patrilineal, Quasi-unilineal, and Unilineal descent
Descent groups, 1–14, 24, 29–30, 114–15, 159
Designative kin terms, 59
Discrete social groups, 4, 52–53, 159–60
Disease, causes of, 43
Divination, 135–36
Divine kingship, 90
Divorce, 57, 75, 104
Djojodigoeno, M. M. M., 88, 162, 163, 166
Double descent, 1
Dowry, 118, 120
Dumont, L., 125, 166
Dutch, 6
Dwellings, 17, 28–29, 53–54, 69–70, 88, 160

Easter Island, 12
Eddystone Island, 12
Education, 28, 38, 89–91
Eggan, F., 5, 13, 24–50, 159, 166
Ellice Islands, 12
Ellipsis, 152
Ember, M., 10, 166
Embree, J. F., 144, 163, 166–67

Endogamy, 9–10, 77. See also Local endogamy and exogamy
English, 6, 59
Eskimo, 6
Eskimo cousin terminology, 3, 6, 14, 31–36, 49, 59, 79–80, 109, 136, 139
Eskimo structural type, 2–7
Evil eye, 73
Exclusive and nonexclusive affiliation, 11
Exogamy, 18, 30, 40, 67, 74, 129, 131, 133–34, 140, 145. See also Local endogamy and exogamy
Extended families, 2, 4, 7, 8, 12, 14, 15, 17–18, 28, 94, 102, 120–21, 132, 133, 140, 145, 153–54

Family, 3, 54. See also Extended, Nuclear, Polygamous, and Stem families
Feng, H. Y., 152, 167
Figures, 19, 31, 32, 35, 62, 78, 82, 83
Filiation, 3, 4, 10, 12, 67
Firth, R., 2, 5, 9–11, 136, 167
Force, R. W., 12, 167
Fortes, M., 3, 9–10, 11–12, 117, 124, 162, 167
Frake, C. O., 3, 51–64, 109, 160, 167
Freeman, J. D., 2, 11, 63, 65–87, 117, 123–24, 138, 160, 161, 167
French, 6
French Canadians, 6
Friendship, 41–42
Funerals. See Mortuary rites
Futunans, 12

Geddes, W. R., 6, 168
Geertz, C., 94, 162, 168
Geertz, H., 88, 110, 168
Generation kinship terminology, 10, 13, 14, 132–33, 134, 136, 138, 140
Geographical environment, 15–17, 25, 51, 65, 88, 117–18, 143–44
Gilbertese, 10, 11, 63
Gluckman, M., 10, 168
Goldman, I., 12, 168
Goodenough, W. H., 2, 5, 10, 12, 63, 136, 159, 160, 168
Graham, D. C., 144, 146, 168

Haida, 4
Handicrafts, 144
Haudricourt, A. G., 17
Havasupai, 8
Hawaiian cousin terminology, 3, 10, 13, 14, 31, 49, 59, 61, 130, 132–33, 140, 146, 151, 162

INDEX

Hawaiians, 11, 13
Hayley, H. A., 118, 168
Headhunting, 28, 77, 133, 138, 141, 164
Headmen, 18, 37, 70, 93–94, 130, 133, 135, 145, 162
Henry, T., 12, 168
Hocart, A. M., 124, 168
Hogbin, H. I., 12, 168
Homans, G. C., 59, 160, 173
Household composition, 28, 53–55, 102–4, 129, 132, 133, 135, 137, 138, 145
Hukundika Shoshone, 13
Hulstaert, G., 12, 168
Hupa, 13
Hutsul, 6

Iban, 2, 3, 63, 65–87, 117, 123, 138, 160–62
Ifugao, 13, 24, 25, 29, 30, 31, 40, 41, 47, 48, 49, 50
Ilocano, 25, 39, 40
Incest, 18, 39, 55, 74, 80, 99–100
Infancy, 42, 79, 96–97
Ingassana, 13
Inggeris, 98, 173
Inheritance, 3, 18, 39, 43, 47, 57, 105–7, 114–15, 117, 118, 120, 122–23, 133, 137, 138, 139
Irish, 6
Iroquois, 116
Iroquois cousin terminology, 7, 14, 124–26
Iroquois structural type, 8
Irrigation, 25, 46–47, 88, 118–19, 138, 144
Islam, 89, 90, 91–92
Ivens, W. G., 12, 169

Jamaicans, 6
Japanese, 6
Javanese, 2–3, 5, 59, 88–115, 162–63
Jen, 17
Jenks, A. E., 27, 169
Jochelson, W., 6, 169
Joking relationships, 21, 80, 122, 155
Jorai, 15, 17
Jukun, 13
Justice, system of, 145

Kachin, 158
Kajang, 65
Kalinga, 6, 25, 29, 30, 31, 37, 46–47, 49, 50, 117, 123
Kanakanabu, 127, 131–32
Kankanay, 25
Karok, 13

Kayan, 65
Keesing, F. M., 6, 27, 28, 31, 45, 50, 169
Kennedy, D. G., 12, 169
Kenyah, 65
Keur, J. Y. and D. L., 6, 169
Kha, 15
Kiangan, 29
Kimball, S. T., 6, 169
Kin groups, classification of, 5, *See also* Descent groups
Kindreds, 3–6, 12, 13, 14, 29–31, 45, 70–73, 114, 137, 139, 142, 146, 159, 160
Kinship behavior, 37–40, 62–63, 68–69, 79–85, 110–14, 122–23, 154–55. *See also* Avoidance, Joking, and Respect relationships
Kinship terminology, 15, 19–23, 24, 31–36, 47–49, 58–64, 77–87, 107–14, 124–26, 130–31, 132–33, 134, 136, 138–39, 140, 147–54. *See also* Bifurcate collateral, Bifurcate merging, Generation, and Lineal terminology, and Crow, Eskimo, Hawaiian, Iroquois, and Omaha cousin terminology
Kiowa Apache, 13
Kirchhoff, P., 29, 48–49, 150, 151, 159, 169
Koentjaraningrat, R. M., 59, 88–115, 160, 169
Koryak, 6
Kroeber, A. L., 24, 47–48, 63, 152, 158, 170
Kung Bushmen, 6
Kutenai, 13
Kwakiutl, 10, 11

La'arua, 127
Labor, division of by age, 38, 98
Labor, division of by sex, 23, 84, 104, 138, 144–45, 164
Lambrecht, F., 29, 50, 170
Land Dayak, 6, 65, 69
Land, property in. See Property
Language, 52
Language styles, 107–8, 111
Lantis, M., 8, 170
Lapps, 6
Leach, F. R., 2, 4, 9, 116–26, 158, 159, 170
Lepanto, 31
Lévi Strauss, C., 18, 158, 170
Levirate, 21, 39, 58, 145
Life cycle ceremonies, 5, 42–45, 79, 94–105, 142
Lillooet, 13
Lineages, 1, 7, 8, 11, 116–18, 129, 131–32, 141–42, 146
Lineal kinship terminology, 3, 6, 14, 34, 61, 79, 109, 130, 139, 140
Lineal kinsmen, 61
Lineal structural principle, 3–4

Lithuanians, 6
Local endogamy and exogamy, 31, 55, 119, 129, 132, 133, 134, 137, 138
Localized kin groups. See Clans
Loeb, E. M., 12, 170
Lounsbury, F. G., 59, 61, 170
Lowie, R. H., 3, 140, 150, 151, 170
Lozi, 10, 11

Maa', 17
Mabuchi, T., 9, 13, 127–40, 163–64, 171–72
Maidu, 8
Maine, H. S., 4, 117
Mangaians, 10, 11
Mangarevans, 12
Maori, 9, 10, 11, 136
Maps, 16, 26, 128
Marriage, age at, 99, 102, 121
Marriage, mode of, 15, 18, 40, 55–56, 75, 99–100, 121–22, 132, 133, 135, 138. See also Brideprice, Secondary marriages, Wedding ceremonies
Marriage, of cousins. See Cousin marriage
Marshall, L., 6, 171
Matrilineal descent, 1, 12, 15, 18, 133–34
Matrilocal residence, 1–2, 7, 15, 18, 19, 56, 102, 133, 146
Mayawyaw, 29
Mayer, L. H., 96, 171
Mazatec, 13
McCulloch, M., 13, 171
McIlwraith, T. F., 10, 171
Meek, C. K., 13, 171
Men's houses, 132, 141
Métraux, A., 12, 171
Miao, 143–55
Mickey, P. M., 146, 171
Midwives, 96, 103
Mixe, 13
Mnong Gar, 15–23, 157
Moi, 15
Moieties, 1, 27
Mongo, 12
Monogamy, 2, 6, 10, 41, 75, 132, 133, 135, 137, 138, 145, 164
Monzon, A., 13, 171
Morgan, L. H., 116, 125, 171
Mortuary rites, 44–45, 105. See also Ancestor cult
Motilon, 7
Murdock, G. P., 1–14, 20, 23, 34, 48, 55, 62, 79, 108, 110, 140, 146, 152, 154, 157, 158, 161, 162, 171–72
Mutual aid, 94

Nabaloy, 25
Names, 101
Naming, 42, 96
Neighbors, 113
Neolocal residence, 2, 6, 14, 56–57, 102, 146–47
Ngoni, 8
Nicobarese, 6
Niueans, 12
Nobility, 90–91, 134–35, 137
Nominals, 59, 62–63
Nuclear families, 2–3, 6, 14, 15, 17, 28, 53–58, 63, 88, 102, 114, 129, 135, 137, 138, 140
Nukuoro, 10, 11
Nunivak Eskimo, 8
Nursing, 96

Occasional groups, 5
Occupations, 89–92, 144
Omaha cousin terminology, 132
Ona, 6
Ontong-Java, 12
Optative affiliation, 11–12, 135–36

Pacyaya, A., 44, 159, 172
Paiwan, 9, 10, 11, 127, 136–38, 139–40
Palauans, 12
Panare, 7
Parsons, T., 2, 162, 172
Patrilineal descent, 1, 118, 125, 131, 146–47, 153–54
Patrilocal residence, 1–2, 7–8, 119–30, 129, 132, 138, 146–47, 153–54
Pehrson, R. N., 6, 172
Pelzer, K. J., 88, 162, 172
Penobscot, 6
Personality development, 41, 97
Phillpotts, B. S., 5, 172
Phratries, 131–32, 141
Pieris, R., 124, 125, 172
Placenta, disposition of, 96
Pnong, 15
Political organization, 18, 28, 52, 63, 70, 77, 90–91, 93–94, 130, 132, 133, 134–35, 138, 139, 145
Polygamous families, 3, 54, 58
Polygyny, 2, 3, 39, 54, 58, 103–4, 145
Polynesian structural type, 10–14
Popoluca, 13
Population, 25, 51, 52, 65, 88–89, 127, 132, 143–44. See also Villages, population of
Pregnancy, 42, 95
Prestige, 43, 75, 94, 120–21. See also Class stratification

INDEX

Primogeniture, 137, 139–40
Property, 17, 47, 54, 57, 66–69, 105–7, 119, 123, 129, 137, 138, 141. *See also* Inheritance
Puppet plays, 97, 163
Puyuma, 9, 10, 11, 127 134–36, 139

Quasi-unilineal descent, 7–9

Radcliffe-Brown, A. R., 77, 85, 161, 172
Ramages, 11–14, 29–30, 105, 114–15, 129, 137–38, 139, 159
Reed, S. W., 88, 172
Rennell Island, 8
Residence, marital, 1, 14, 28, 56, 102, 139. *See also* Ambilocal, Avunculocal, Matrilocal, Neolocal, Patrilocal, and Unilocal residence
Respect relationships, 20–21, 41, 62–63, 80, 97, 111–13, 152, 154–55
Rhadé, 17, 21
Ritual groups, 129–31, 135–36
Rivers, W. H. R., 3, 9, 12, 161, 172
Ruey, Y. F., 143–55, 172–73
Rukai, 127, 136–38, 139
Ruopp, P., 93, 173
Russians, 6
Ryan, B., 117, 173
Rykyu Islands, 6

Sagada Igorots, 2, 3, 5, 24–50
Saisiyat, 127, 129–30
Samoans, 10, 11
Sapir, E., 50
Schneider, D. M., 59, 160, 173
Schrieke, B., 98, 173
Scott, W. H., 25, 27, 159, 173
Scots, 5, 10
Secondary marriages, 43, 58, 145. *See also* Levirate, Sororate
Sedang, 17
Sedeq, 127, 129–31, 134
Segmentary lineage system, 141
Selung, 6
Septs, 11
Settlement patterns, 17, 23, 25, 27–28, 46, 53, 69, 76–77, 93, 119, 131–32, 134, 136–37, 138, 145
Sexuality, premarital, 40–42, 98–99, 146
Shasta, 8
Sherbro, 13
Shryock, J. K., 152, 166
Sibs, 1, 5, 15, 17, 18–19, 129, 131–32, 133–34, 141, 146

Sinhalese, 7–9, 116–26
Sinkaietk, 13
Siuslaw, 8
Skewed kindreds, 5
Slavery, 23
Socialization, 38, 97–99, 154
Sororate, 21, 39, 58, 100
Soul, 43
Spencer, R. F., 6, 173
Spier, L., 8, 34, 173
Spirits, 17, 43
Spoehr, A., 6, 173
Stem families, 2, 4, 66–68, 81, 102
Subandrio, H., 88, 96, 173
Subanun, 2–3, 7, 51–64
Succession, 5, 70, 93–94, 135, 137, 139
Sugbuhanon, 6, 7
Sumner, W. G., 153, 173
Swaddling, 96

Taboos, 95–96, 131
Tagalog, 6
Tagbanua, 6
Tahitians, 12
Tambiah, S. J., 118, 124, 125, 173
Tamil, 125
Tax, S., 152, 173
Teit, J. A., 13, 173
Tekeisonymy, 152
Teknonymy, 38, 40, 151–52
Terena, 13
Tewa, 6
Tikopia, 5
Tinguian, 25, 49
Tirtawinata, R., 88, 162, 163, 166
Tiwa, 6
Toilet training, 42, 97
Tongarevans, 13
Totonac, 13
Trukese, 12
Tsou, 127, 131–33, 141

Ukun Surjaman, 88, 173
Ulawans, 12
Unilineal descent, 1, 12, 24, 46, 49, 85, 116–17, 139
Unilocal residence, 1, 8, 14
Ute, 13
Utrolateral, 11, 67–68, 138, 160
Utrolocal, 67, 160
Uxorilocal. *See* Matrilocal residence

Vengeance, 5, 39, 46, 141

Villages, population of, 15, 18, 25, 69, 93, 118, 129, 133, 134, 136, 138
Virilocal. See Patrilocal residence

Wapishana, 7
Ward organization, 27–28, 45–46
Weaning, 42, 96
Wedding ceremonies, 40–43, 56, 100–2, 121–22
Wei, H. L., 141–42
Wergild, 5, 50
Whitaker, I., 6, 174
Widjojo Nitisastro, 103, 162, 174
Wittfogel, K. A., 118, 174

Women, status of, 104, 122–23

Yabarana, 6
Yahgan, 6
Yalman, N., 118, 174
Yami, 2, 3, 127, 138–39, 140, 142
Yaqui, 13
Yekuana, 7
Yugoslavs, 6
Yurok, 13

Zapotec, 13